REALISTIC STILL LIFE IN

COLORED PENCIL

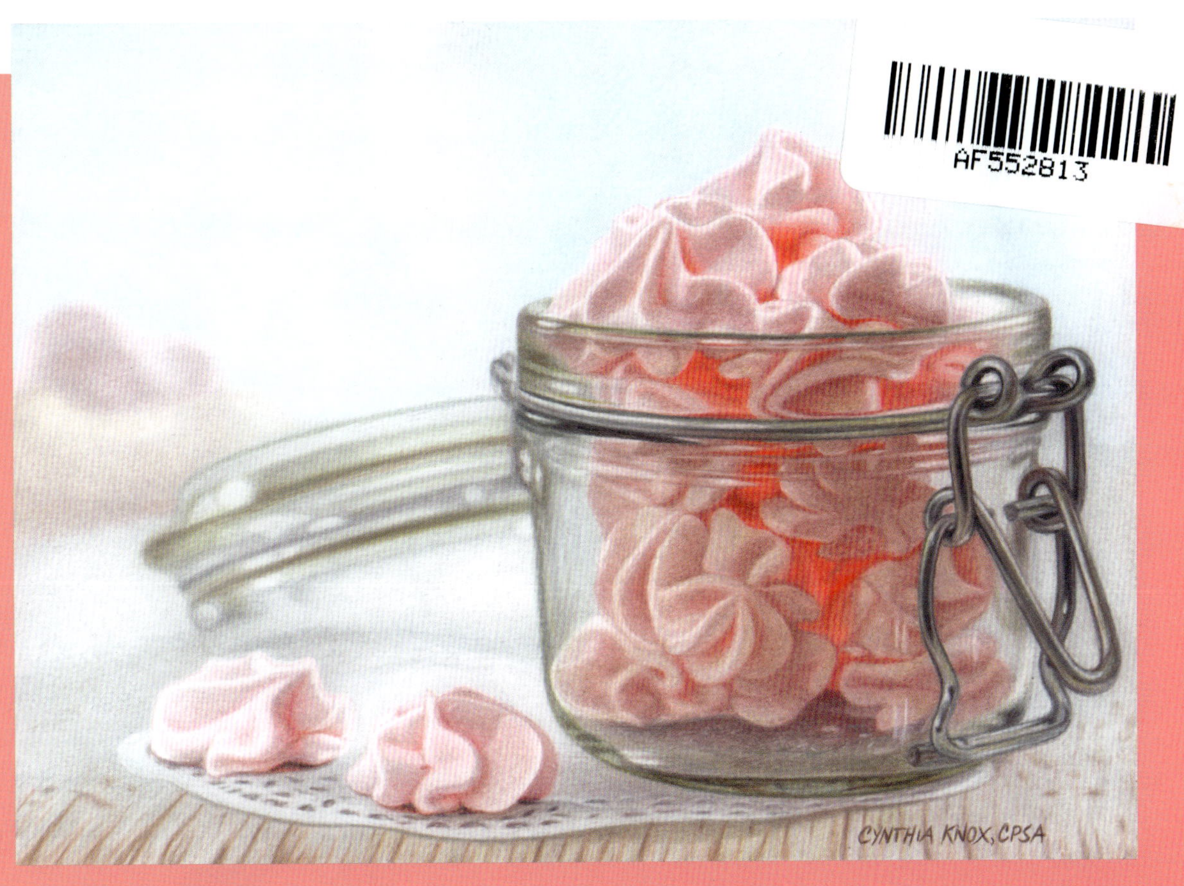

CYNTHIA KNOX

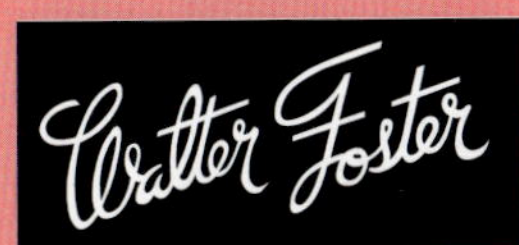

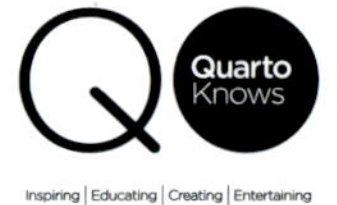

Brimming with creative inspiration, how-to projects, and useful information to enrich your everyday life, Quarto Knows is a favorite destination for those pursuing their interests and passions. Visit our site and dig deeper with our books into your area of interest: Quarto Creates, Quarto Cooks, Quarto Homes, Quarto Lives, Quarto Drives, Quarto Explores, Quarto Gifts, or Quarto Kids.

First published in 2020 by Walter Foster Publishing, an imprint of The Quarto Group.
26391 Crown Valley Parkway, Suite 220, Mission Viejo, CA 92691, USA.
T (949) 380-7510 **F** (949) 380-7575 **www.QuartoKnows.com**

Walter Foster Publishing titles are also available at discount for retail, wholesale, promotional, and bulk purchase. For details, contact the Special Sales Manager by email at specialsales@quarto.com or by mail at The Quarto Group, Attn: Special Sales Manager, 100 Cummings Center, Suite 265D, Beverly, MA 01915, USA.

ISBN: 978-1-63322-868-9

Digital edition published in 2020
eISBN: 978-1-63322-869-6

Printed in China
10 9 8 7 6 5 4 3 2 1

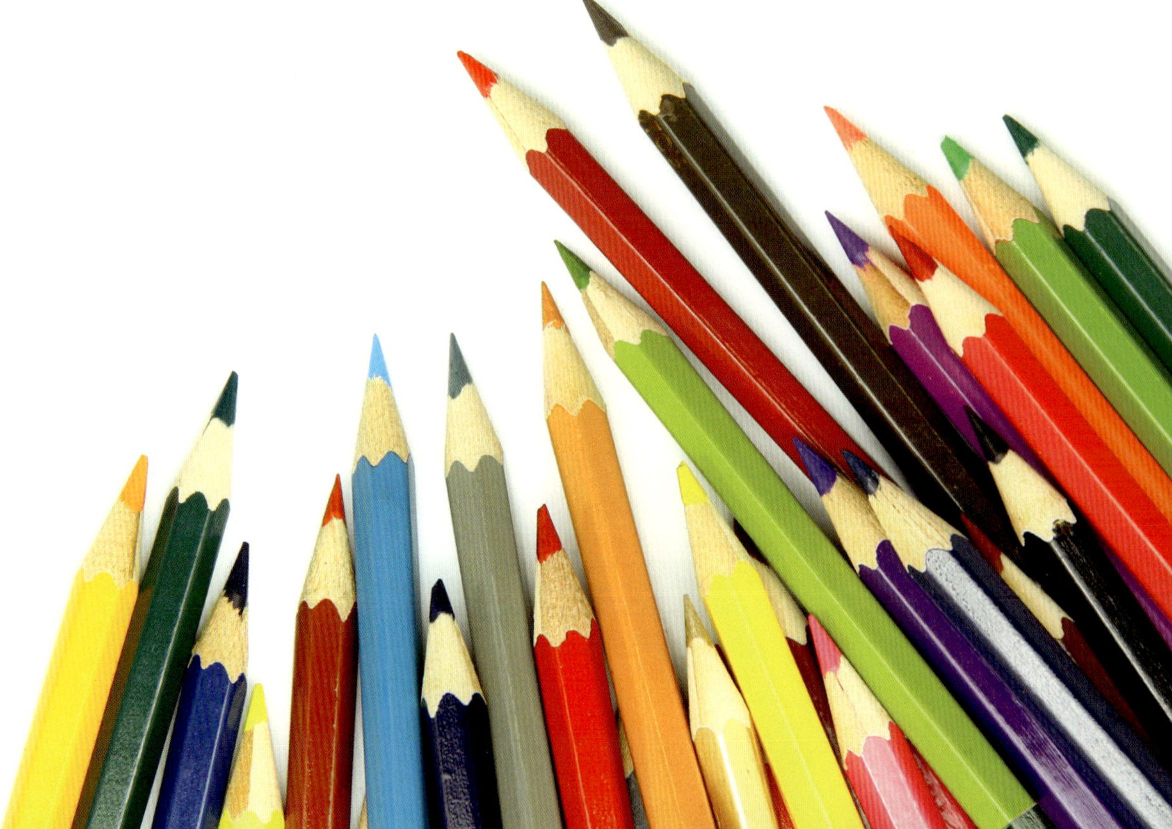

TABLE OF CONTENTS

Introduction

"Just do it." A dear friend encouraged me to take the next step in my art journey. I had been drawing with graphite pencils and felt comfortable in my world of gray, but I knew that there was more out there. I decided to transition into all things color but didn't know where to start—so I procrastinated. Have you ever done this? You want to move forward into something exciting that holds promise, but you feel a bit stuck? My friend motivated me to leave my doubts behind and embrace color, and I turned to the colored-pencil medium to do just that. I was particularly attracted to still-life compositions, and that's when it all came together for me.

My new goal was to learn the painterly technique of colored pencil and create beautiful still-life artwork with an emphasis on vivid color and extreme detail. Several artists became my mentors via their books, workshops, online classes, and personal instruction, and I'm truly grateful for them and the techniques they shared. They have inspired me to teach my own techniques and show people how much fun colored pencils can be.

Over time, my artistic style has evolved and it now leans toward realism with vibrant colors, a variety of textures, and smoothly blurred backgrounds. I love a challenge, and many still-life subjects certainly present one.

In this book, we'll work together to create beautiful flowers and fruit, elegant antiques, intricate lace, tinted glass, delectable pastries, and so much more. Join me as I show you how to create your own personal masterpieces step by step throughout the pages of this book. Your friends and family will exclaim, "That's colored pencil?!" when you show them your work, and you'll be amazed at how quickly it all comes together for you. Now let's get started!

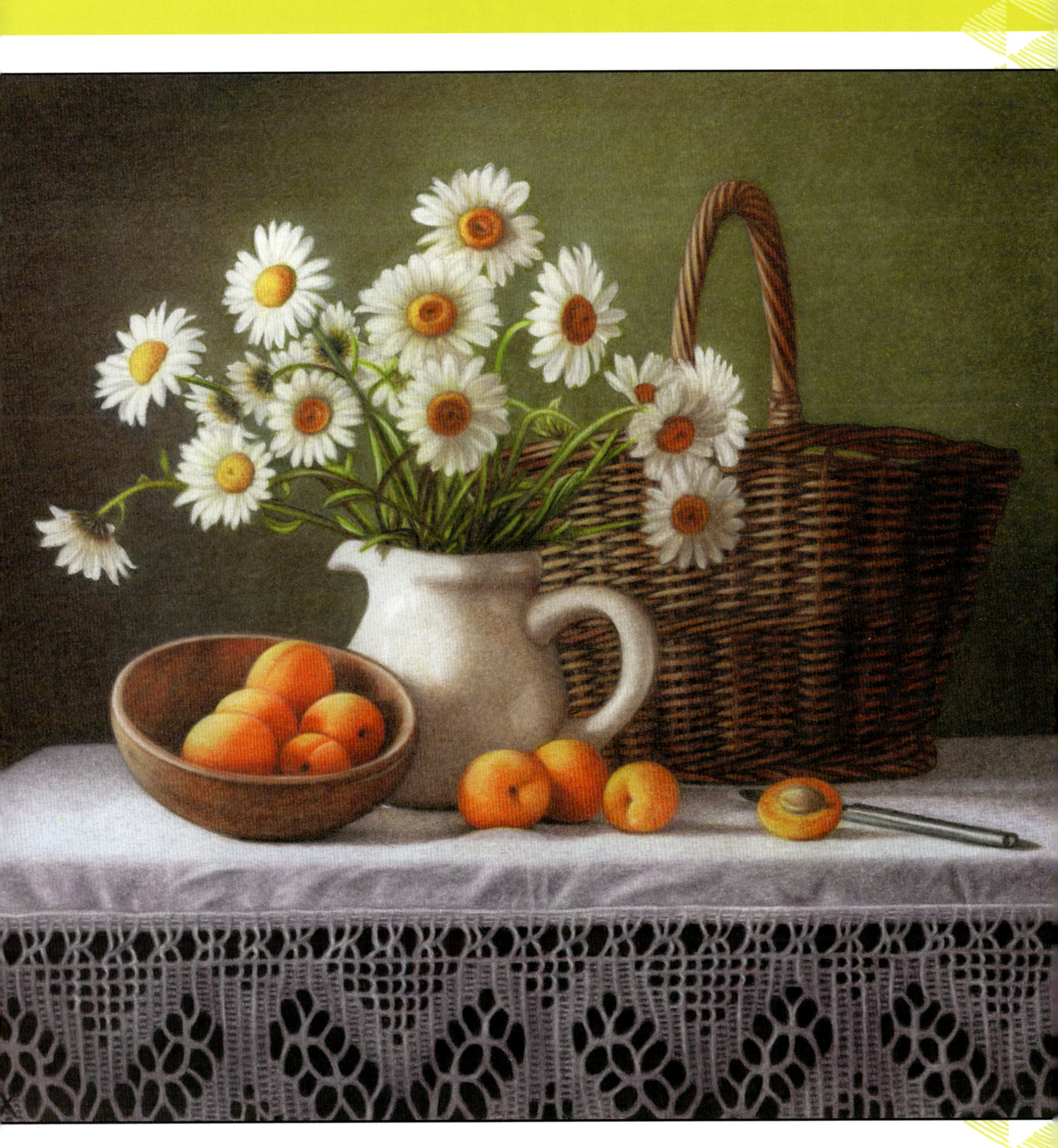

Tools & Materials

Colored-pencil artwork is affordable to create and requires only a few supplies. However, I strongly recommend that you purchase the best-quality materials possible. This is particularly important with pencils and paper. Invest in the good stuff, and your artwork will last for many years after you create it.

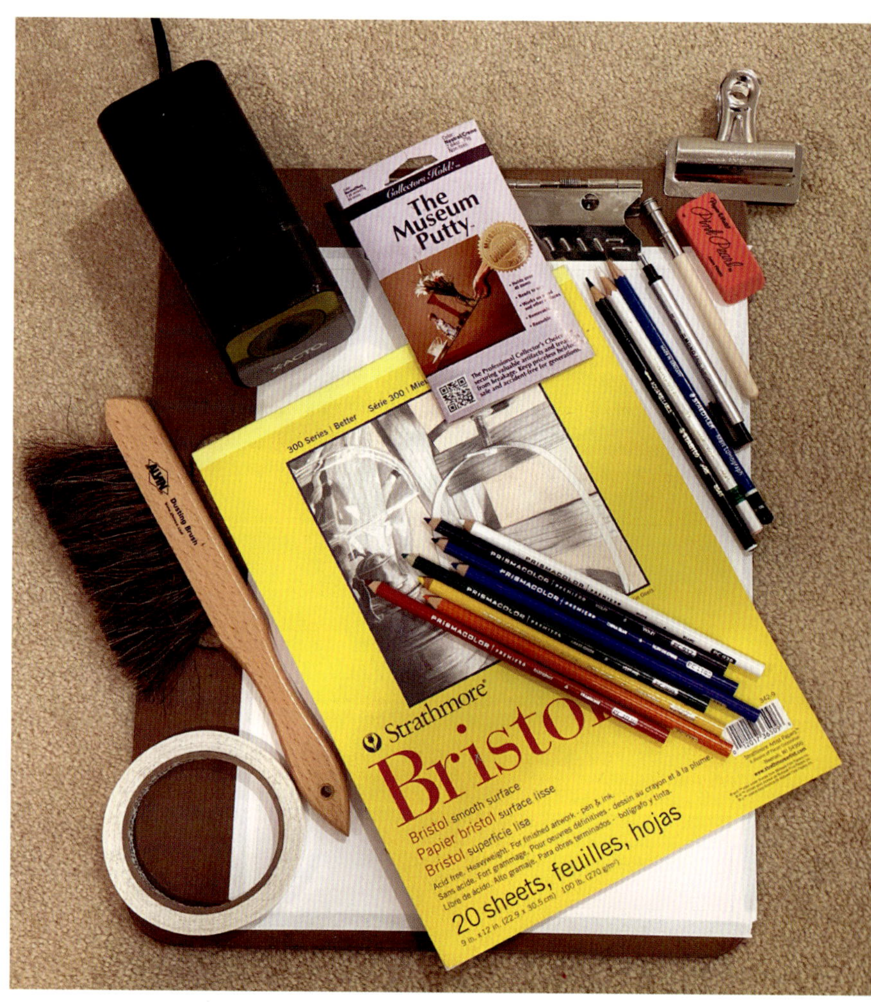

COLORED PENCILS

To create beautiful pieces of art, I recommend purchasing professional-grade colored pencils. These are a step up from student-grade pencils. A few leaders in the industry include Prismacolor®, Faber-Castell®, Derwent®, and Caran d'Ache®. Their pencils are sold in sets as well as individually online and in stores in most countries.

Quality professional colored pencils have thin cores of pigment within their casings. These cores are wax- or oil-based, or water-soluble with watercolor effects. I recommend that you try a few pencils of each type to see what appeals most to you. It is possible to combine pencil types, and when using oil- and wax-based pencils together, it's best to use oil-based pencils first with foundational layers of wax-based pigment applied over that. Either may be used effectively over a water-soluble foundation.

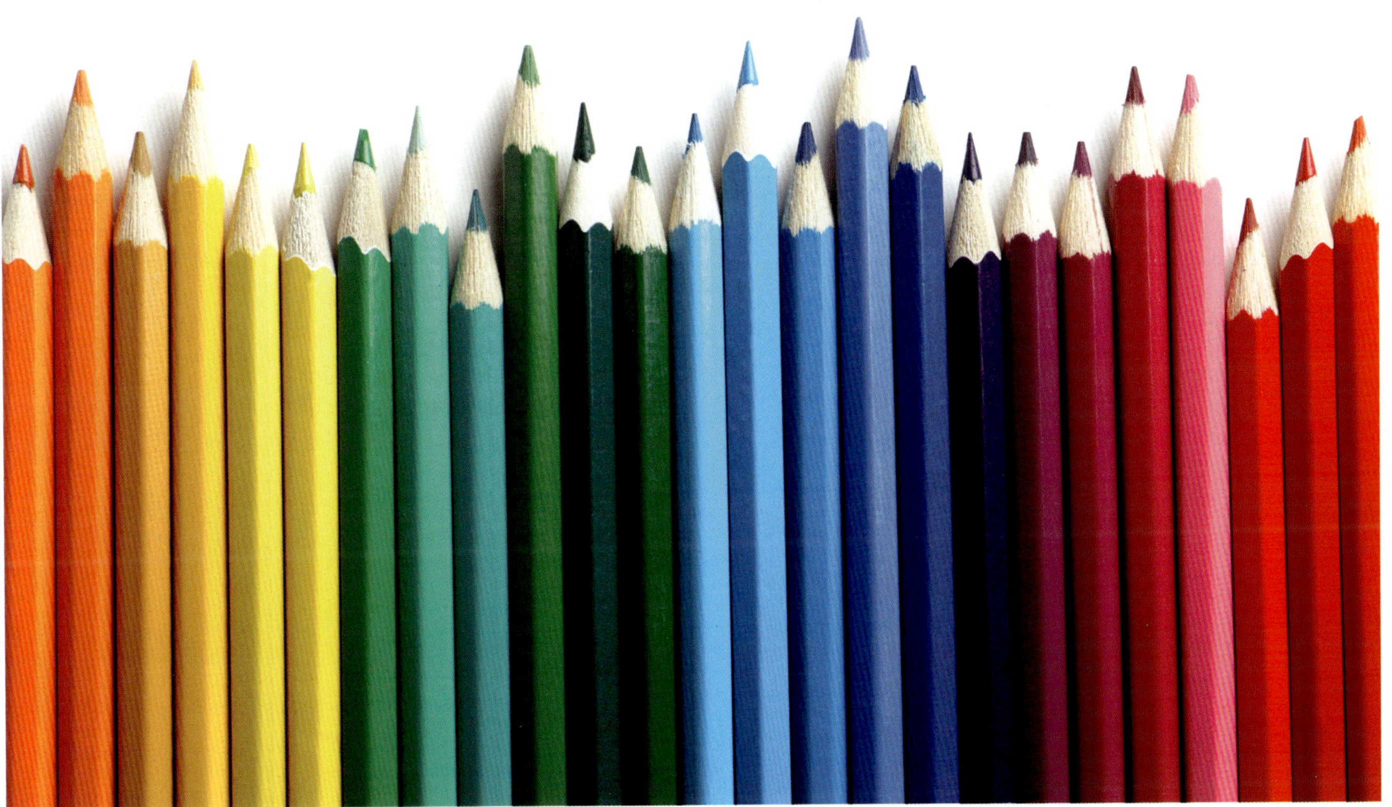

WAX-BASED PENCILS are extremely creamy, and I love working with them. They deliver pigment to the paper surface with smooth consistency and are easy to layer and blend. Their pencil points are somewhat soft and prone to breakage; however, with the right touch and application angle, breakage is minimal. A good pencil sharpener also reduces the possibility of breakage. If waxy buildup occurs, you can easily remove it with the sweep of a tissue or clean cloth. A fixative spray prevents the recurrence of waxy buildup.

OIL-BASED PENCILS also deliver pigment smoothly, but they are not quite as creamy as wax-based pencils. They produce generous color with very little breakage and lay down pigment nicely, especially if used with a light touch. There is no wax buildup and little pencil debris. They sharpen well and last longer than wax-based pencils.

WATER-SOLUBLE PENCILS are essentially watercolor pencils that can be used wet or dry with impressive results. Many artists will create a watercolor base with these pencils, and then add dry detail with them. Backgrounds and foundational color for subjects can be accomplished quickly with water-soluble pencils.

STABILO® ALL pencils are water-soluble, and the Black and White ones have become staples in my artwork. The Black pencil yields extremely dark black pigment and becomes even blacker with the addition of water. When used with water and a small paintbrush, the White pencil enables me to paint bright highlights over my colored pencil layers.

Something to consider with your choice of colored pencil brand is its “lightfast” rating. This indicates how pigment may fade or change its hue over time when exposed to light. A pigment that is lightfast resists fading.

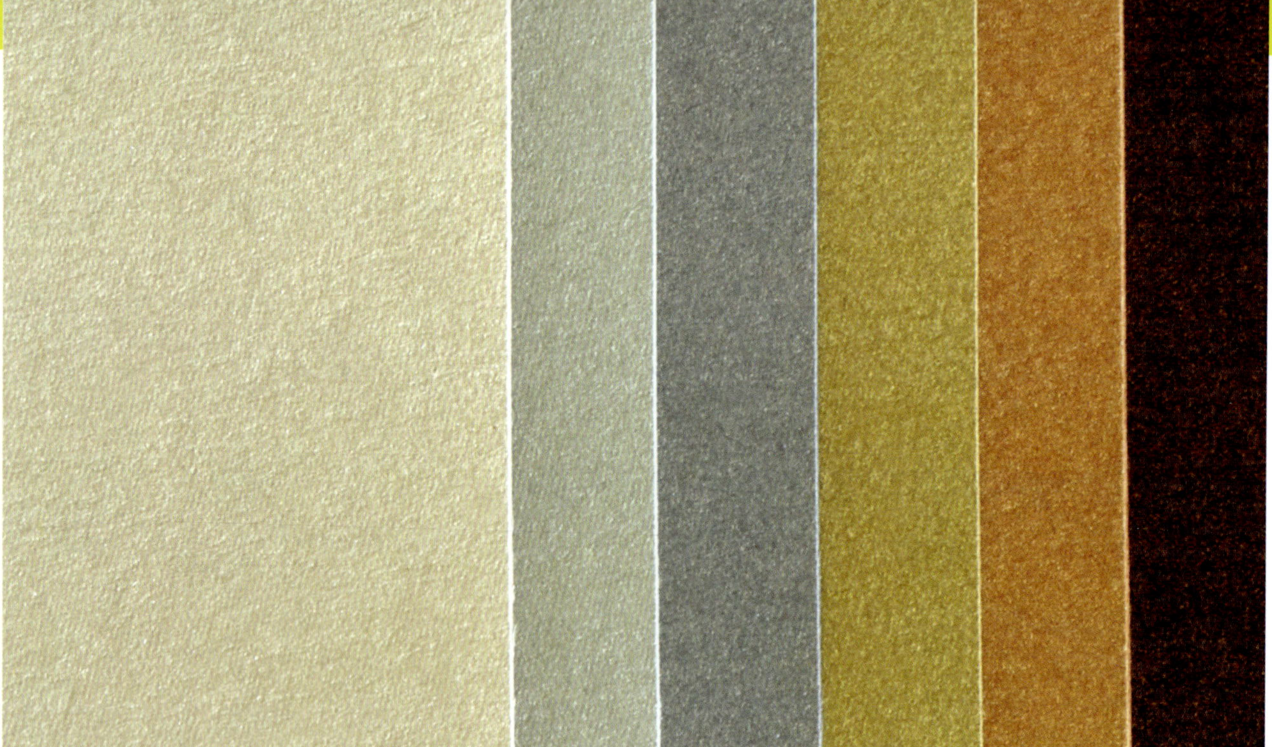

SURFACES

Colored-pencil artists work on everything from smooth white paper to grainy wood to create their works of art. There is a great deal of surface variety to choose from, and I'll briefly touch on the characteristics of a few favorites.

Paper textures are identified by their "tooth" and are primarily considered "hot pressed" or "cold pressed" based on how they are made. Tooth describes the little hills, valleys, and ridges that can be felt when you slide your finger across the surface.

HOT-PRESSED PAPER has very little tooth and a smooth texture. Strathmore® smooth Bristol paper is a hot-pressed paper and my personal favorite due to its sleek texture. Vellum Bristol has a bit more tooth and is also popular with colored-pencil artists.

COLD-PRESSED PAPER has more tooth and a discernible texture. Artists using water-soluble pencils enjoy cold-pressed paper for its ability to deposit pigment nicely within the variegated surface of the paper. Use light pencil pressure to convey a "drawn" look or firm pressure to flatten and depress the tooth and create a "painted" look. More paper tooth generally enables you to apply additional layers of pencil.

When working with paper, make sure to check out the brand's archival qualities. Archival paper is higher quality, durable, and acid-free, and it will stand the test of time. This is especially important if you are creating keepsake pieces or selling your artwork to clients.

Stonehenge paper is popular among many artists because of its smooth texture, affordability, and excellent archival properties. It can receive many layers of pencil.

Many artists today enjoy drafting film as a surface. Not only does its smooth texture offer luxurious pigment application, but both sides can be used for a more enhanced appearance to the artwork.

PASTELMAT® paper is available in pads with a range of gorgeous colors. The surface is smooth for easy application, yet it is comprised of cork grain, which ensures longevity. I have seen stunning people and animal portraits created on PASTELMAT, with the colored paper backgrounds complementing the colors within the artworks.

With suede mat board, pigment glides nicely over the velvety texture. Light pencil layers can be applied over darker ones without being affected by the deeper colors.

I recommend that you experiment with different surface types, colors, and textures to determine what works best for you with the colored-pencil brands that you have chosen.

PANPASTELS

PanPastel® products are containers of pressed pastel. When used with sponge applicators, their application is soft and smooth and covers a lot of territory in a short amount of time. I love how the different colors blend and have used them to establish dark backgrounds and base colors quickly.

> To apply colored pencils over the pastel pigment and still achieve a smoothly blended appearance, use White Prismacolor Premier first, and then work with the remaining colored pencils for smooth and even color transitions.

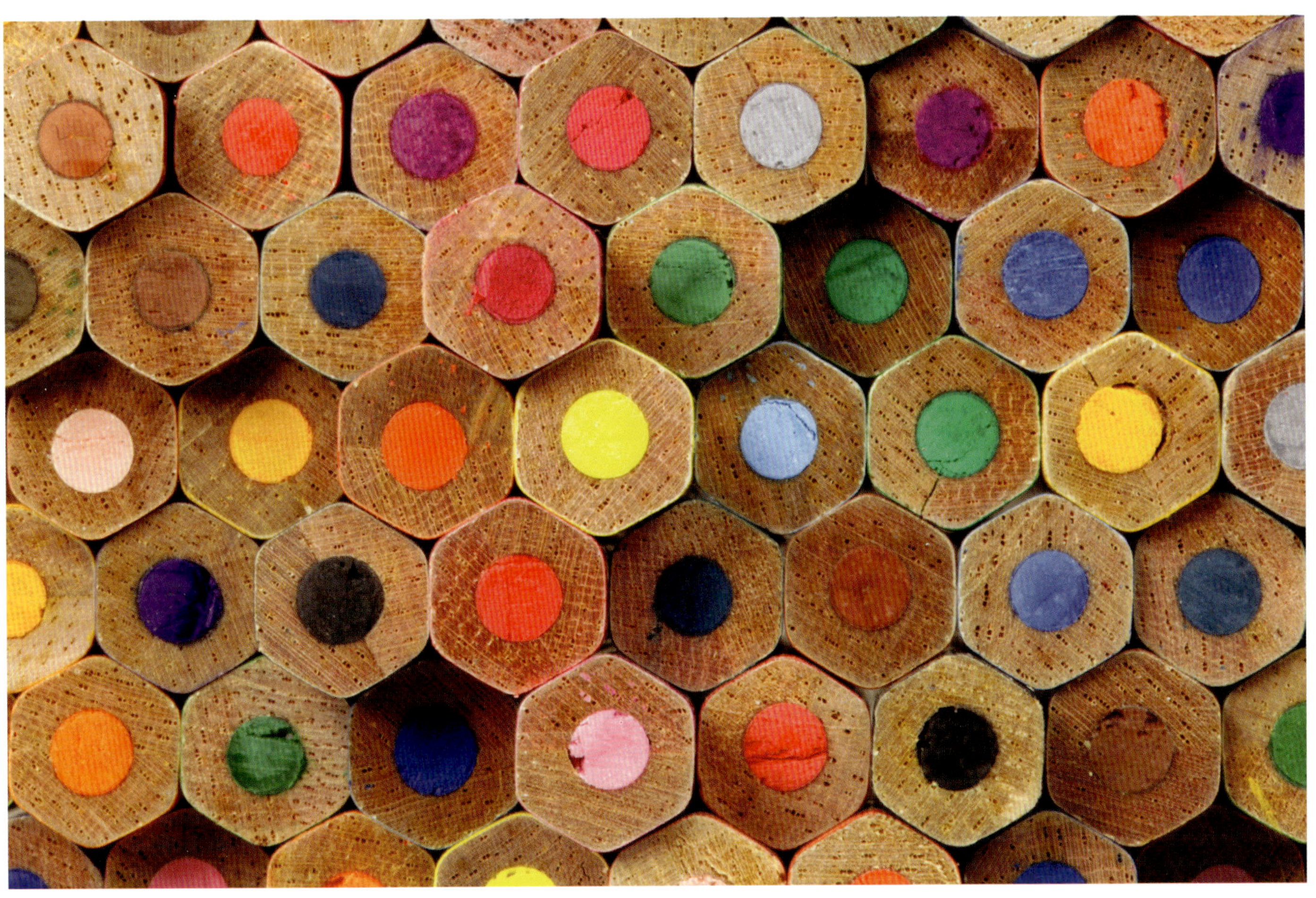

ADDITIONAL TOOLS

DRAWING BOARD My drawing setup is fairly simple. I sit in a comfortable recliner with a small table next to me that holds my pencils, sharpener, and a few other supplies. I tape my artwork to a portable drawing board with a sheet of blank, smooth Bristol paper taped under it to the board. You can find drawing boards in a variety of sizes at any art store and online. Mine has a handle for carrying, and I attach the photo reference I'm working from with a bulldog clip to the upper-left side of the board.

PENCIL SHARPENER A good sharpener is important to get a clean, sharp point. My personal preference is an electric X-ACTO® model that is heavy enough to stay put on my table while sharpening.

TIP

Sharpen a graphite pencil occasionally to reduce wax buildup.

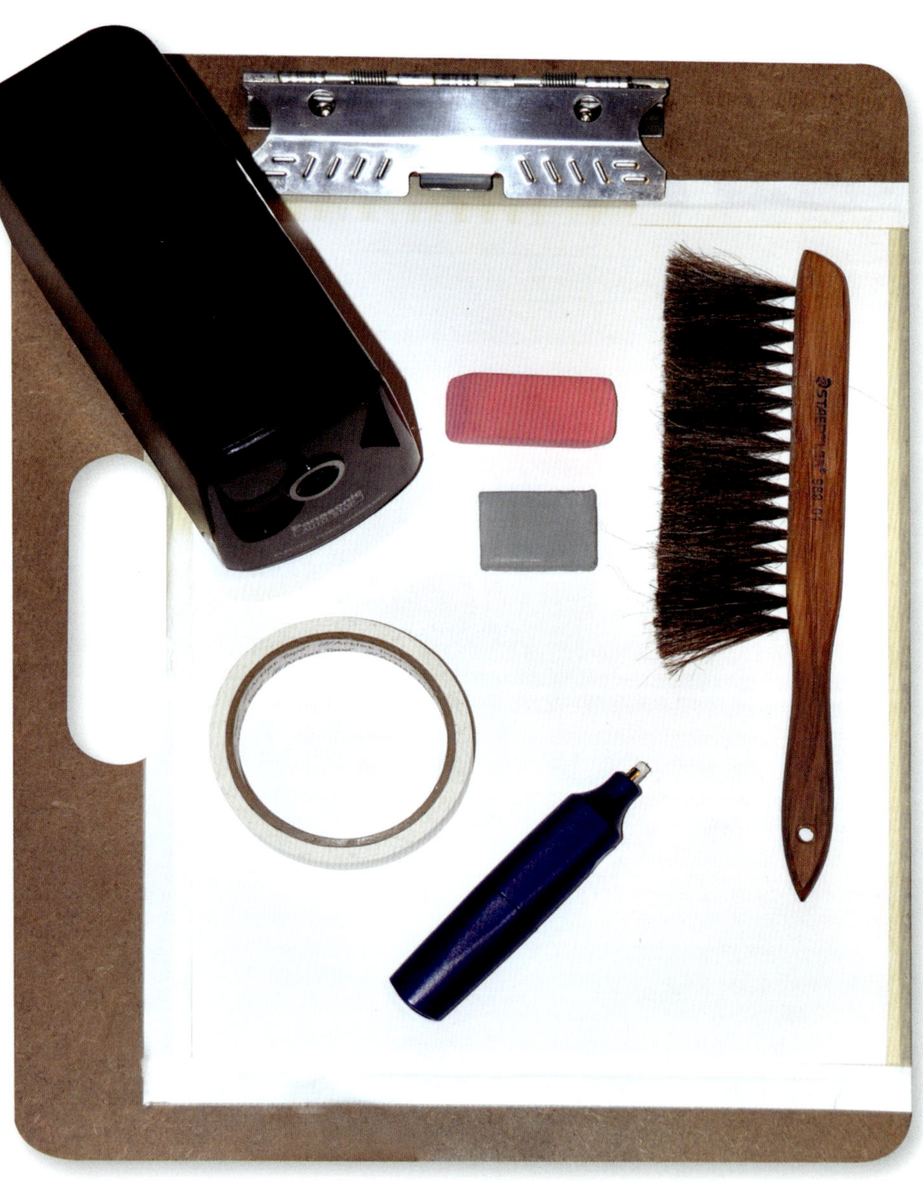

ERASERS Unlike graphite, colored-pencil pigment does not erase fully, especially after layers have built up; however, a few erasers can do a remarkable job. Pink and White Pearl® erasers are excellent for removing smudges and lifting one or two layers of colored-pencil pigment. Tombow® MONO Zero erasers are exceptional for erasing pigment within tight areas. Sometimes I'll "draw" with my eraser and lighten specific areas to create unique shapes. Lastly, battery-operated erasers are great for reducing color quickly and significantly. However, I recommend using these with caution because they can wear down the tooth of your paper or even rip right through it.

DRAFTING BRUSH It's important to sweep away the pencil dust left behind after sharpening and drawing. I use two soft-bristled drafting brushes made by Alvin® to keep my paper clean. I keep one next to my pencil sharpener and wipe newly sharpened pencil points across its bristles. The second one is next to my left hand and is used to sweep pencil crumbs off my working surface.

ARTIST TAPE Artist tape looks and applies like masking tape, but it is white and peels off easily without leaving anything behind. I tape all four sides of my smooth, blank Bristol cushion paper to my board with this tape, as well as my actual artwork over that. Peel the tape up slowly whenever removing your artwork from the board to ensure that no colored-pencil pigment comes up with it.

MOUNTING PUTTY & REUSABLE ADHESIVE These products are great for removing a few layers of color. To use, peel a section from the packaging and roll it into a ball. Then dab that ball against your colored-pencil surface with some pressure and observe how it lifts pigment. This can be done after many layers have been applied and you simply want to lighten an area, or to remove the last few undesired layers. It also works well for lifting specks of dirt, debris, or pigment off your paper without smudging.

PENCIL EXTENDERS As a pencil becomes shorter, these small holders allow you to get more life from the pencil, right down to the nub. They attach easily and will reduce your pencil expenses.

SPRAY FIXATIVE Spray fixatives seal your artwork while still allowing you to make color changes. They prevent smudging and wax bloom from occurring. Before using, gently remove any wax bloom with a tissue or soft cloth. Make a few test sprays to avoid any spitting; then hold the can about six inches from your artwork and spray in a smooth, horizontal motion. Repeat in a vertical motion. Be sure to do this outside, as fixatives are usually toxic.

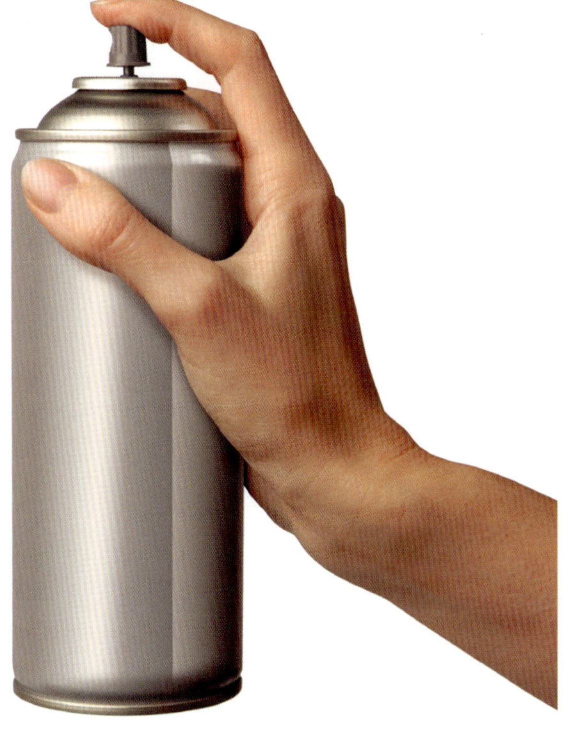

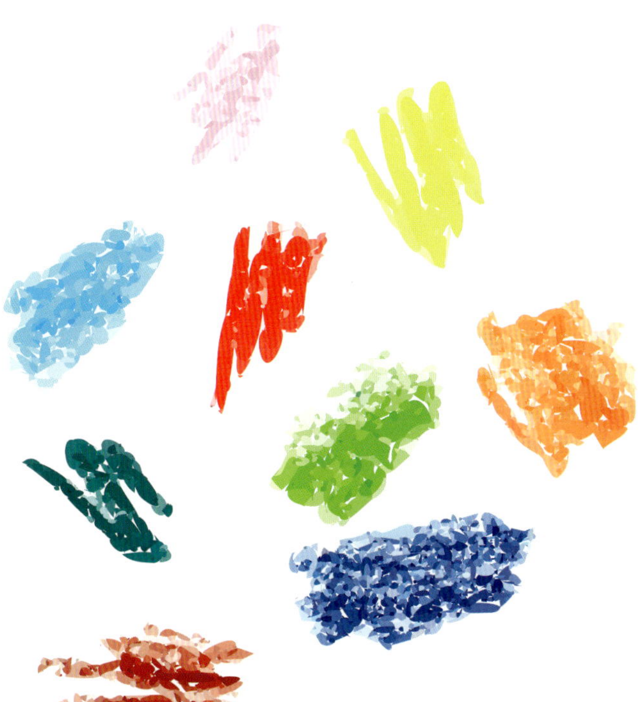

Techniques

Colored pencils are easy to work with, portable, and affordable, and they can produce a diverse mix of textures, color densities, and finished looks. If you prefer a looser, sketched look to your artwork, use cold-pressed paper (page 8) and bolder strokes with less layering to allow the paper surface to peek through. If you lean toward a more painterly appearance, choose hot-pressed paper (page 8), layer extensively, and apply firm pressure to achieve a polished finish.

With unlimited subject and style possibilities, colored-pencil artists can achieve stunning results with just a few techniques. We concern ourselves with pencil pressure, stroke direction, and color layering. It's really as basic as that! Pressure affects whether our artwork looks light and ethereal or glossy and polished. Strokes create texture and can suggest the dimpling of a lemon or the smoothness of a flower petal. Desired color and gorgeous results can be achieved by combining two or more pencils, even with a limited pencil palette. As you practice, you will determine your own style and technique.

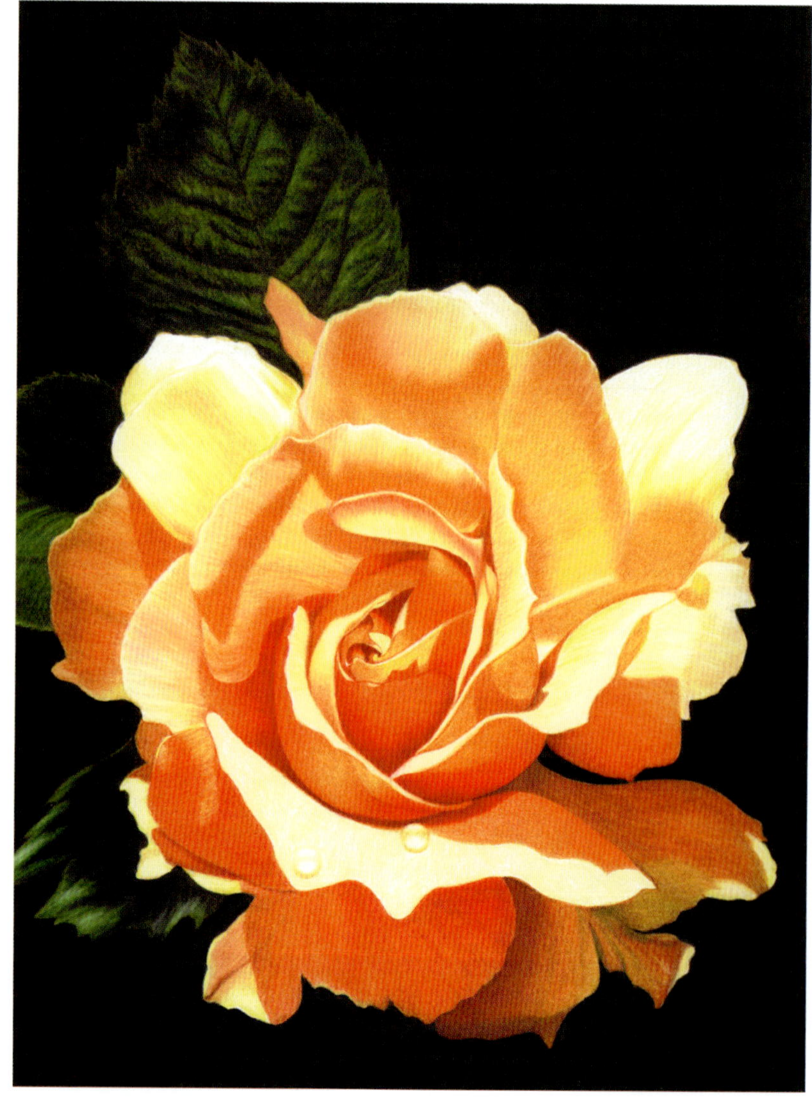

STROKES

There are several types of strokes for laying down color. How you hold your pencil and the direction of movement determine the outcome of your finished piece. The most popular strokes are rounded and linear.

I usually use rounded strokes, where I create rounded or elliptical circles in an overlapping manner with a sharp pencil point. As layers build up, you can achieve a smooth consistency without visible lines. This provides a foundation for establishing directional detail, such as leaf veins, pottery patterns, and raised fabric stitching.

Use horizontal, vertical, and diagonal strokes when a subject has a linear form. Examples include wood tables and backgrounds, stems arranged in a tall vase, and woven basket strips. To increase density, use techniques called "hatching" to place parallel lines and "crosshatching" to apply parallel lines over the initial set of lines. These two techniques help to quickly cover large blocks of paper with color.

When I begin a project, I use loose and directional strokes—rounded or linear. After applying a few layers of color, I focus on specific areas to bring forth detail and realism. My strokes become smaller, controlled, and more intentionally placed.

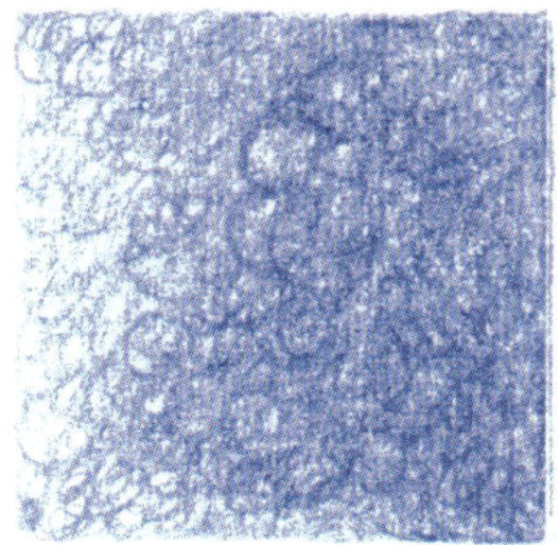

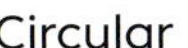

Circular

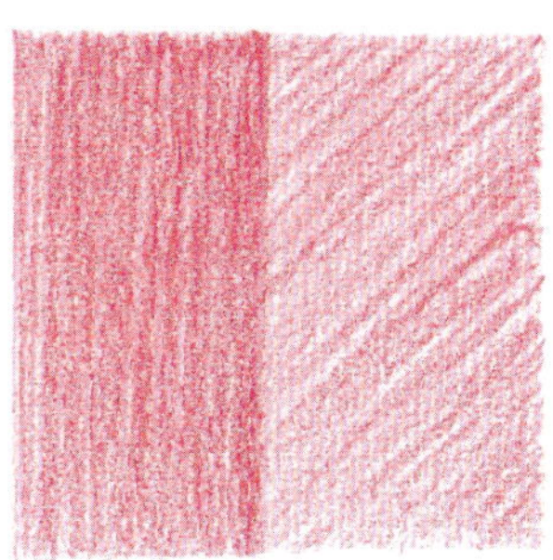

Linear

Hatching

PRESSURE

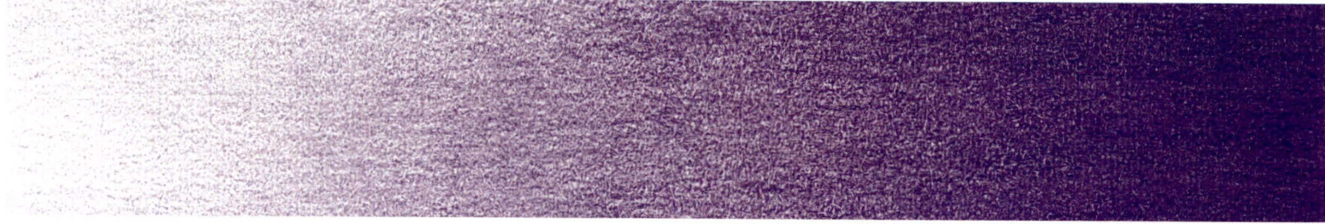

Pencil pressure will determine whether you create a colored-pencil drawing or a colored-pencil painting. If you consistently use light pressure, your finished piece will look soft and airy. Discernible strokes with some paper showing through contribute to a loosely drawn appearance. On the other hand, heavy pressure with lots of layering and burnishing will yield a painted look that many prefer.

You can initially control your color intensity by how firmly you press the pencil point into the paper's tooth. I recommend starting with a light to moderate touch and then increasing pencil pressure with additional layers. Final layers with firm pressure will create a burnished, painterly appearance, especially when the underlying paper is no longer visible.

PENCIL PRESSURE SCALE

In the tutorials in this book, I suggest pencil pressures for each stage using a scale from 1 to 5.

1: Lightest pressure is 1; your pencil point will skim the paper very lightly.
2: Moderate pressure is 2; this is how I usually begin my first few layers.
3: Medium pressure is 3 and similar to the pressure used when writing your name.
4: Firm pressure is 4 and used to blend all existing layers together with a top layer, resulting in a sleek and polished appearance.
5: Very firm pressure is 5 and used only when necessary to eliminate all underlying paper specks or to establish a very glossy finished layer.

Note that when using wax-based pencils, firm to very firm pressure often causes the point to break. I never worry about this and just continue using the dull side of the pencil to complete the section I'm working on. Additionally, a sharp, jagged point is excellent for "carving" through existing layers to establish markings such as vein lines, wood grain, fruit dimples, lace holes, distressed leather accents, and more.

TIP

To get the feel for applying color with increased pencil pressure, create a pressure bar using your favorite color. This will help you develop wrist control and a smooth progression from light to dark.

BLENDING & LAYERING

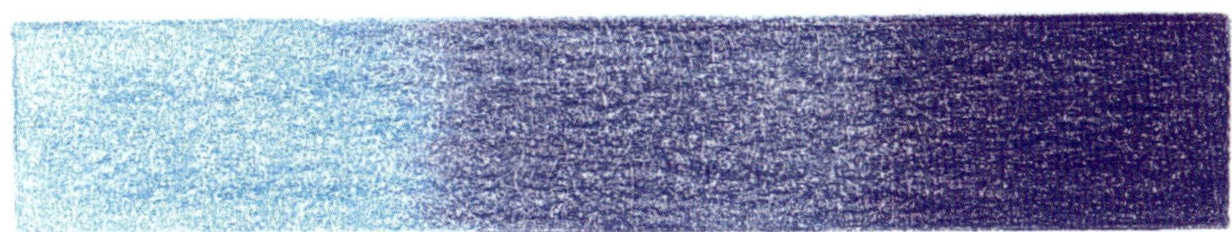

Layering & blending

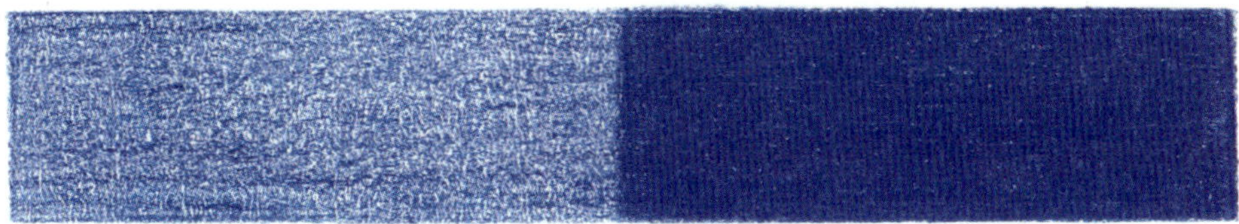

Blending & burnishing

While painters use a palette to mix their colors, colored-pencil artists apply one color on top of another to achieve desired shades and intensity. The more colors you use, the richer the outcome. For example, a combination of deep reds and purples with a touch of black will yield a densely rich, dark background with lovely color accents that are visible but not overpowering.

Depending on your pencil pressure, there may come a time when you are no longer able to apply pigment—the pencil point will simply skate across the layered surface. This usually happens toward the end of a project, but don't worry. Simply sharpen your pencil point and apply color diagonally across the area with light to moderate pressure. The pigment will adhere, and then you can add another layer or two to finish that section. This works especially well with darker pencils, such as deep reds, purples, blues, greens, and black.

Practice layering and blending by starting out with a rectangular bar shape. Fill it in with a solid color throughout. One-third of the way into it, layer the remaining two-thirds with a second color. Lastly, use another color for the last third. Use light to medium pressure at all times with consistent application. Compare the new colors to the original color of each pencil.

Practice blending and burnishing by filling in a bar with two layers of color and then applying a third color over the right side with firm pressure.

BURNISHING

Burnishing is my favorite technique because it transitions a drawing into a painting. This process is quite simple and involves the application of firm pencil pressure during the final steps of color layering. The firm pressure flattens the tooth of the paper and results in a lovely sheen over the finished area. The friction created by the firm pencil pressure warms up the existing pigment and melds underlying layers together beautifully. If there are enough layers on the paper, this technique can even coax the pigment to spread out a bit, similar to moving oil or acrylic around on a surface. I have found that the White Prismacolor Premier pencil delivers the magic for me during this process.

Typically, I will establish three to four layers of color in an area with moderate to medium pressure. Then I burnish with my White Prismacolor pencil using firm pressure. At this point, I know I'm close to finished and will then restore color with a few more pencil layers and light to moderate pressure.

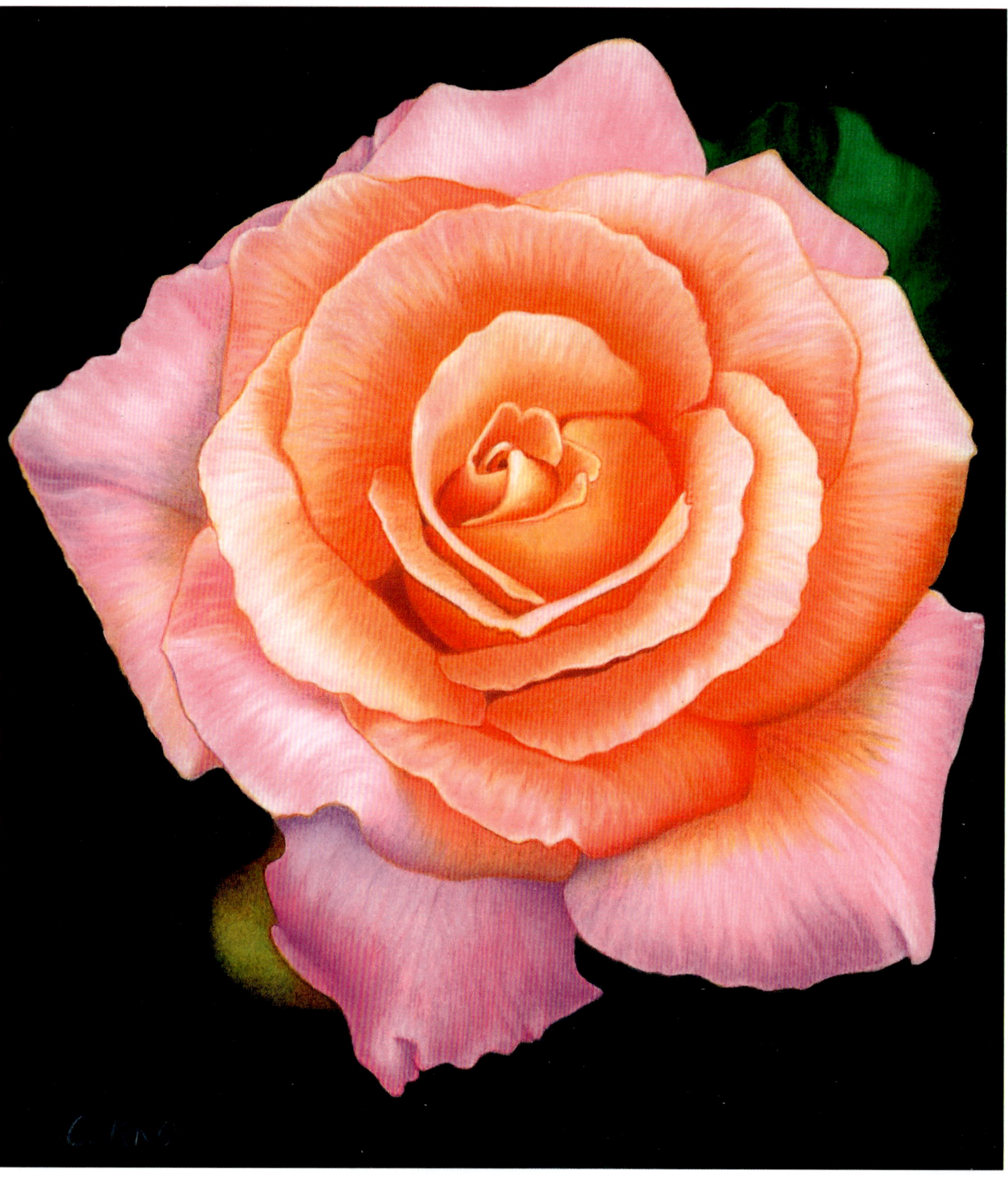

Here, I used white to burnish in the light areas and blend overall.

WATERCOLOR EFFECTS

Water-soluble pencils can create traditional colored-pencil pieces when used dry, as well as loose, watercolor pieces when mixed with water. The simplest technique is to lay down several layers of dry color from a pencil, and then lightly add water with a small brush. Instead of oversaturating your brush at once, build color with repeated brushings. After the area dries, you can restore color and add detail with dry color application.

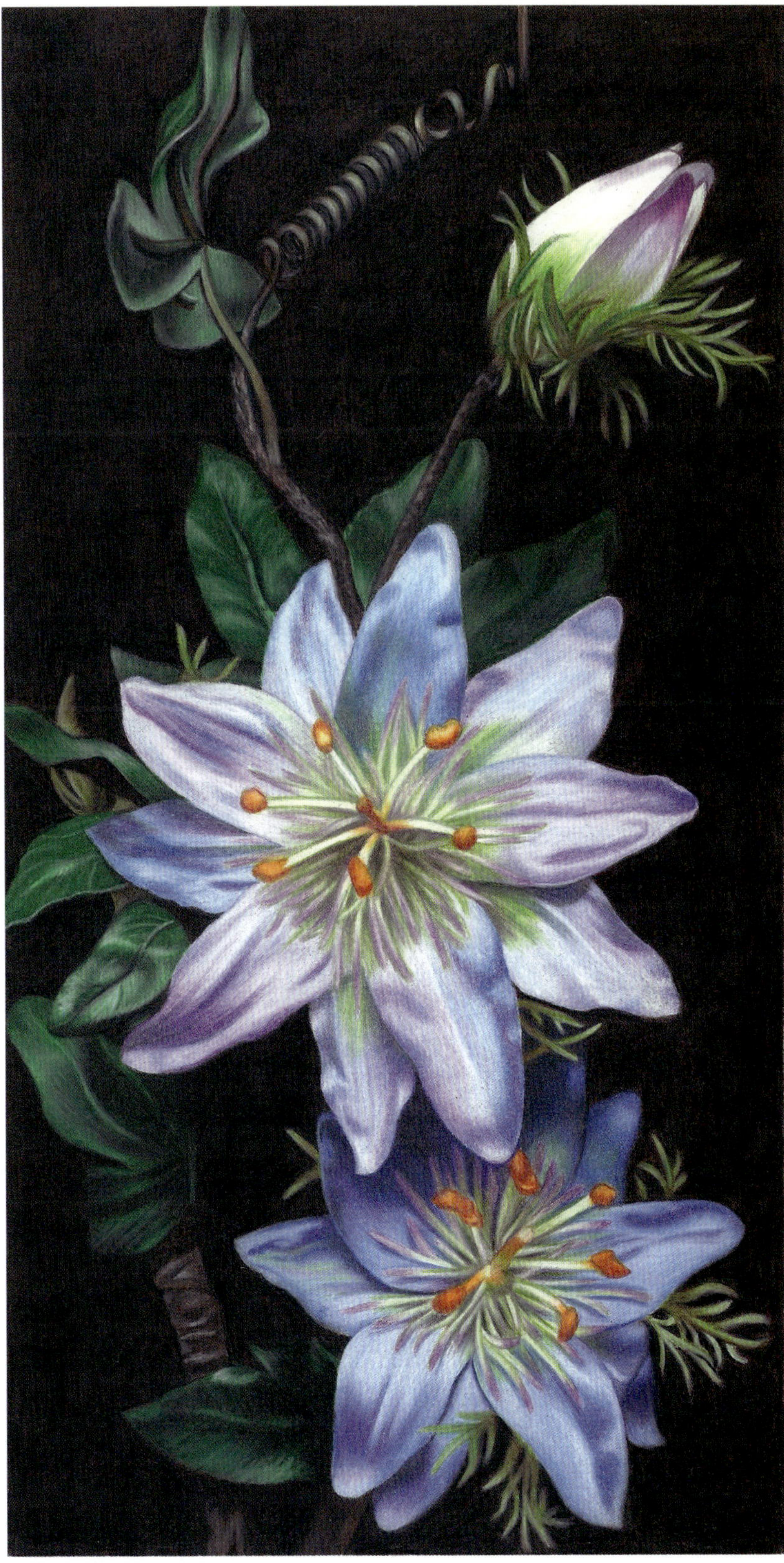

Wax- and oil-based pencils can also create watercolor effects with the use of solvents and brushes, which blend and smooth pigment nicely. I prefer odorless mineral spirits (OMS) over household oils, such as baby oil or vegetable oil, for the integrity and longevity of my artwork. OMS products are safe to use but should be handled with caution to avoid spilling. Solvent blender pens can be effective when applied over smaller sections of pigment. Always test a product on sample swatches of your surface.

DETERMINING VALUES & SELECTING COLORS

Often when selecting a reference photo, I will observe the values—lights and darks—of the entire visual. Is it overly dark in its presentation? That lends itself to a dramatic and moodier finished artwork. Perhaps it is light and airy with few dark shadows. This is more uplifting and conveys a happy, joyful sense of well-being. Maybe there is a nice balance within the value spectrum and there are dark shadows, attractive midtones, and bright highlights.

This decision is made instinctively when looking at potential project photos. Values can be observed easily when you squint your eyes. You can quickly see the darks, midtones, and highlights, and a simple technique explained at the end of this section will ensure your accuracy in conveying these values.

Value viewers help you select colored pencils to match your photo references.

This book includes moodier projects with deep colors and dark backgrounds, as well as brighter projects with pastel colors and light backgrounds. While you are probably attracted to some more than others, I encourage you to observe the different value shifts throughout all of them.

Along with value determination comes color selection. I am often asked how I figure out which pencils to use and in what order to layer them. Is there an actual formula? Are there many options or just a few to create the colors observed in the photo reference? Do I use one brand of pencil or a few?

Value viewers, or two small pieces of white card stock about two inches long with a hole punched in the middle, immediately reveal the photo's value and color in each subject. First, I place one value viewer over an area of color in my photo. Then I choose three to four pencils and layer them onto a sheet of practice paper to somewhat resemble what I'm seeing in the photo. Next, I place the second value viewer over my swatch to see how the color matches up to the color isolated in the photo. I keep playing with the color combinations on my scrap paper until it similarly matches the colors in my photo. Then I write down the pencil names in the order that I used them.
I continue this process until I have identified all of the pencils I need to complete the project.

COLOR REMOVAL

With the initial application or two of an undesired color, you can erase pigment and layer new color over that area with little to no problem. Use firm pressure with your eraser and the pencil replacing the color. You can also lift undesired color with a dab of rolled mounting putty/reusable adhesive or tape (see page 11).

After several layers are down and I realize that I have made a more serious mistake—either with the shape of an object, color choice, or placement of detail—I will use my Prismacolor Premier White pencil and very firm pressure to burnish over the undesired section. This effectively erases that area.

If the area is small, use the sharp point with precision to lift color. These techniques will whiten or lighten the area so well that you can apply new color or detail with absolutely no trouble. Of course, the pencil point may break during the process, but the broken tip works perfectly to push even more white pigment into the affected area. Then you can finish that area with new color or detail choices. The more layers of existing pigment you have, the easier it is to lift undesired color with the White pencil and begin again. It doesn't work well with only one or two layers of color down; use an eraser for that.

If absolutely nothing is working, use your battery-operated eraser with caution or make an artistic change to your piece, such as adding a shadow or new detail in that area. Perhaps you have a strange-looking mark on a piece of pottery that just won't come up? Try darkening the pottery overall or randomly place similar marks over the pottery to create a pattern. Think outside the box!

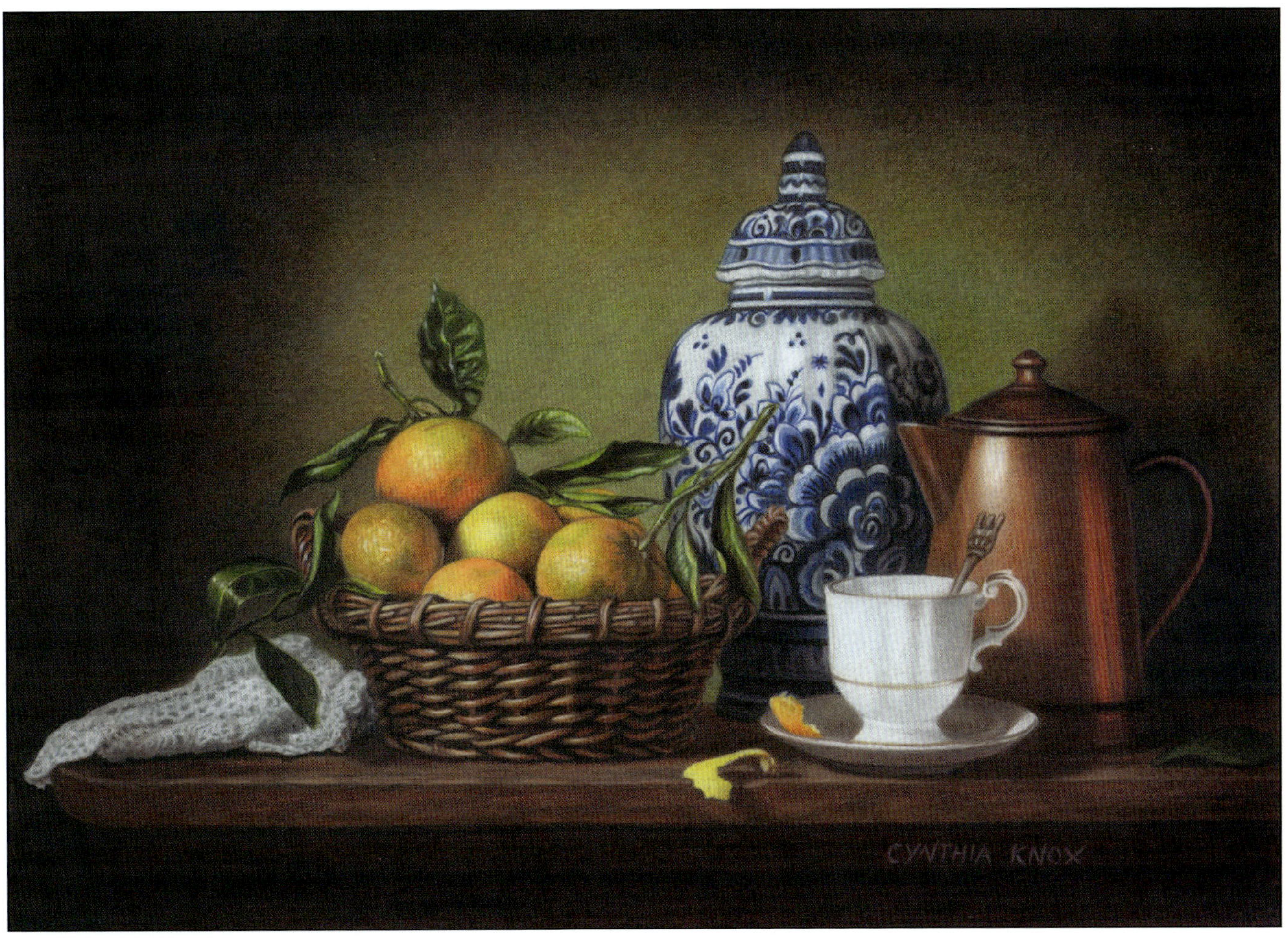

Color Basics

Colored pencils are transparent by nature, so instead of "mixing" colors as you would for painting, you layer colors on top of one another to create blends. Knowing a little about basic color theory can help you tremendously in drawing with colored pencils.

The primary colors (red, yellow, and blue) are the three basic colors that can't be created by mixing other colors; all other colors are derived from these three. Secondary colors (orange, green, and purple) are each a combination of two primaries, and tertiary colors (red-orange, red-purple, yellow-orange, yellow-green, blue-green, and blue-purple) are a combination of a primary color and a secondary color.

COLOR WHEEL

A color wheel is a useful reference tool for understanding color relationships. Knowing where each color lies on the color wheel makes it easy to understand how colors relate to and react with one another.

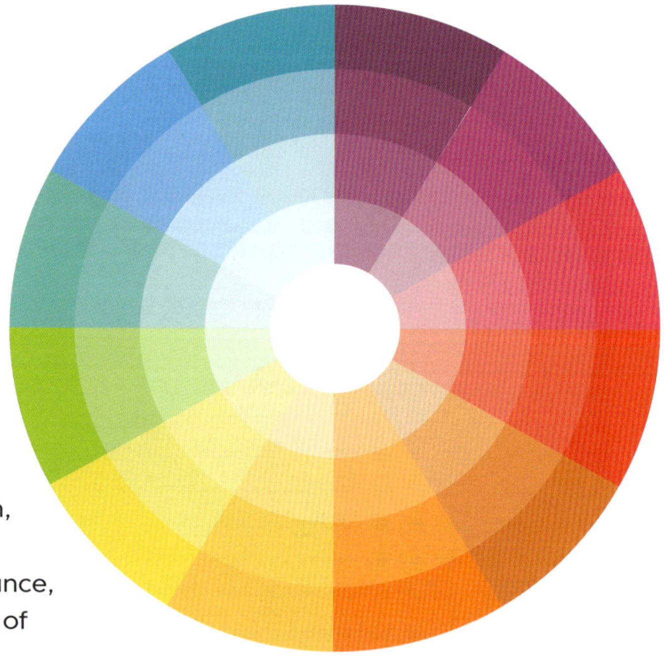

COMPLEMENTARY COLORS

Complementary colors are any two colors directly across from each other on the color wheel (such as red and green, orange and blue, and yellow and purple). You can see combinations of complementary colors in nature—for instance, if you look at white clouds in a blue sky, you'll notice a hint of orange in the clouds.

USING COMPLEMENTS

When placed next to each other, complementary colors can create lively, exciting contrasts. Using a complementary color in the background will cause your subject to seemingly "pop" off the paper. For example, you could place bright orange poppies against a blue sky or draw red berries amid green leaves.

COLOR PSYCHOLOGY

Colors are often referred to in terms of temperature, which can be understood by thinking of the color wheel divided into two halves: The colors on the red side are warm, and the colors on the blue side are cool. Colors with more red or yellow in the them appear warmer, and colors with more green or blue in them appear cooler. For instance, if a normally cool color (like green) has more yellow added to it, it will appear warmer. If a warm color (like red) has a little more blue, it will seem cooler. Another important point to remember about color temperature is that warm colors appear to come forward and cool colors appear to recede; this knowledge is valuable when creating the illusion of depth in a scene.

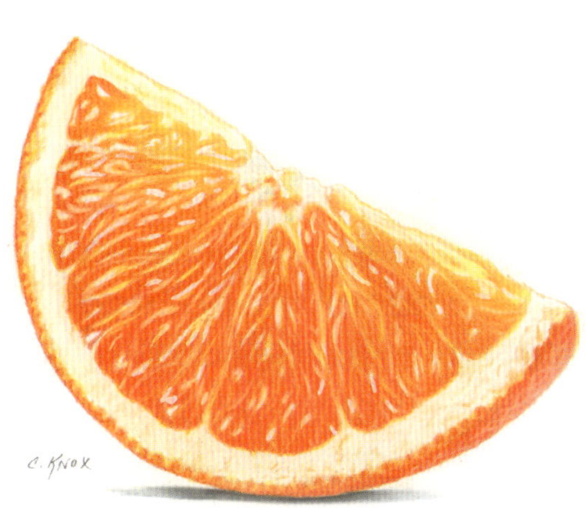

Warm

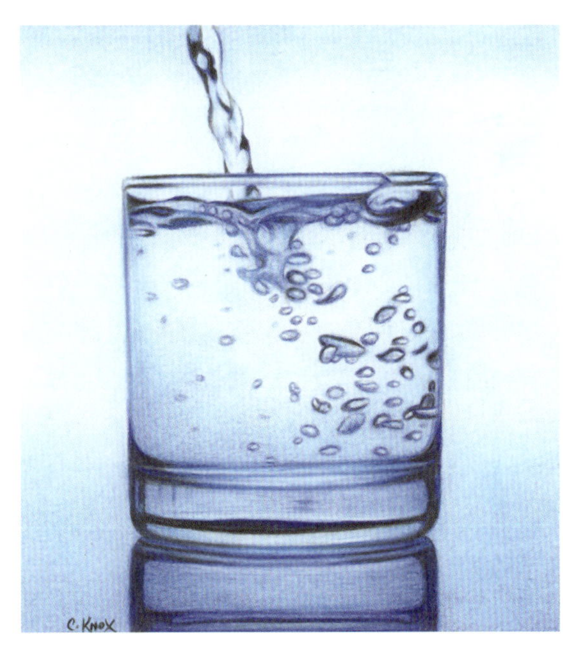

Cool

TINTS, SHADES & TONES

Colors can be tinted with white to make them lighter, shaded with black to make them darker, or toned with gray to make them more muted. Here each color was applied using graduated pressure—light, then heavy, then light. Black was applied at the top and white at the bottom to tone and tint the colors, respectively. To tint a color without muting it, apply the white first and then the color.

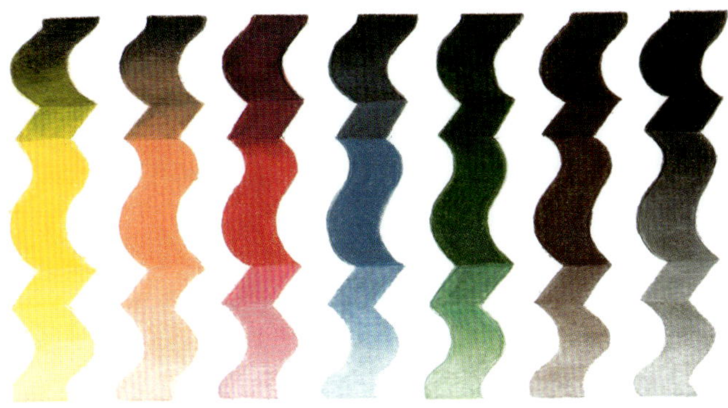

Creating a Pleasing Composition

From an artistic perspective, "composition" refers to the placement or arrangement of objects to convey a theme, message, or mood. There are various factors to consider when creating a still-life composition or choosing a still-life photograph to work from.

In my earlier days of working with colored pencils, I frequented antique shops and specialty stores to find just the right china, glassware, patterned scarf, and flowers to create a beautiful still-life setup. Sometimes I would ask a silk-flower expert to fashion a unique arrangement, and then I would pair it with a special teapot and lovely piece of linen or lace. My photography skills were sufficient that I could take a respectable photo, and then work from that to create what I hoped would become a masterpiece.

When I began working with Walter Foster Publishing to author instructional art books, I was introduced to the stock-photo world. It was a huge treat to be invited to peruse galleries of superb images and then encouraged to create tutorials from a few of them. That still brings me joy, and I have combined my love of photography with my enthusiasm for viewing online photos to share some favorite artworks (old and new) with you in this book.

Here are some considerations to keep in mind when selecting a successful still-life composition.

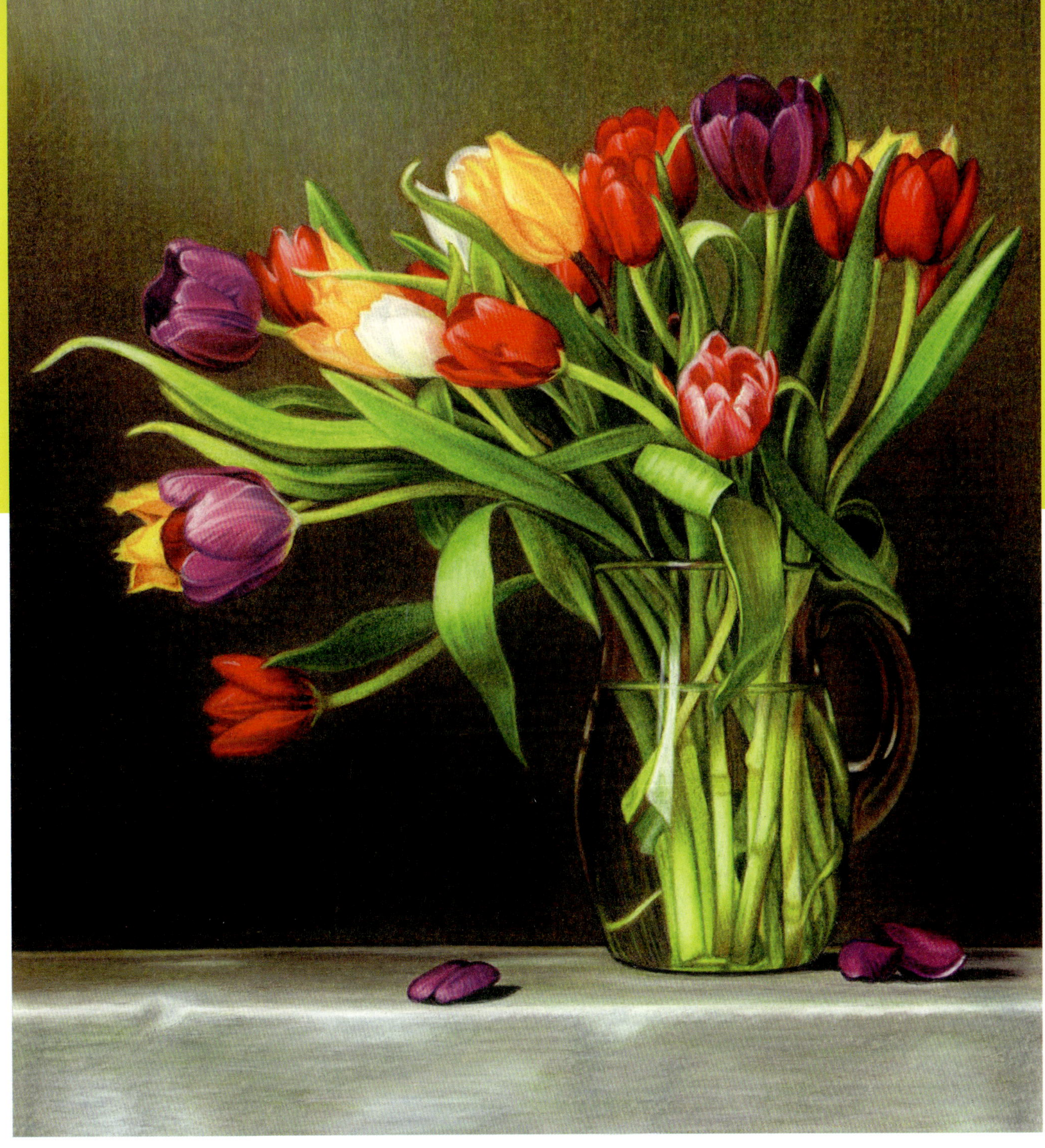

THEME Determine the theme or message that you want to convey to your viewers. Are you interested in exotic flowers, plants, or foods? Perhaps you love antiques and want to juxtapose charmingly aged objects against sparkling new ones. Nautical and beach themes delight vacationers, and shells with a blue and white color palette are quite popular in seaside communities. I am particularly fond of floral and fruit themes with colorful and abundant flower bouquets. I also favor unique containers, vibrantly colored fruits, and attractive fabrics.

COLOR SCHEME Color choices affect the mood of an artwork. Bright and bold jewel tones with vivid hues suggest drama and excitement. Earth tones, neutral colors, and authentic outdoor objects can be used to create a soothing or striking nature composition. Pastel colors and whimsical objects are perfect for lighthearted compositions that encourage viewers to smile. Color patterns are important as well. Monochromatic color schemes are often used for simplicity or to make a statement, and complementary color schemes create impact and contrast even though we may not know why. Consider your color choices carefully; they may be even more important than your theme or the objects you use within the composition.

COMPONENTS & PLACEMENT What and how many objects will you use to create your composition? Are they similar in size or is there a height range? Will you place them equidistant apart or weight the composition in one primary area to convey visual tension? An appealing arrangement involves a triangular structure. This creates balance, height, and visual appeal. It doesn't have to look like a pyramid; a loose triangular presentation works well and can include symmetrical or asymmetrical objects.

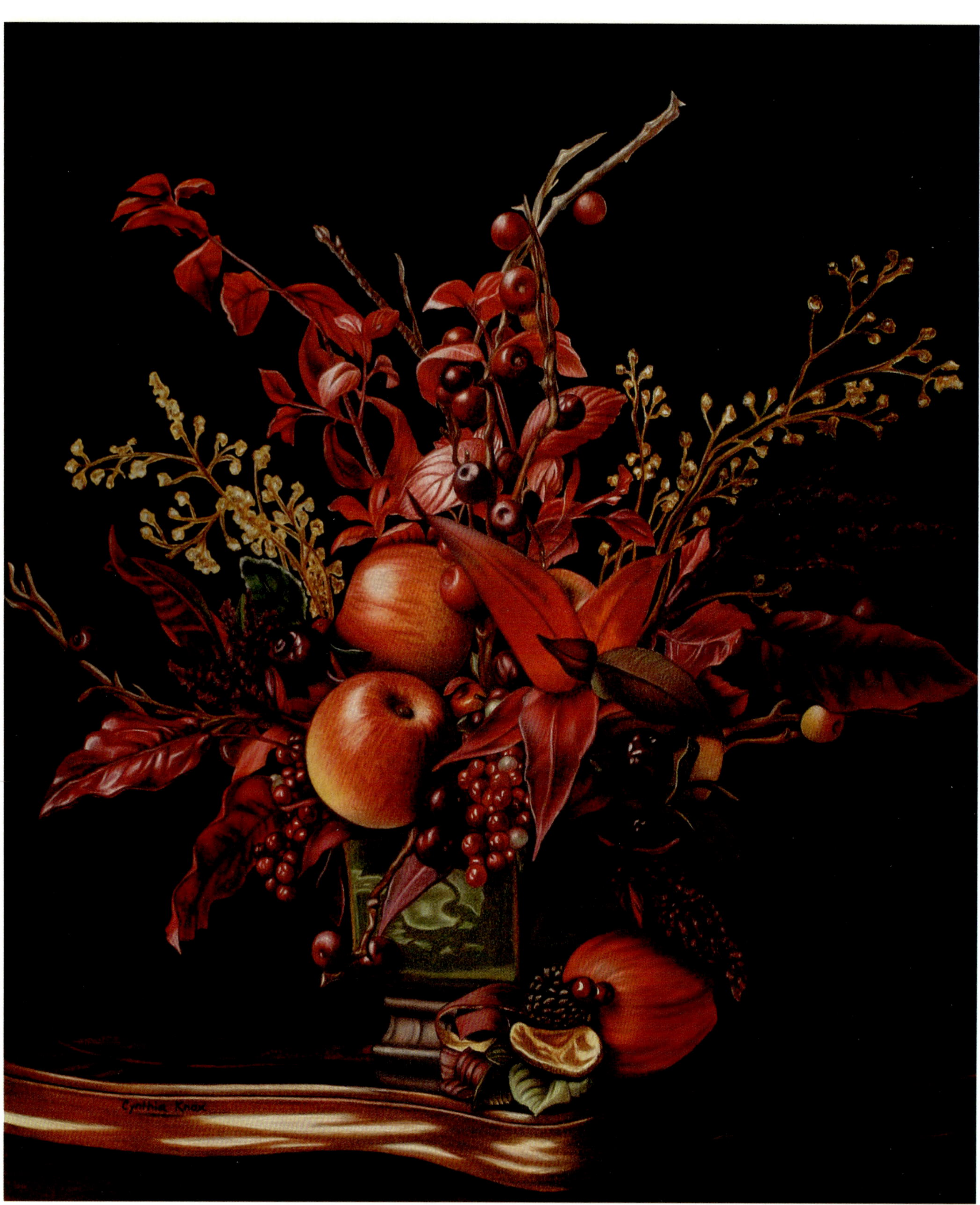

FOCAL POINT Often, the theme or message of a still-life composition is communicated through one focal point. Our eye is drawn to that focal point, and we contemplate its value in relation to the entire setup. The remaining objects near or around it serve as props to stage the primary subject.

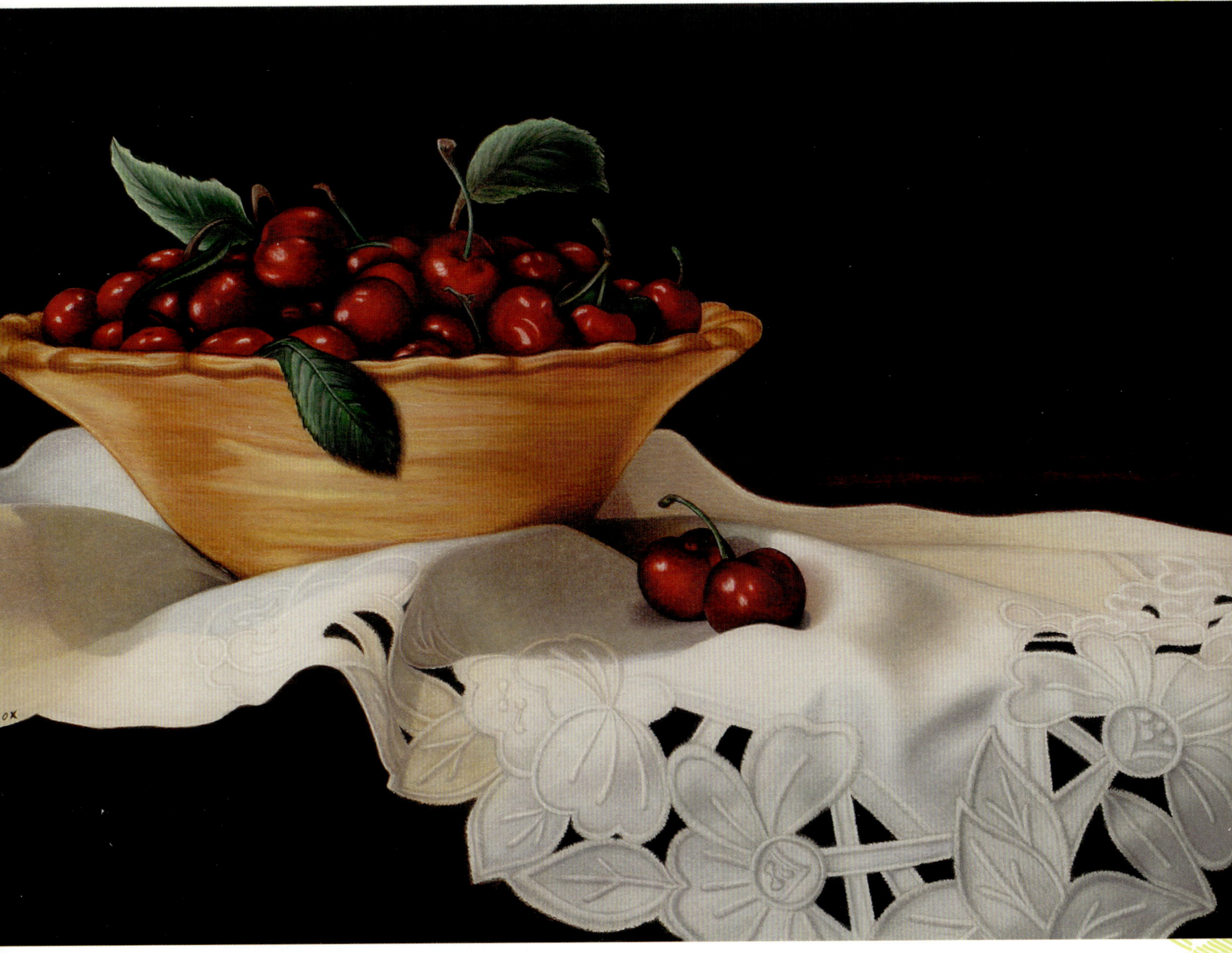

LIGHTING Without attractive lighting, your still life will appear dull and flat. Sometimes this is addressed with an overall wash of general light that brightens almost everything in the composition, or perhaps a singular beam of light is used to draw the viewer's eye to one section of the still life. The direction of light is important too. Front lighting illuminates a subject straight on. Sidelighting creates a three-dimensional appearance and emphasizes texture and object forms. Backlighting produces spectacular glowing effects that dramatically rim components within the setup. Diffused lighting is soft without bleached highlights or harsh shadows and flatters object hues. You can use indoor or outdoor light when arranging your still life, and I encourage you to try both.

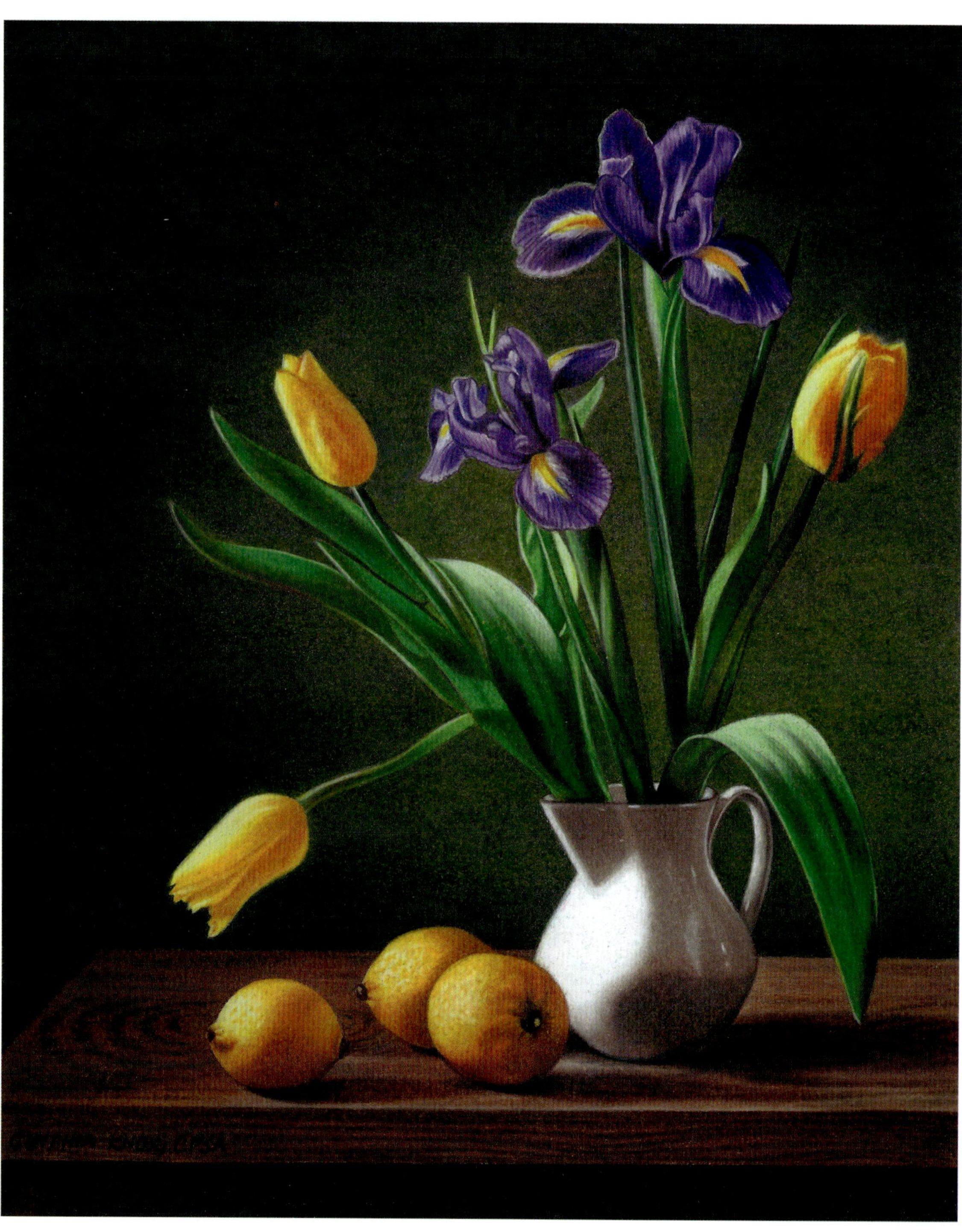

VISUAL PERSPECTIVE Are viewers looking up, down, or directly at your still life? The most common perspective is from eye level; however, the other two angles can also be impressive when done correctly. Remember that objects in the back may appear to be smaller than they are, and objects in the immediate front will often appear larger.

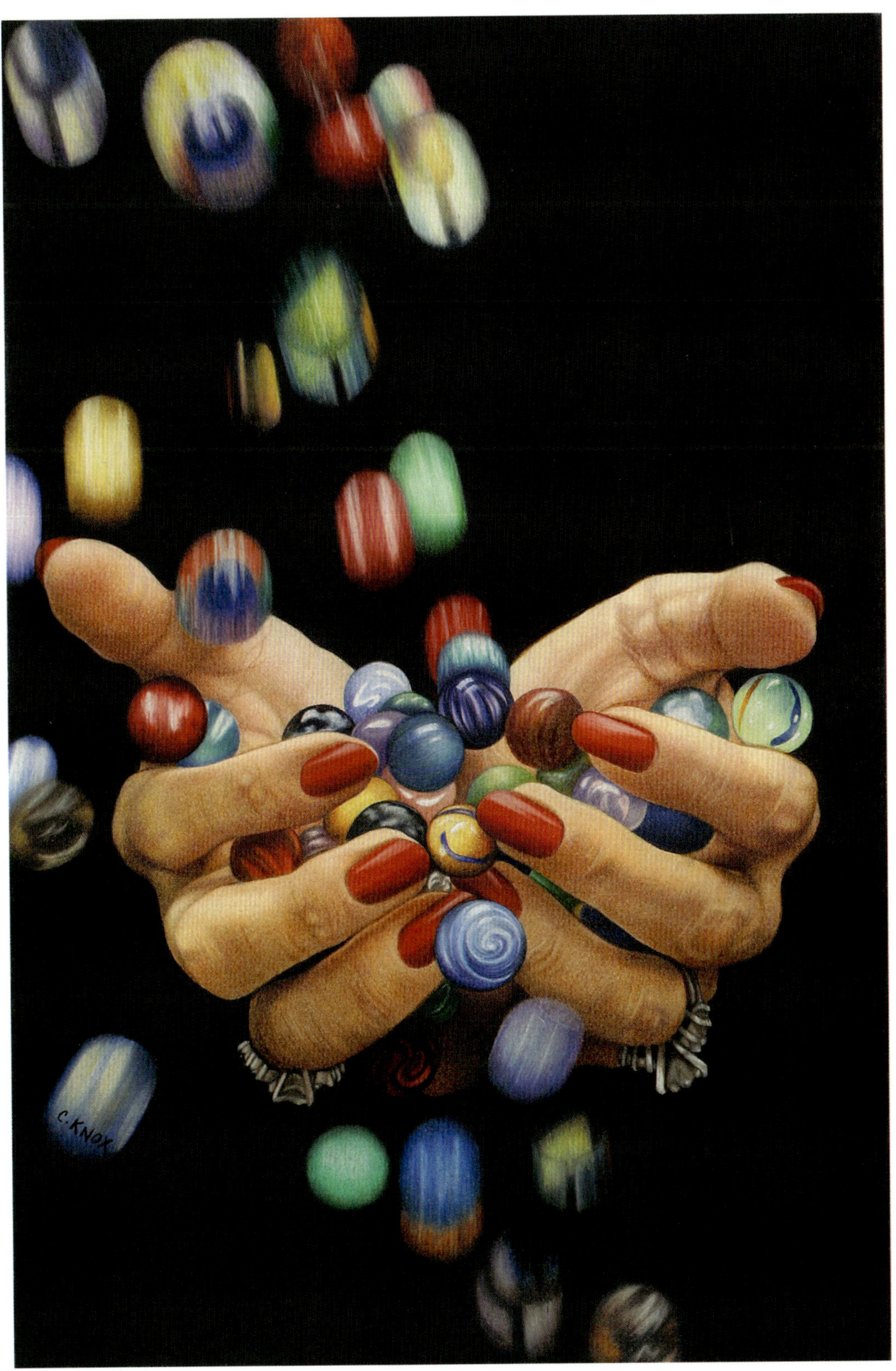

DETAIL How complex would you like your still-life composition to be? Will you include objects with patterns, fabrics with repetitive textures, or baskets with many woven strips? While still-life artworks are rarely considered simple, they may be viewed as simplistic. This means that they are uncluttered with only a few objects, significant space, and an uncomplicated color scheme. With respect to detail, I personally prefer more versus less because it adds interest and presents technical challenges to me.

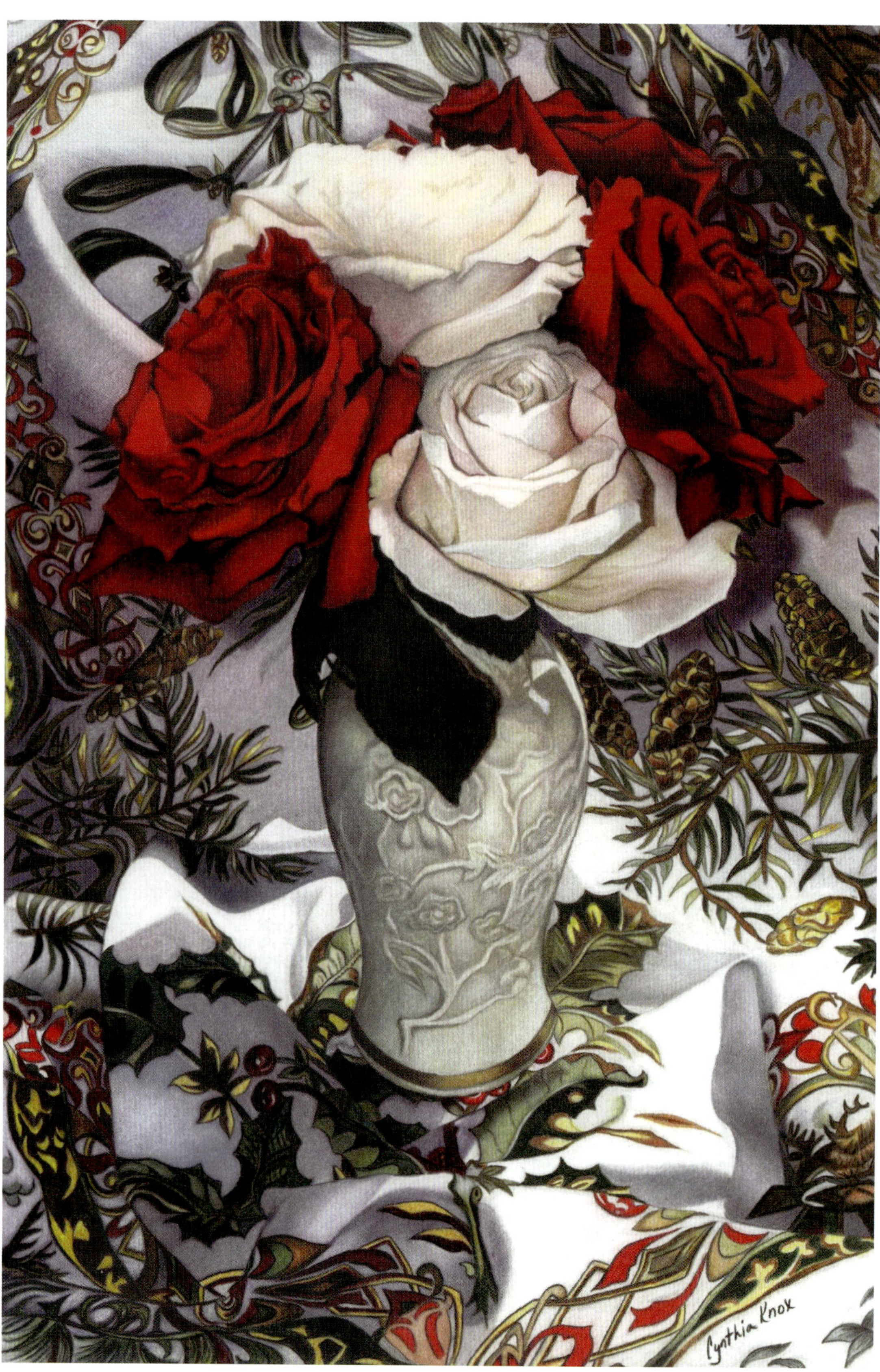

BACKGROUND & FOREGROUND Will you choose a monochromatic backdrop for your composition, detailed and focused staging, or blurring with the suggestion of other background objects? Perhaps you like a wood foreground with every knot and grain rendered in detail or, conversely, a shadowed and faded surface in the front. Many of my still lifes feature wood or concrete surfaces, and I favor sidelighting. This means that there is grain or chipped detail evident in the illuminated areas—back and front—and only a mere suggestion of detail in the shadows.

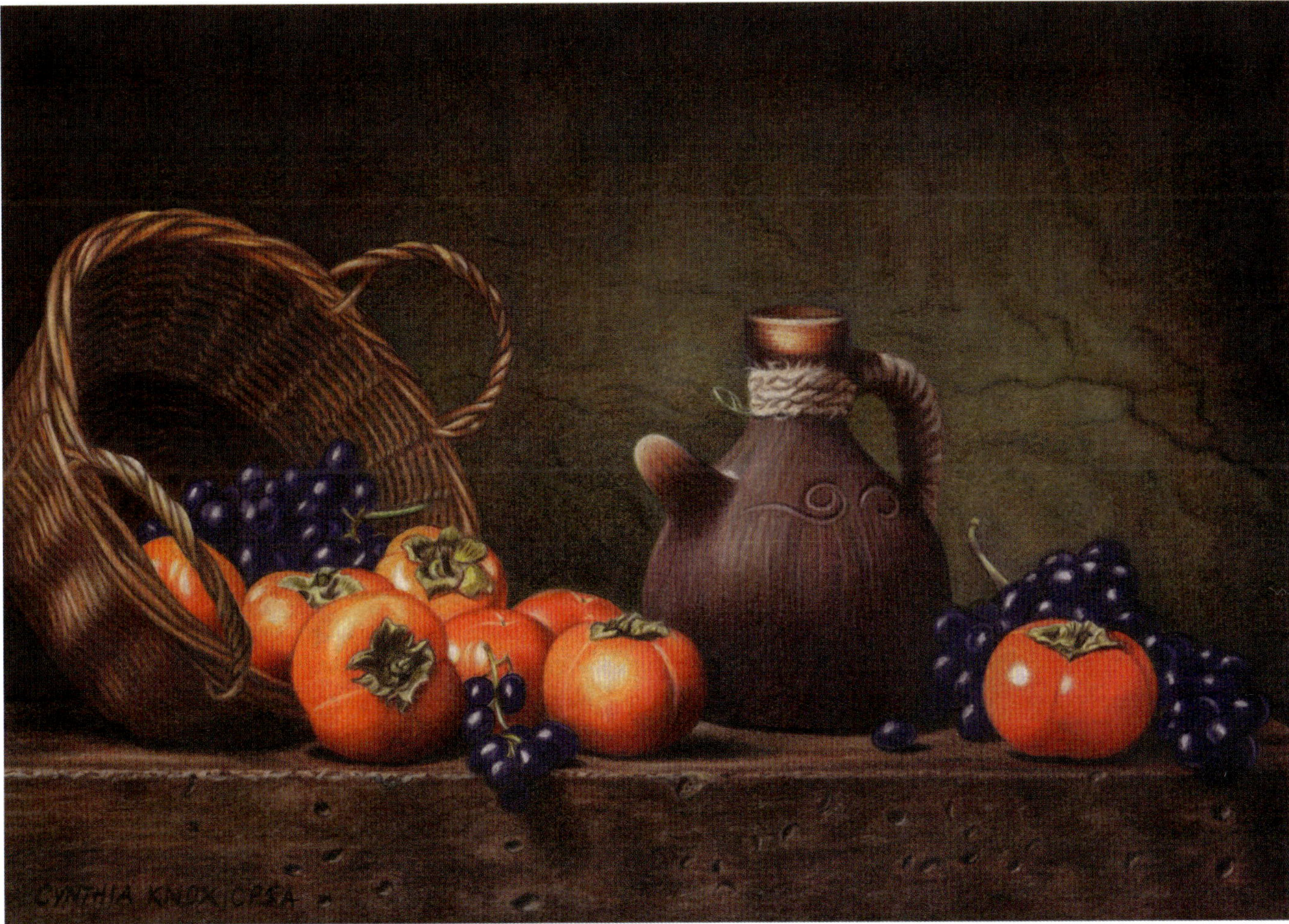

The considerations for creating pleasing compositions can be overwhelming, and I understand that. My best advice is to go on a stock-photo or other social-media site like Pinterest™ or Instagram™ and do a search for still-life images. Notice what appeals to you and determine why. Then incorporate those particulars into your next photo session or look specifically for them when reviewing others' pictures to draw or paint from. This will help define your unique and individual style as you create your own portfolio of still-life artwork.

Working from Photographs

Like many artists, I prefer to use photos to create my still-life artworks. This works best for me because flowers and fruit have a relatively short life, and I'm a slow artist. When using photo references, you'll need to make several decisions, and I'll briefly address them here.

TAKING THE PHOTO If you decide to use your own camera and set up the still life yourself, congratulations! That's often the hardest part of the creative process. Factors to consider include composition, lighting, and backdrop, and you'll want to take photos from different angles to determine the optimal perspective. Familiarity with your lens and camera controls is important, specifically when focusing and choosing your settings. I prefer to dial in my camera's aperture priority mode to alternate between a crisp background and a blurred one. This mode works with the camera's "F-stop" settings. The lower the number, the softer and blurrier the area around your focal point, including the background and foreground. As you select the desired F-stops, your camera will automatically adjust the other elements to create different yet pleasing photos.

CHOOSING THE PHOTO If you have taken your own photo, you're all set and don't need to be concerned about copyright and permissions. However, if you are using another photographer's photo, be sure to get documented permission to use that image, including payment receipt. My publishers and I are comfortable working with stock-photo sites where there are clear stipulations and reasonable pricing. There are also copyright-free photo sites on the Internet. Make sure to comply with their rules.

EXAMINING THE PHOTO Now that you have identified the photo for your artwork, ask yourself a few questions. Is the quality good enough so that an enlargement will be clear and not pixelated? Is all of the detail crisp and manageable to draw? Are the colors and lighting attractive? Show your photo to a few trusted people and ask if it impacts them as much as it did you. Listen to what they say, and hopefully their excitement will match yours and you can move forward.

EDITING THE PHOTO I have rarely encountered the perfect photo and usually make a few minor corrections using Adobe® Photoshop® Elements, including brightening and contrasting color, sharpening blurry edges, cloning out undesirable elements, and cropping for a tighter composition. Then I save it in my computer and print out a couple copies on quality photo paper.

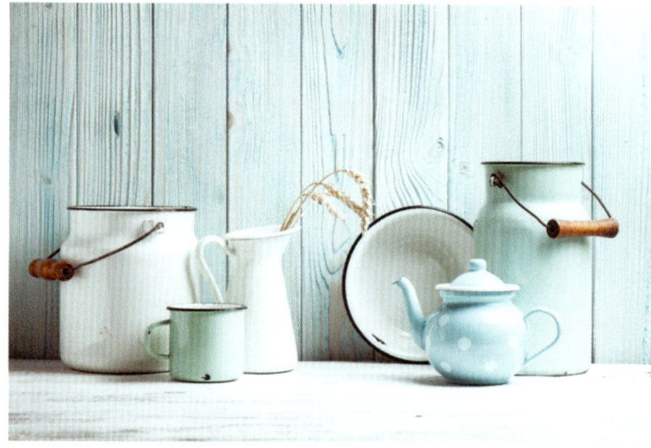

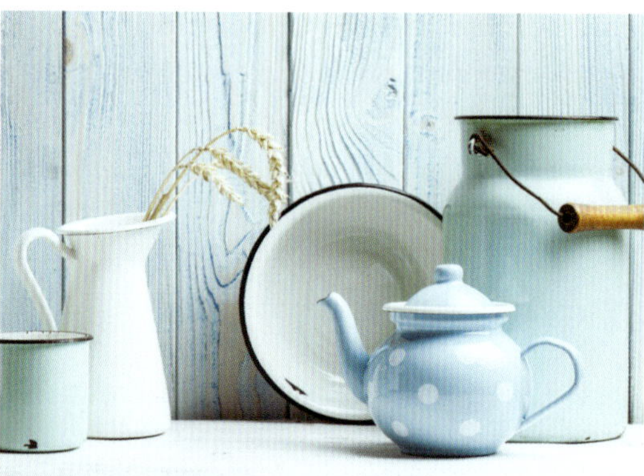

Here I cropped the original image, cloned the left side, darkened slightly, added contrast, and enhanced the blue color.

PRINTING THE PHOTO I recommend using a large photo for visual ease and detail clarity. I attach one photo to my drawing board with a bulldog clip on the left side so that the photo is in front of me as I draw. I study the second photo in my spare time when I'm not working on the project. The more I look at the image, the greater its impression becomes in my mind. This makes it easier to understand how to draw each component of the composition. I tend to address the trickiest sections later in the drawing process. After hours and hours of observing the overall visual—while drawing and studying it—I find that tackling the hard stuff goes quicker than anticipated.

TRANSFERRING THE PHOTO There are several good options for creating a quality line drawing on your art surface. You can sketch it out freehand (be careful with proportions); trace it against a bright window, light box, or projector; draw a grid on both the photo and the art surface and sketch the composition from box to box; or use transfer paper to impress the basic outlines of the photo or your sketch onto your art surface. Two popular options are discussed below.

- **Grid method:** This method enables you to sketch out your line drawing in small segments using squares. First, photocopy your photo onto printer paper and draw a grid of one-inch squares over the photocopy with a pen and ruler. Then very lightly draw the same grid of one-inch squares with a graphite pencil (B or HB preferred) on your final drawing surface. Starting from left to right, draw what you see in each square. Erase the grid. Maintain a light touch with the pencil so that no grooves are impressed into the paper. Lightly erase all lines so that they are visible enough for you to see the outlines but not dark enough to compete with your colored-pencil pigment.

- **Transfer method:** On a sheet of thin drawing or tracing paper, sketch or trace your composition. Tape a piece of graphite transfer paper over the white paper surface you have chosen for your artwork. If your surface is colored, use white transfer paper. Next, tape your drawing or tracing paper over the transfer paper. Using a ballpoint pen or stylus, impress the outlines of your drawing with medium pressure. Before you begin applying color, lightly erase the graphite lines so that they are visible enough for you to see but not dark enough to compete with your colored pencil pigment.

ENHANCING THE PHOTO As you proceed through the stages of completing your colored-pencil artwork, you may decide to change a few things. That's OK! We have artistic license to create whatever we desire, and I encourage you to embrace that freedom. Enjoy the process from start to finish, and you'll have the added benefit of learning along the way.

LOSING THE PHOTO Once you have completed your artwork, celebrate and show your friends and family. If they ask to see the photo to compare it to your artwork, politely decline—your masterpiece is better than the photo, anyway! Enjoy the moment and then begin planning your next still-life project.

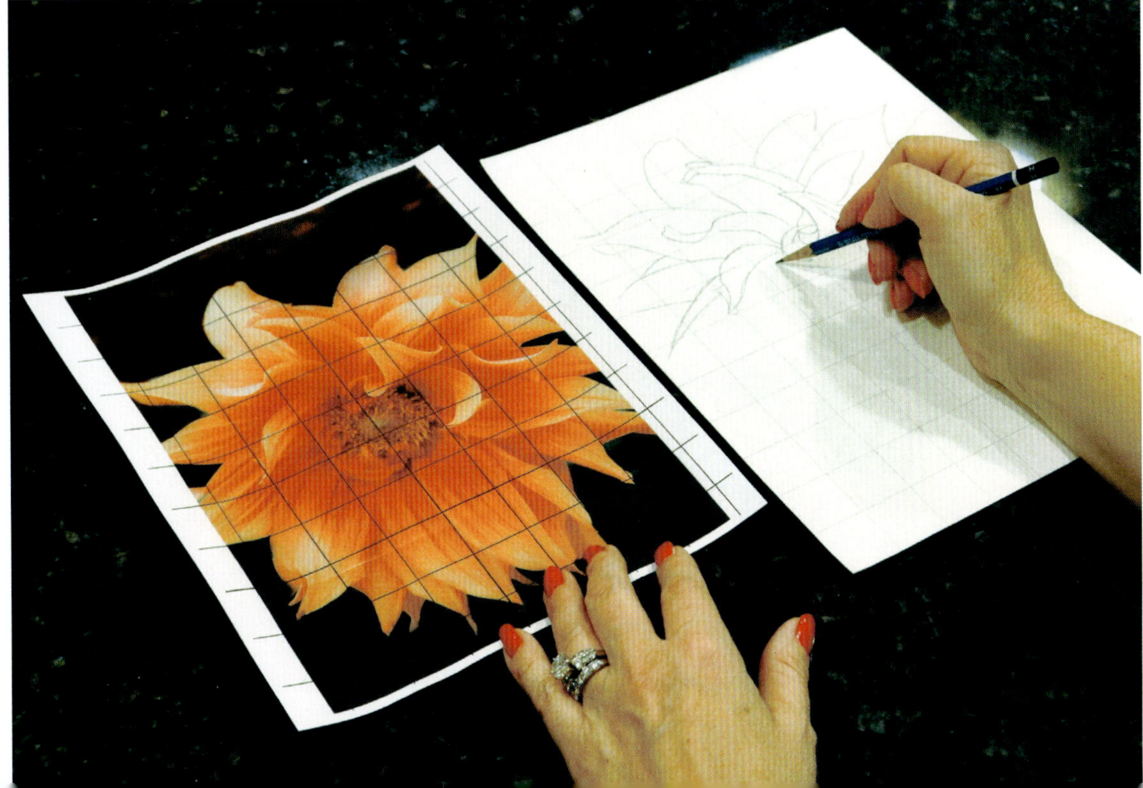

Creating Realistic Still-Life **Textures**

Using a small collection of pencils with a few directional strokes, it's possible to draw delicate flower petals, reflective glass and waterdrops, aged and new leather, intricate wood grain, dimpled fruit, lace fabric, and so much more. Whenever an object is challenging for me to draw, I remind myself that it's just a shape, color, and value. It has a form and a particular color, and its lighting is dark, medium, or light.

Over the years of drawing and painting still-life artworks, I have come to favor a collection of objects that are fun to arrange or look for in a still-life composition.

GLASS & WATER

Flower arrangements are often placed in clear or frosted glass containers with water. The key to depicting the water is to carefully observe and create the very thin top rim of the water. It will have highlights and shadows based on the lighting and the objects within the glass. There may be waterdrops and bubbles as well; those are simply rounded or elliptical shapes with dark and light colors inside. Frosted glass usually involves working with the Cool Grey and White pencils and creating a blurred effect. Tinted glass receives an overall sweep or skimming of one or two pencil layers at the end to approximate the glass color.

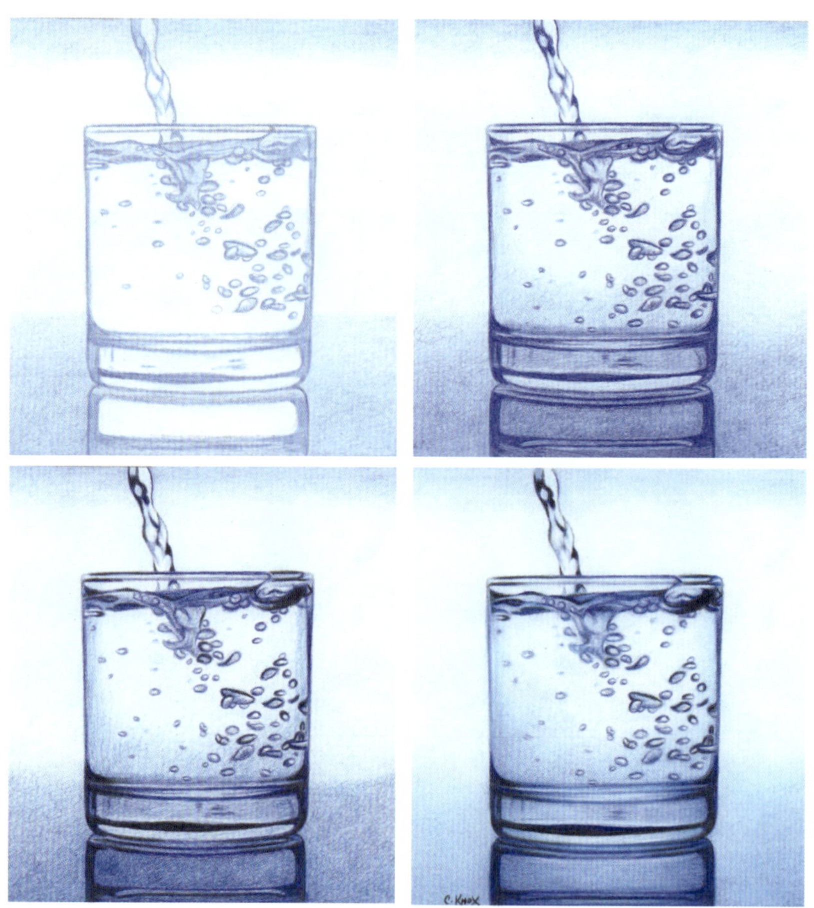

WOOD GRAIN

Start by layering all of the wood with the lightest color you see. Build color density from light to dark with multiple layers of beiges, light browns, and dark browns, stroking in a linear fashion. Establish the darkest shadows with Black and use a light neutral or White to achieve the light highlights; then install your grain lines. Once done, use several of those pencils over the grain lines to soften, diffuse, and blend into the wood. Diagonal strokes work well. Repeat until satisfied.

FABRIC

I love the effect of linen and lace in a still life. They add a lighter value, a classic touch, and the opportunity to create nice detail. Determine the hole pattern and use a light gray or graphite pencil to lightly outline and color in those holes. Build up the colors and values of the surrounding fabric with its highlights and shadows, and then finish darkening the holes—usually with browns and black. Some holes will be darker than others, depending upon the surface beneath the fabric. Sketch patterns within printed fabric, such as silk scarves, with an emphasis on the larger shapes. I never worry about getting the pattern perfect. Rather, I'm concerned with the essence of it. Work section by section to completion and be sure to skim dark gray, dark brown, black, or any other color observed in the photo over the shadowed areas to suggest realistic shading. You can finish with a final application of each area's color over the dark shadows to blend it all out.

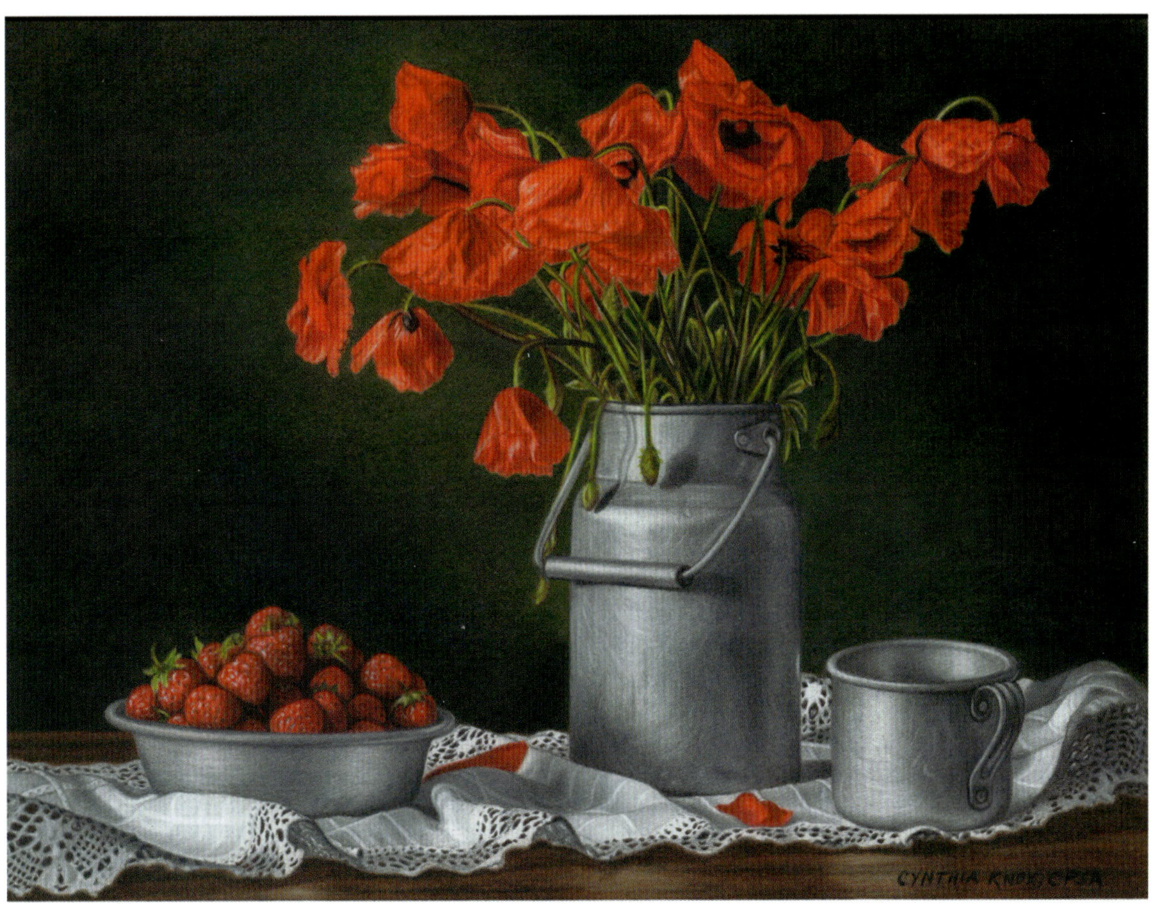

FRUIT

Smooth fruit, like apples, grapes, cherries, and plums, are relatively straightforward to draw and usually are brought to a high shine using firm pencil pressure and White for highlights. Peaches, pears, and kiwis are blended softly and without any burnishing to convey diffused highlights. Pay attention to curved striations of color, shadows, and highlights, and observe stems and their dark indentations.

Convey dimpled fruit with tiny, curved lines that are slightly darker than the surface color. Then "carve" little curved shapes within those lines using a sharp White or light pencil with firm pressure. Skim a light pencil over the entire small area to soften and diffuse. Slices of fruit have juicy, reflective, and membranous textures. Outline the largest light sections, color around them, complete those light sections with White or a light pencil for shine, and then "carve" a few thin, light streaks randomly over the colored areas to suggest juiciness.

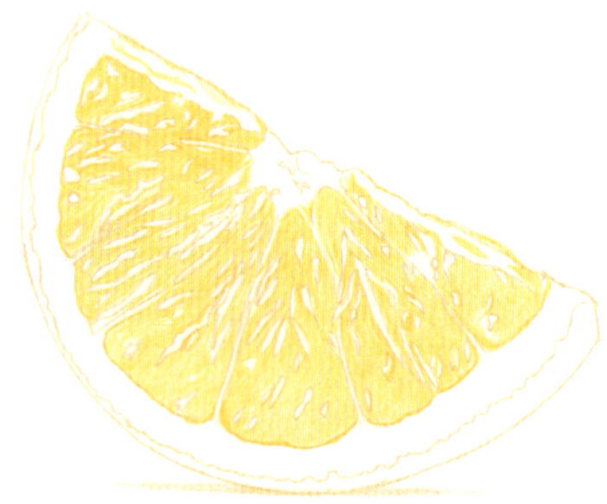

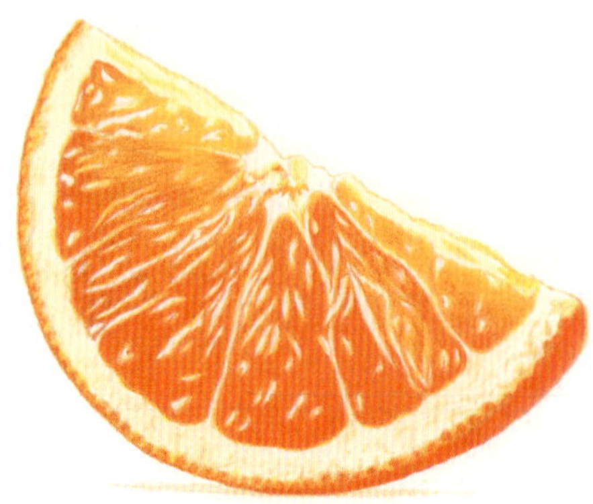

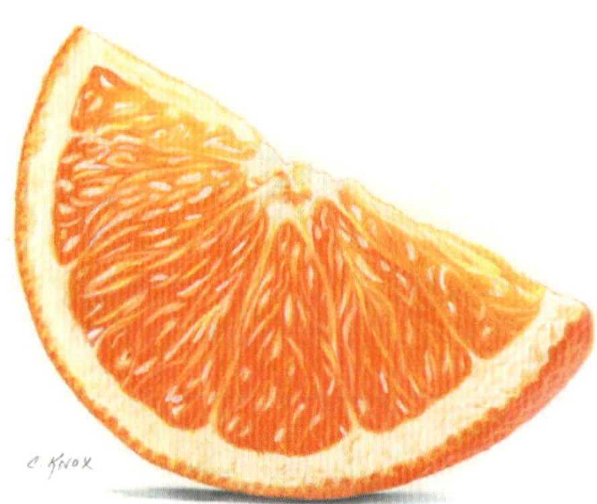

LEAVES & STEMS

Use long, linear strokes to render these. I like to start with the lightest color observed in a leaf and build density in darker areas. Once you've established the foundation of greens and browns within both leaves and stems, draw in their detail, such as veins, nubs, and tiny filaments extending off the edges.

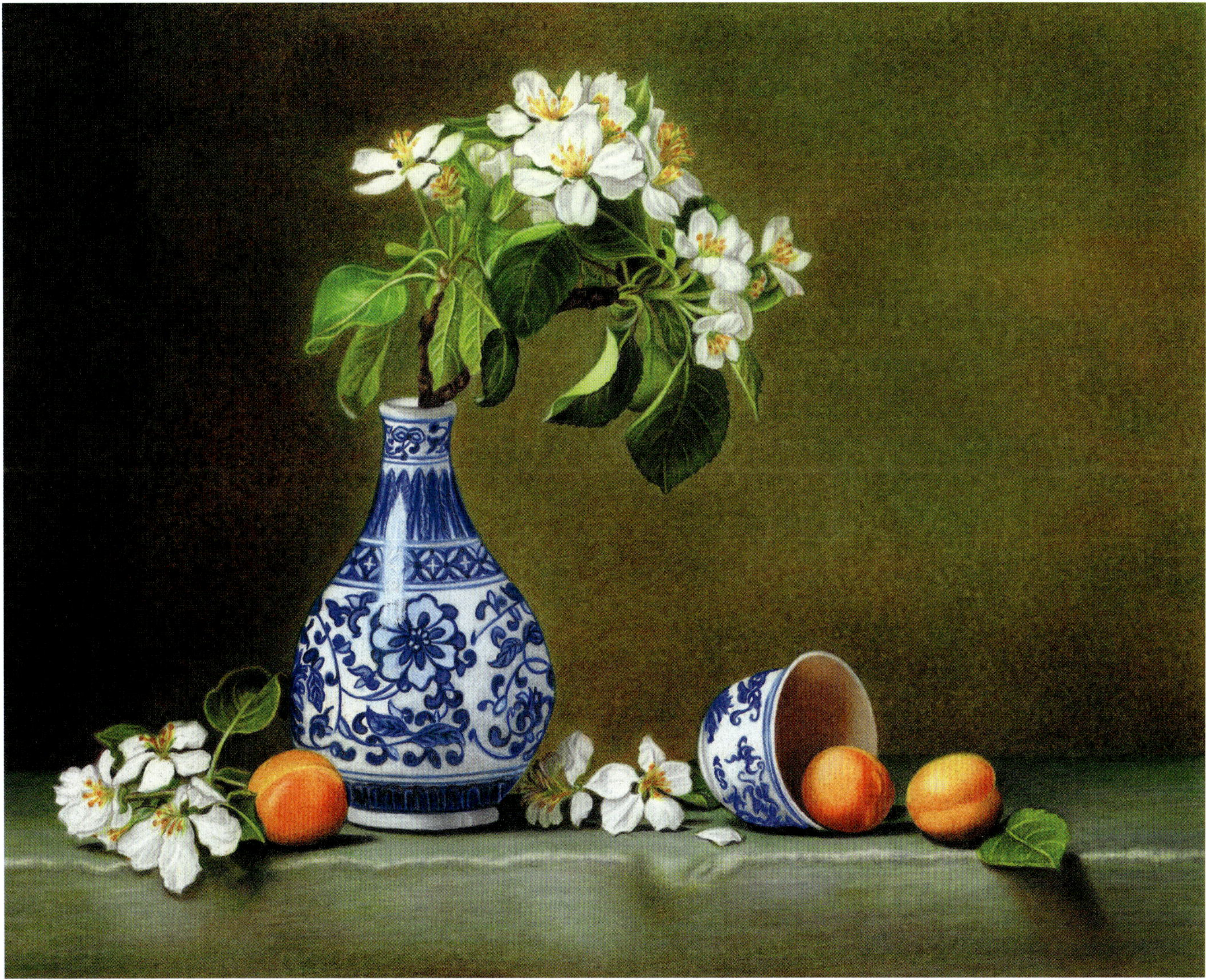

FLOWERS

Roses, lilies, and tropical blooms are my favorite flowers to draw, and their vibrant colors are a joy to develop. Typically, I do not establish the petal veins and detail until after the base has been layered, blended, and burnished with circular strokes. Then I'll lightly draw in petal detail and reinforce it with another layer or two using firmer pressure. A final softening of color completes the petal. When there are interior structures like filaments and anthers visible, those are individually rendered and colored. Smooth color and value transitions across each petal are important to avoid a choppy, uneven appearance. The White pencil is excellent for this.

LEATHER

This texture can appear aged with wrinkles and a soft, buttery look or new and tightly stretched with no blemishes or marks. After completing the overall color, highlights, and shadows, use the sharp point of a lighter pencil to "slash" straight and curved lines across aged leather. Soften and diffuse with a final pencil or two skimmed over the areas. Depicting detail, such as laces, stitching, and wear patterns, is important. Perfection is not necessary; just identify the pattern and be consistent in drawing it. New leather is a bit easier to create. It usually has a shine and no distress markings.

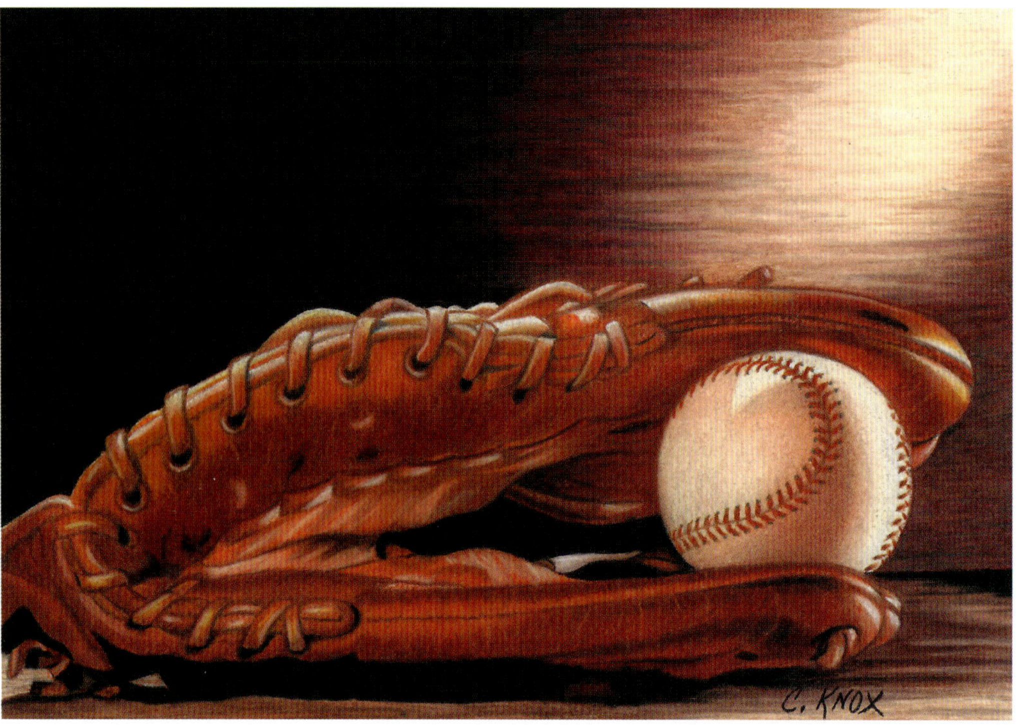

POTTERY

From simple white pitchers to elaborately designed vases, pottery is a definite favorite in still-life compositions. The complicated patterns must be lightly sketched within your line drawing. Develop the colors within the pattern by blocking in the darks and preserving the lights. Once you are pleased with the final pattern, work on the surrounding pottery from light to dark. Pay attention to where the shadows and highlights are and blend, blend, blend for smooth color and value transitions. Lastly, deepen the shadows over the pattern areas with your darker pencils, such as dark grays, dark browns, and black. This is the only way to establish shadowed realism. Squint and see if you need to continue darkening the pattern. Then use your previous pencils and skim over the dark shadow areas to restore color, soften, and finesse to completion.

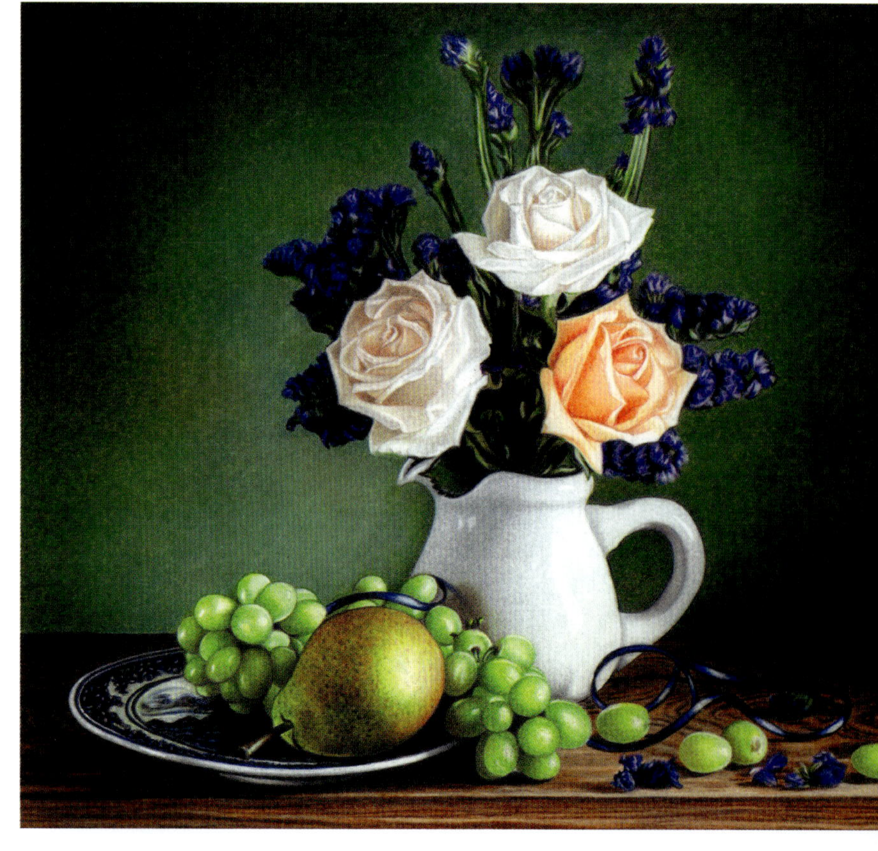

Putting It All Together

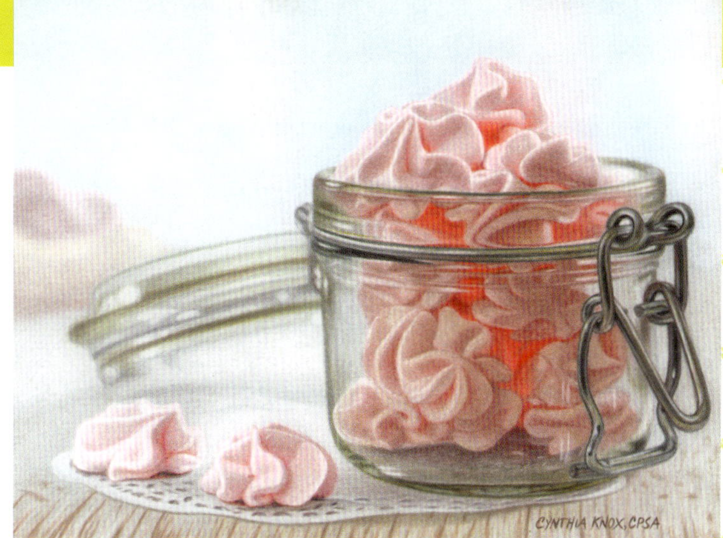

Now that we have covered some introductory material, let's put it to practical use! Each project in this book includes a list of pencils to enable you to create these still-life artworks along with me. We'll proceed step by step, and there are detailed instructions and clear illustrations for you to follow. My hope is that you'll enjoy the experience, learn some new things about the colored-pencil medium, and create beautiful artworks of your own. Be sure to show me your artwork! I would love to see it and can be reached through my website at www.cynthiaknox.com.

Within the step-by-step instructions in each project, I describe pencil pressure using a scale of 1 to 5. To familiarize yourself with these numbers and their corresponding pressures, make sure to read page 14 before beginning any project.

For each project, you'll need the following:

- 9" x 12" smooth Bristol paper (white)
- 13" x 17" drawing board with paper cushion taped over it
- Light box or sunny window
- Tracing paper and transfer paper if not tracing image onto Bristol paper
- Pencil sharpener
- Two drafting or soft brushes to remove pencil dust
- Erasers
- B or HB graphite pencil for line drawing
- Artist tape to attach artwork and cushion paper to drawing board
- Plain sheet of paper to place under your hand
- Workable or final fixative to seal in pigment

Project 1:

Poppies

This beautiful still life evokes thoughts and perhaps memories of rural living and farmhouse décor. You'll enjoy creating the numerous textures in this composition. The delicate folds of the poppy petals and the pitted surface of the strawberries provide a contrast that's still manageable to render. The overlapping flower stems, distressed markings of the antique metallics, delicate lace pattern, and highlighted table grain will keep you busy with a variety of pencil strokes, colors, and values. Lastly, the softly blurred background stages the main subjects beautifully.

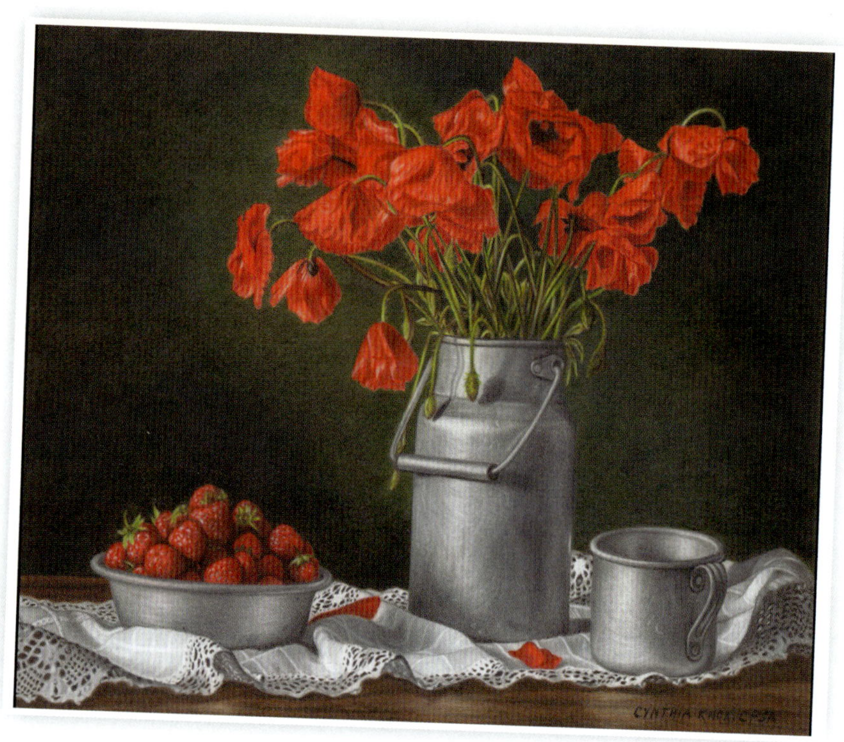

PALETTE

Prismacolor Premier:
911 Olive Green
912 Apple Green
918 Orange
922 Poppy Red
924 Crimson Red
935 Black
937 Tuscan Red
938 White (x2)
941 Light Umber
946 Dark Brown
947 Dark Umber
989 Chartreuse
1005 Limepeel
1061 30% Cool Grey
1063 50% Cool Grey
1065 70% Cool Grey
1067 90% Cool Grey
1082 Chocolate
1083 Putty Beige
1091 Green Ochre

STABILO All:
8046 Black
8052 White

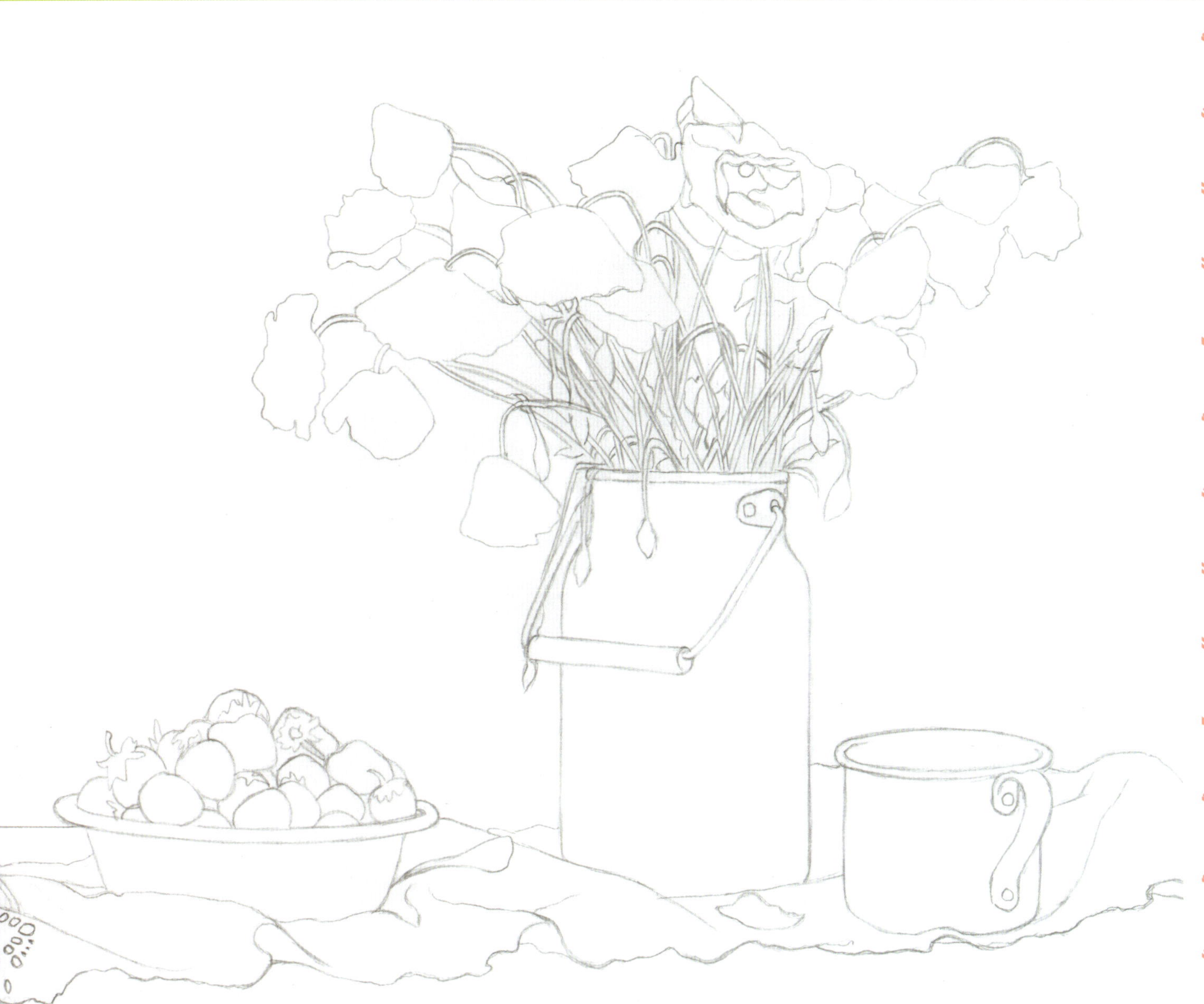

Transfer or trace this line drawing onto your choice of paper. Feel free to enlarge or reduce the size by scanning. I recommend using a graphite B or HB pencil for the outlines, and keep them light to avoid competing with the colors.

Note: Use of the STABILO pencils is specified as Black STABILO or White STABILO. For all other Black and White references, use Prismacolor pencils.

1 Outline and color in the poppies with a sharp Poppy Red using moderate pressure (2) and small, rounded, overlapping strokes.

2 To separate the petals, increase your pressure on the overlapping petal edges. Your goal is to establish smooth layers of color before introducing the linear detail. Observe the overlapping stems and color between the lines accordingly.

3 Color in the stems with Chartreuse using moderate pressure (2) and linear strokes.

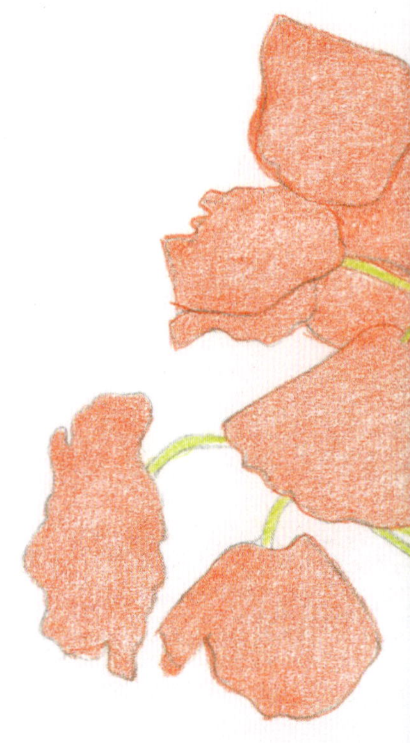

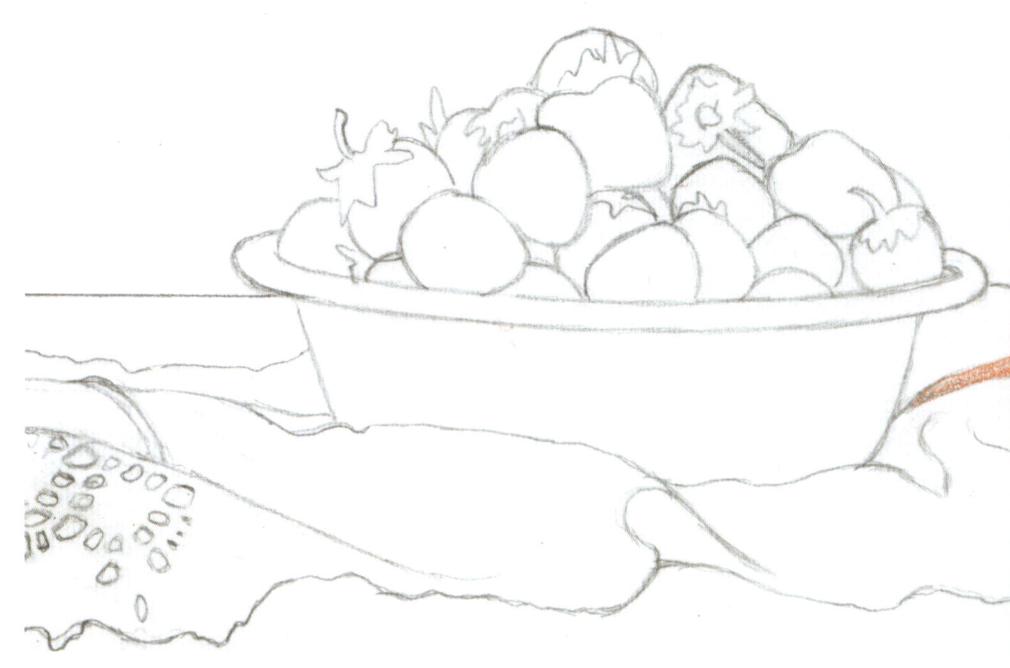

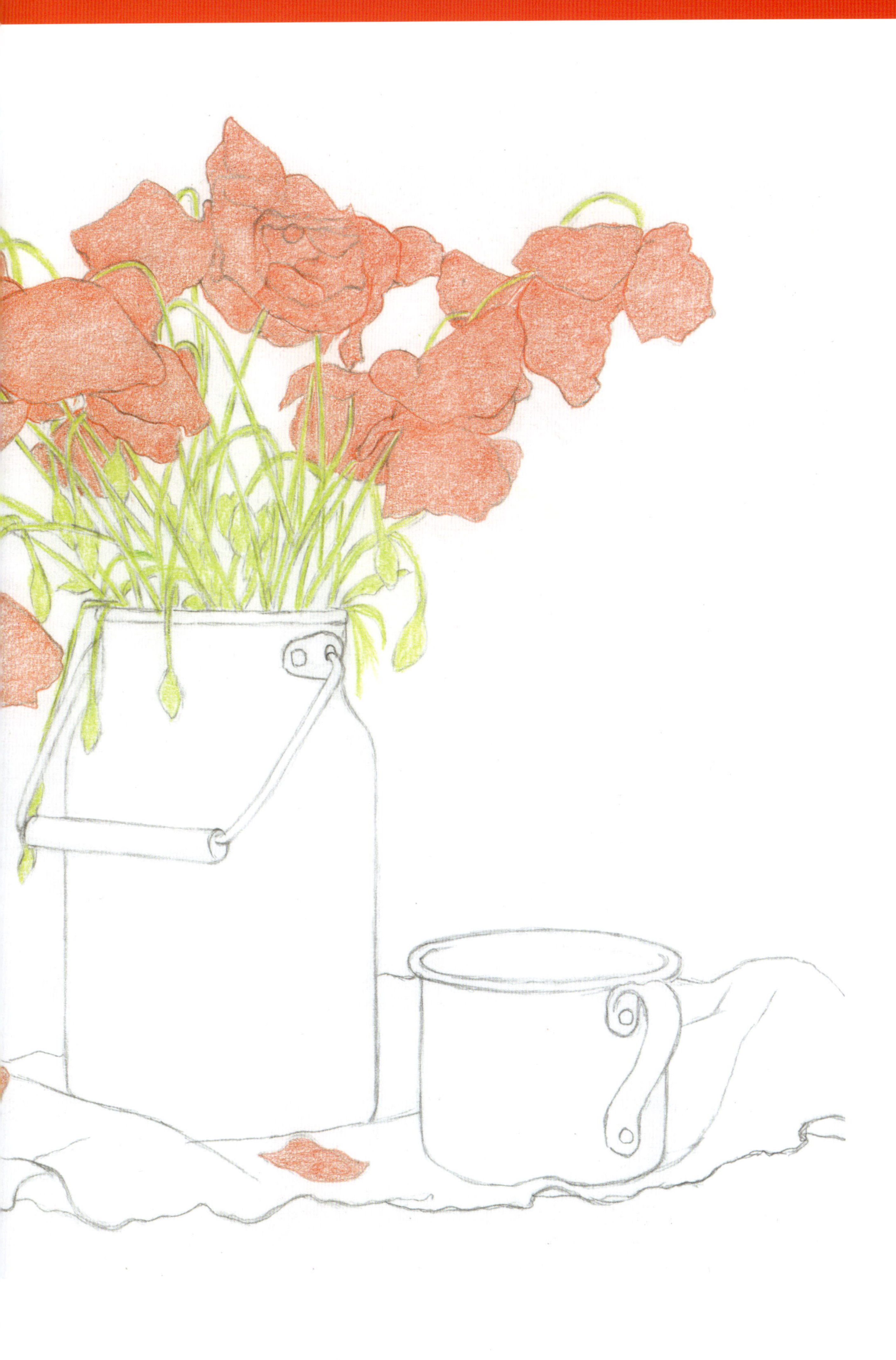

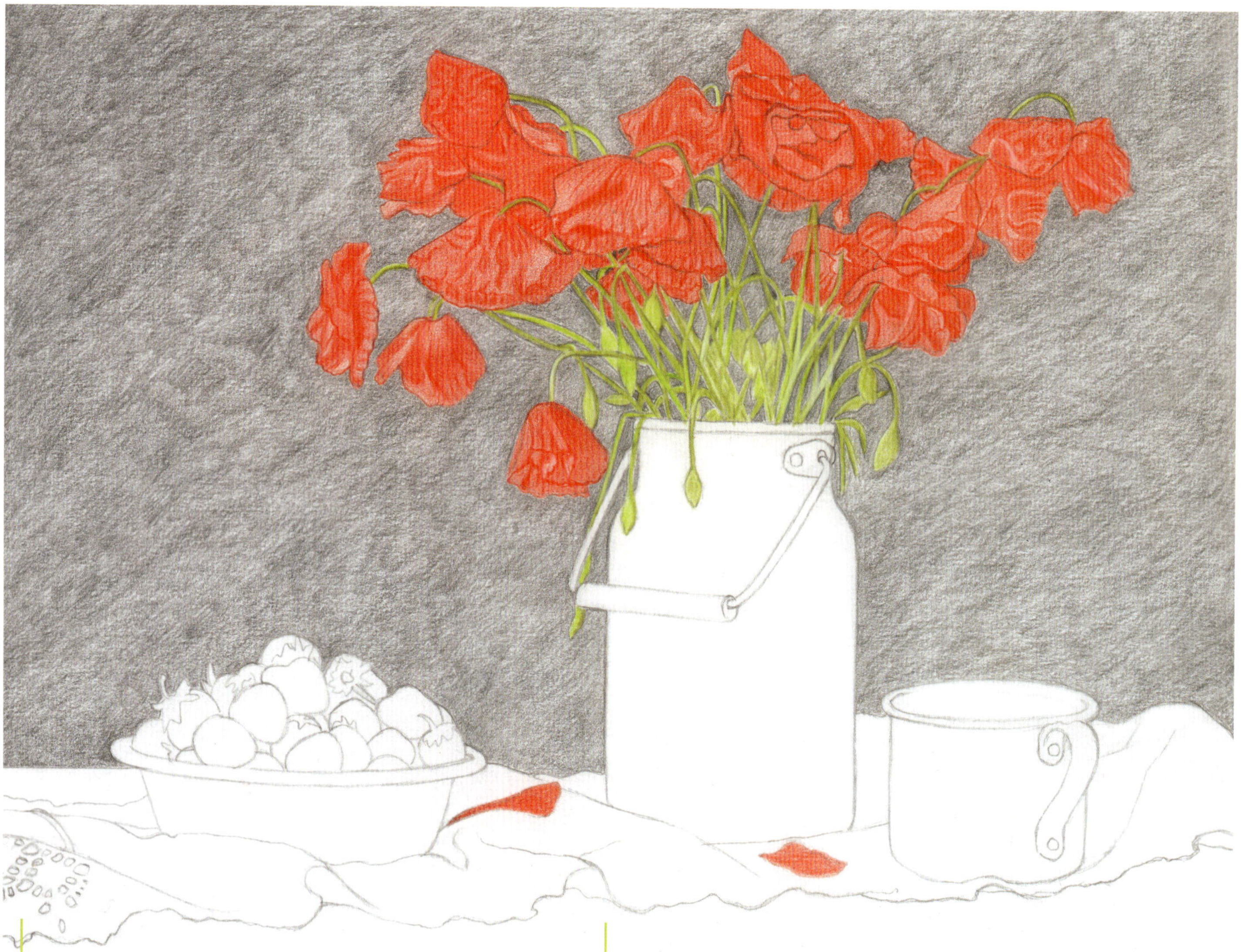

POPPIES

1 Intensify the red color using Crimson Red and moderate pressure (2).

2 Increase your pressure to medium (3) or firm (4) to block in the deeper reds.

STEMS

1 Work with just two pencils for now: Chartreuse and Limepeel. Over every light-green stem, color in with Chartreuse again. Over any darker stem, use Limepeel. Begin at the left side and work methodically toward the right.

2 Use a sharp White to lighten, straighten, and/or make corrections. If it gets confusing, use Chartreuse.

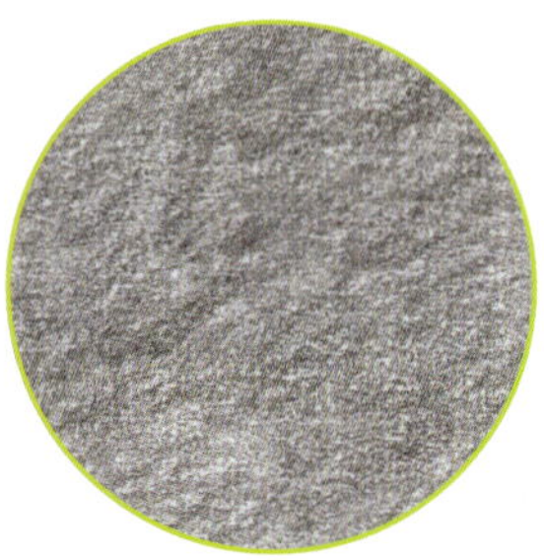

BACKGROUND

1 Begin with a layer of Black using diagonal strokes and moderate pressure (2). Bring Black almost, but not quite, to the outlines of the poppies and stems.

2 Once the majority of the background is complete, finish bringing pigment right up to the borders of the poppies and stems to ensure crisp edges and precise detail.

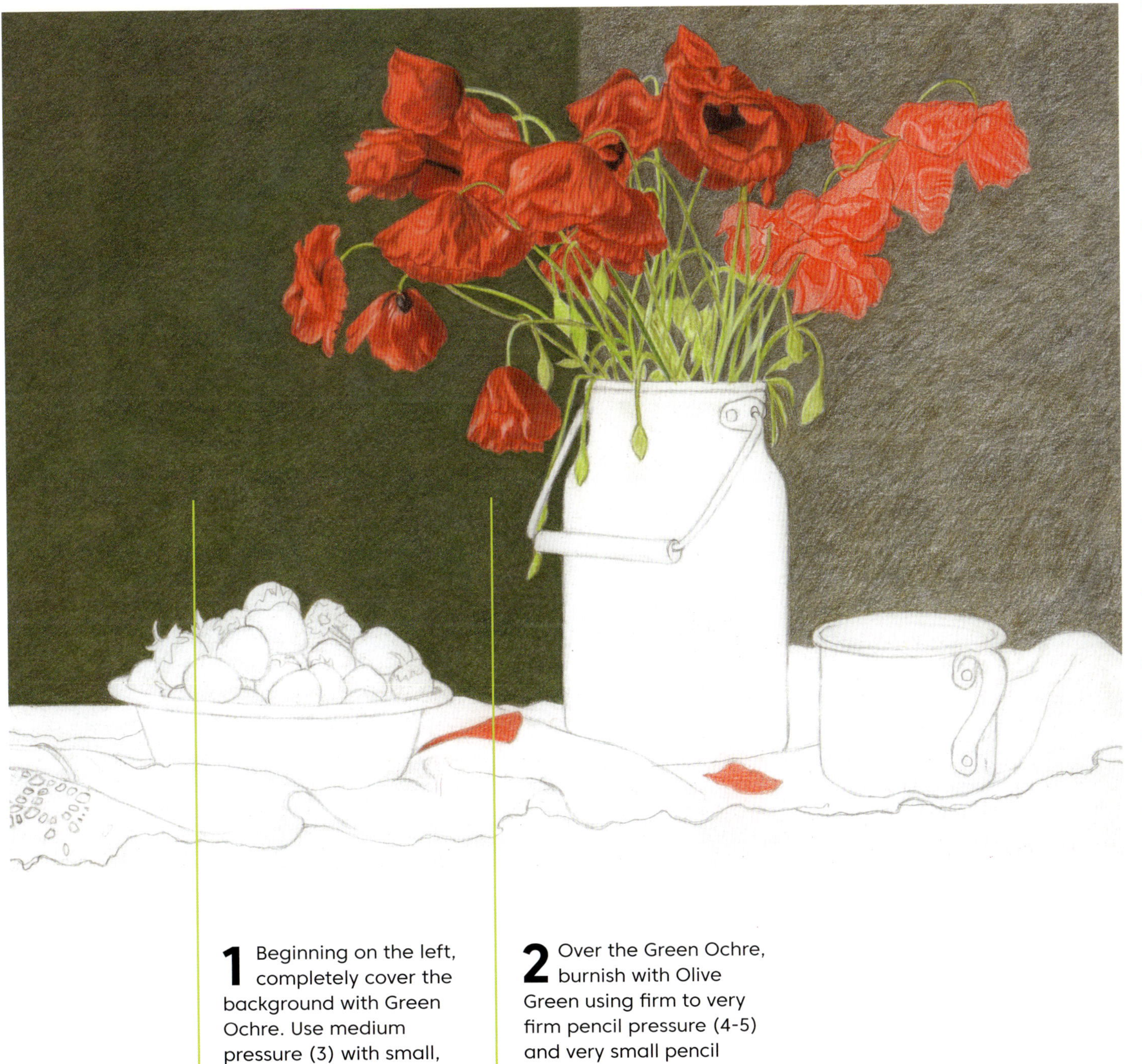

1 Beginning on the left, completely cover the background with Green Ochre. Use medium pressure (3) with small, linear, and overlapping strokes that move upward and diagonally.

2 Over the Green Ochre, burnish with Olive Green using firm to very firm pencil pressure (4-5) and very small pencil strokes that overlap and move in the same diagonal direction.

To continue layering over the poppies on the left, see page 45.

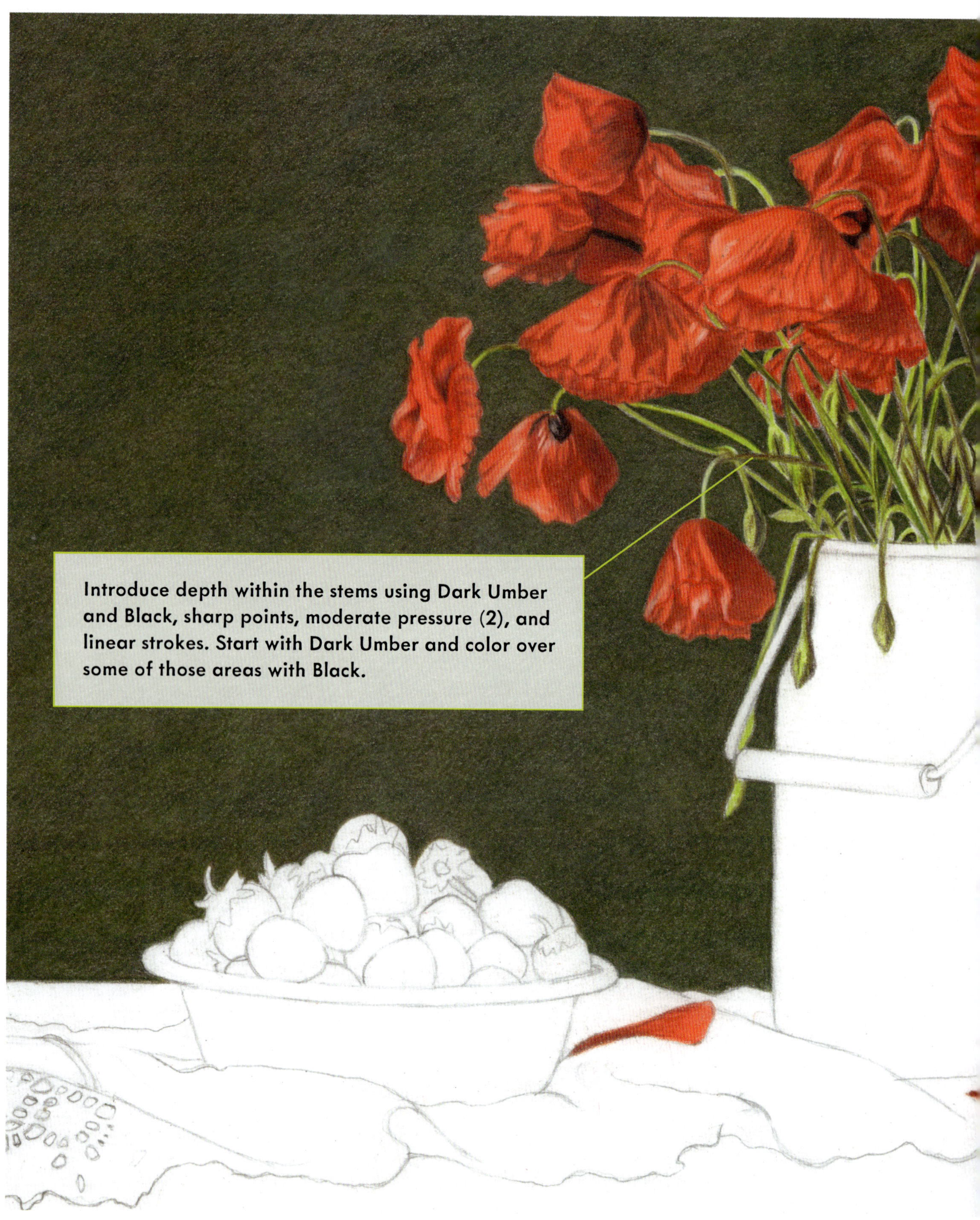
Introduce depth within the stems using Dark Umber and Black, sharp points, moderate pressure (2), and linear strokes. Start with Dark Umber and color over some of those areas with Black.

1 Deepen the shadow hues in the poppies using Tuscan Red; tiny, directional strokes; and medium to firm pressure (3-4).

2 Brighten the poppies with Orange over all of the red areas using medium to firm pressure (3-4).

3 Use a sharply pointed Black with a light touch (1-2) to enhance the shadow areas. Increase your pressure in the centers of the poppies.

4 Use a sharp White to preserve the tiny highlights throughout.

TIP

Placing darks directly over or behind the lighter greens immediately creates depth.

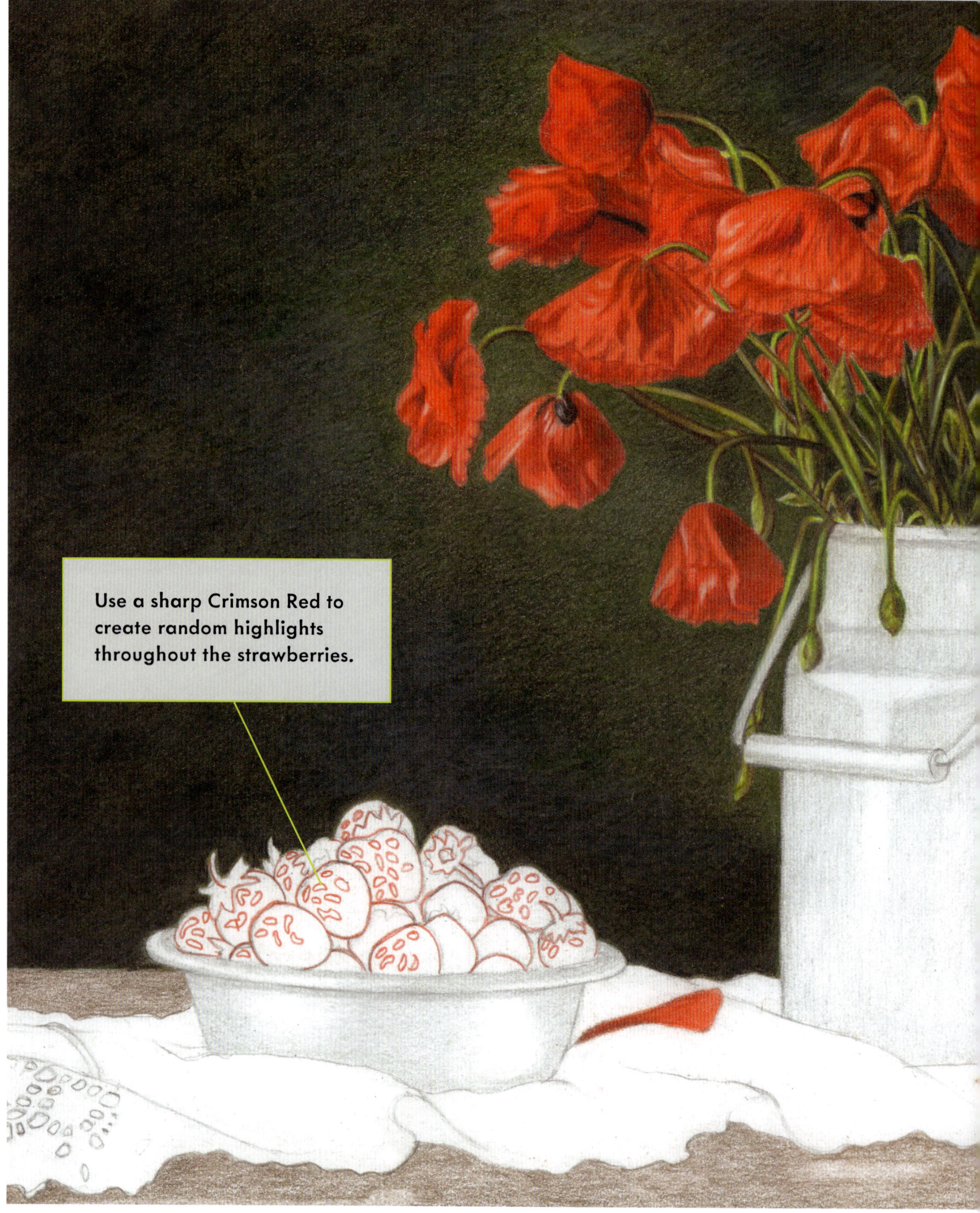

POPPIES

1 Work with the greens, Dark Umber, Black, and White to complete the foliage.

2 Use Chartreuse and Limepeel for the light and dark lime-green hues within the stems. Apple Green colors the sweeter greens, and Olive Green deepens the darker greens. Dark Umber and Black create nice depth and dimension in the darkest areas.

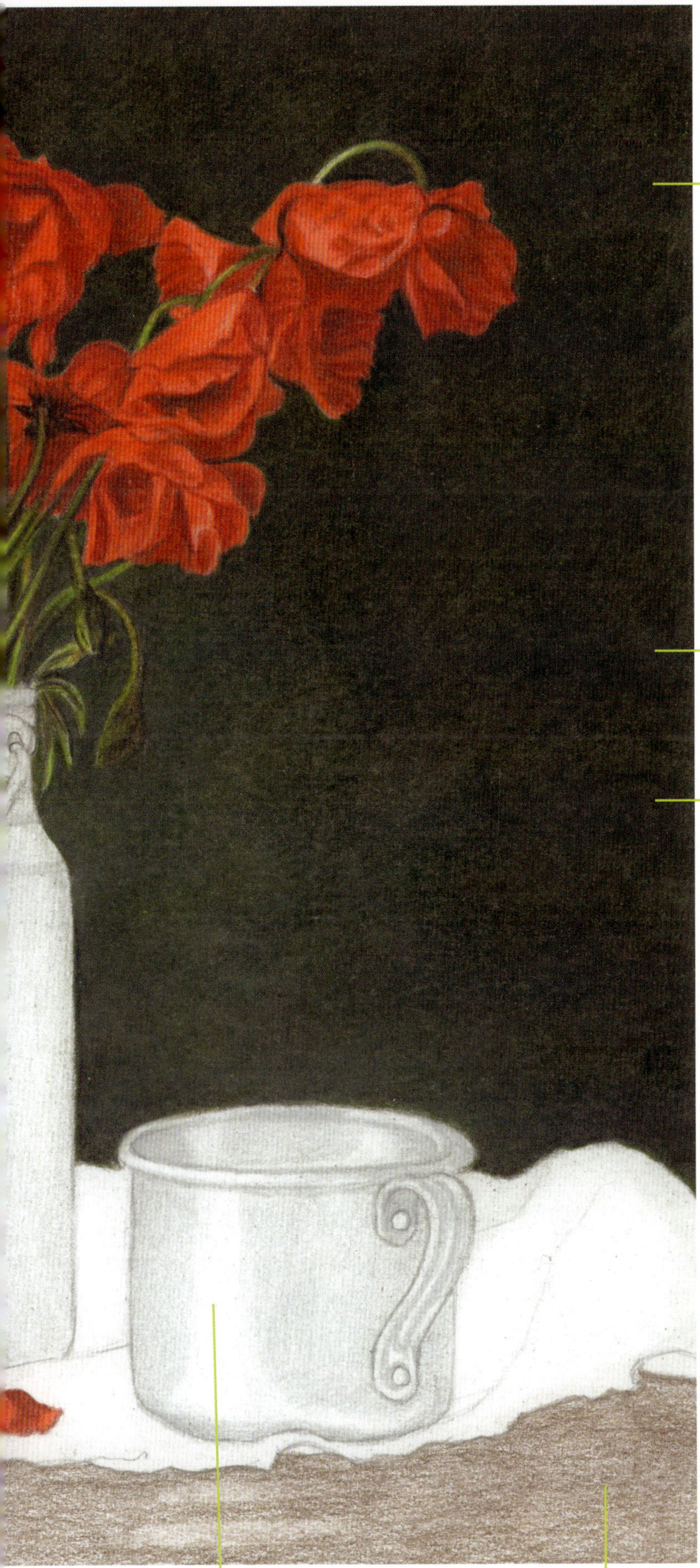

1 Complete the poppies with a layer of Crimson Red applied over all of the petals. Use moderate to medium pressure (2-3).

2 Review each poppy. Do certain areas need to be darker? Add Tuscan Red. Darker still? Lightly apply Black. Do you have all the little white highlights in place? If not, carve through existing waxy layers with White.

BACKGROUND

1 To achieve seamless color transitions in the background, start by applying Black around the perimeters. Use firm to very firm pressure (4-5) and small, overlapping strokes to ensure that no paper specks show through.

2 Use White to connect the green area immediately next to the milk can into the black areas. Then work with Olive Green over the White and Black to blend.

3 Use a sharp pencil point (Olive Green, Black, or White) to scrape through or skim off waxy blips. Changing the direction of your pencil stroke will help eliminate these blips.

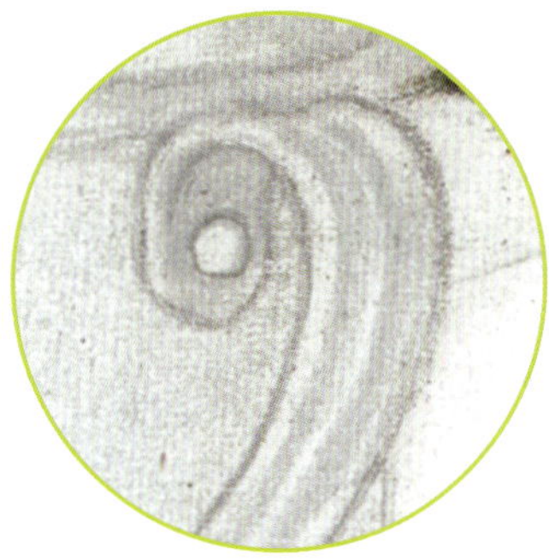

Apply an initial layer of 30% Cool Grey over the gray areas of the metallic objects. Leave the extreme highlights white for now. Use moderate pressure (2) and vertical strokes for the milk can and exterior cup, and horizontal strokes for the bowl and interior cup.

Create highlights with an eraser if necessary.

Begin the table with two horizontal layers of Dark Brown using moderate pressure (2).

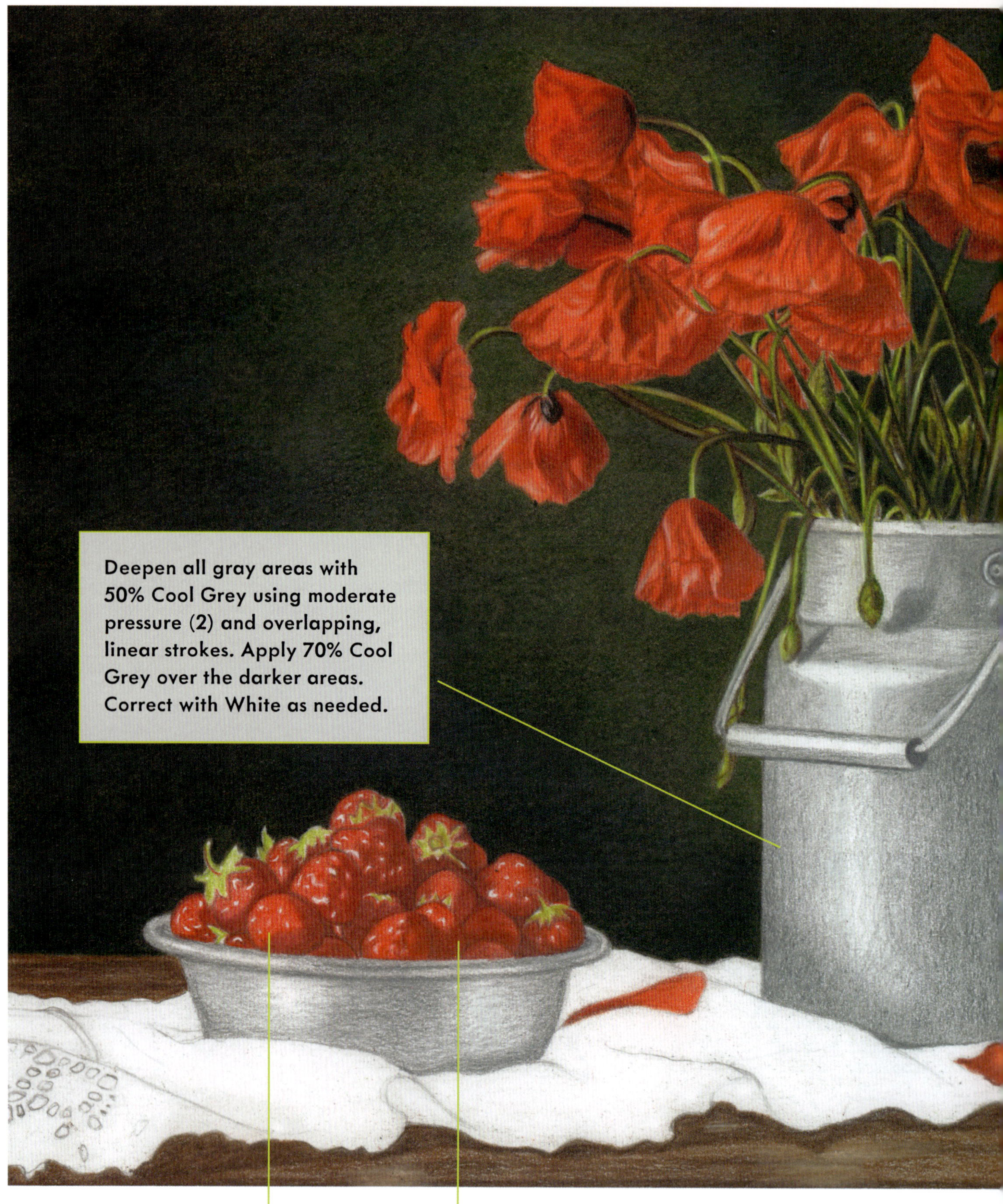

Deepen all gray areas with 50% Cool Grey using moderate pressure (2) and overlapping, linear strokes. Apply 70% Cool Grey over the darker areas. Correct with White as needed.

1 Color Crimson Red around the white sections of the strawberries using tiny, rounded, overlapping strokes and moderate pressure (2).

2 Apply Tuscan Red in the shadowed areas using tiny, rounded strokes with medium to firm pressure (3-4).

3 Color in the stems with Chartreuse and moderate pressure (2).

1 Develop the table with a layer of Chocolate overall, including the lighter highlights, using linear strokes applied with moderate pressure (2).

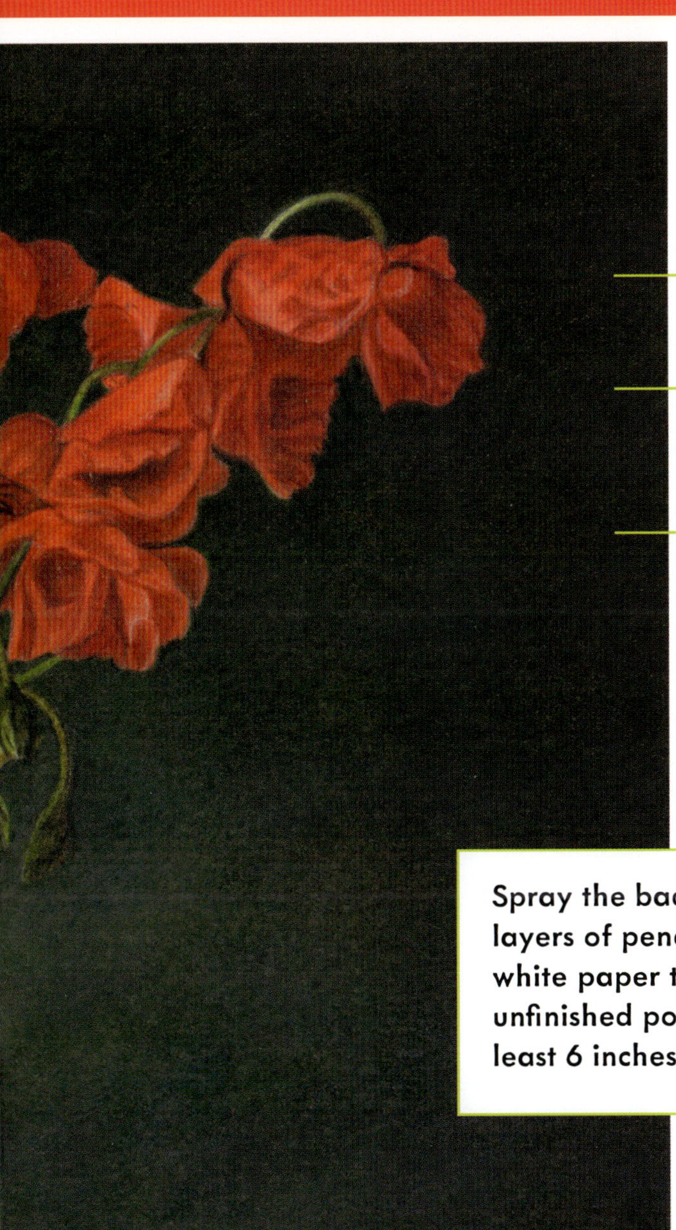

BACKGROUND

1 Work with Black and Olive Green to complete the transition from dark into light around the poppies and milk can.

2 Add a bit of Limepeel on the left side.

3 For random waxy blips of Black, use a sharp Olive Green or White, moving in different directions to cross through and eliminate the blips.

4 Finish the black area on the right with tiny, rounded, overlapping strokes and the Black STABILO pencil. Lighten your touch as you get closer to the green interior. If necessary, work Olive Green over some of the Black STABILO.

Spray the background with a workable fixative to seal in the layers of pencil. To spray just the background, rip up pieces of white paper to cover the poppies, metallic objects, and lower, unfinished portion of the artwork. Shake the can and spray at least 6 inches from your artwork; then repeat.

TIP

If the background looks waxy, sweep a soft cloth over it using moderate pressure and a circular motion.

2 Follow with Dark Umber applied as separate grain streaks in the back-left corner and in the front. Also use Dark Umber for the dark shadows under the lace using medium pressure (3).

3 Use firm pressure (4) and short linear strokes with Putty Beige to restore the highlights throughout the table.

STRAWBERRIES

1 Create the shadows on the strawberries with a sharp Black and tiny, rounded strokes. Start with one of the darkest areas and medium pressure (3); then increase to firm pressure (4) to darken.

2 Move to a lighter shadow and reduce your pencil pressure to moderate (2). You may need to lightly (1) skim Black over a strawberry.

3 Burnish Crimson Red over everything to smooth out the Black pigment. Use medium to firm pressure (3-4) with tiny, rounded strokes.

4 Intensify the color of the berry stems with Olive Green and Dark Umber in the shadows.

5 Brighten and touch up color overall with Chartreuse and White. Use medium pressure (3) with these pencils.

To burnish the grays in the metallic objects, begin with a sharp White and use medium pressure (3) and very small strokes in the direction of previous color application. The goal is to establish a smooth blend of gray midtones into the highlights and shadows.

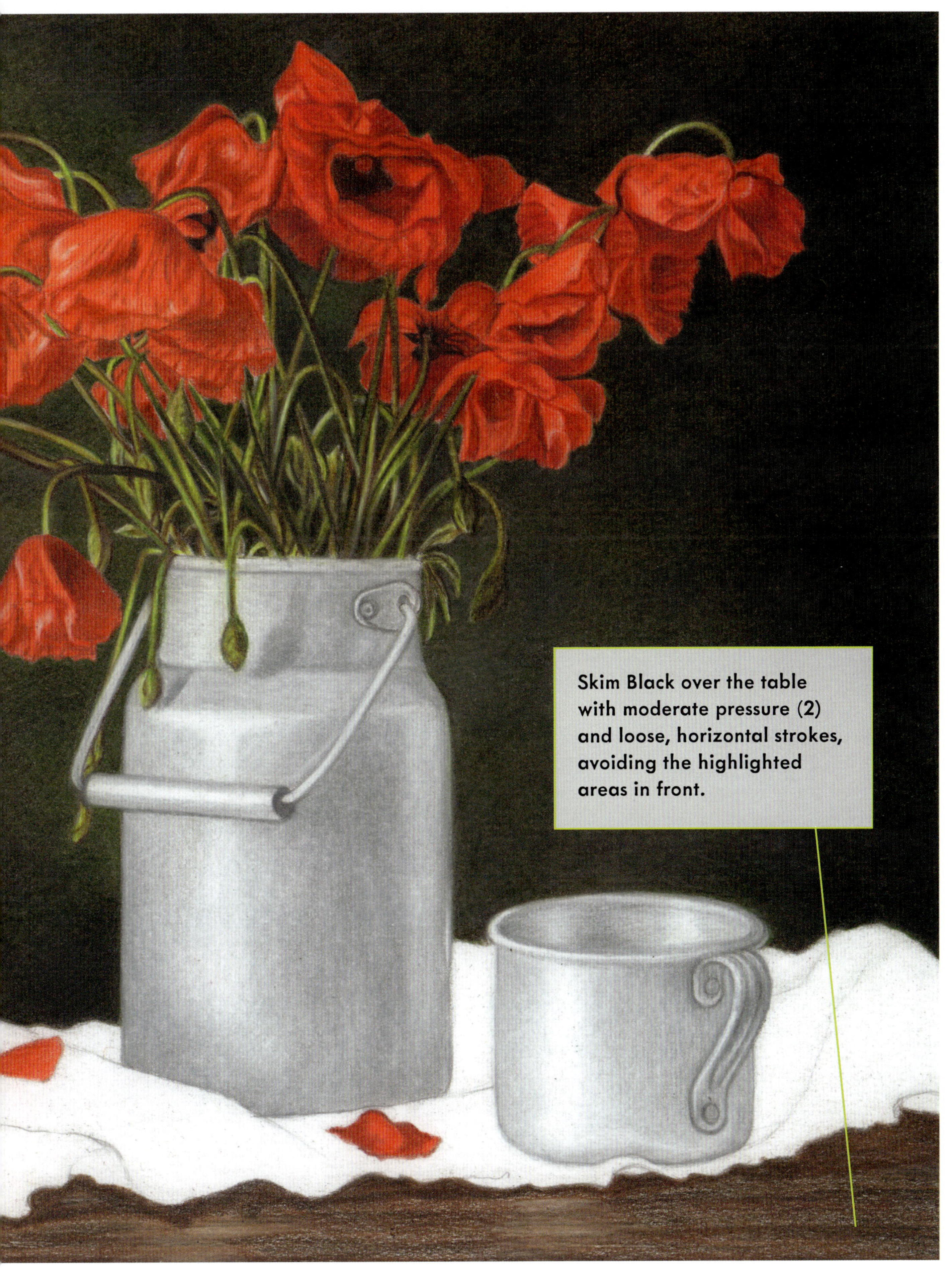

Skim Black over the table with moderate pressure (2) and loose, horizontal strokes, avoiding the highlighted areas in front.

STRAWBERRIES

1 Minimize the bright white highlights with a sharp Crimson Red.

2 Deepen the very black crevice shadows with the Black STABILO pencil using moderate to medium pressure (2-3). Lightly skim it over the darkest areas of the strawberries and softly blend with Crimson Red.

3 Create the remaining tiny white highlights with White STABILO and a 000 paintbrush. Dip the paintbrush in water, flick off excess drops, and sweep the tip back and forth across the point of the pencil. Then dot the paintbrush tip over the brighter areas of each strawberry.

4 Sharpen your Olive Green and use medium pressure (3) to install the small and often curved green markings above some of the white dots.

5 Within the deeply shadowed areas, apply random dark dots with the Black STABILO pencil.

6 Look at your values; you may need to deepen the darks a bit. Skim Black over that area. Touch up the reds overall with Crimson Red and Tuscan Red.

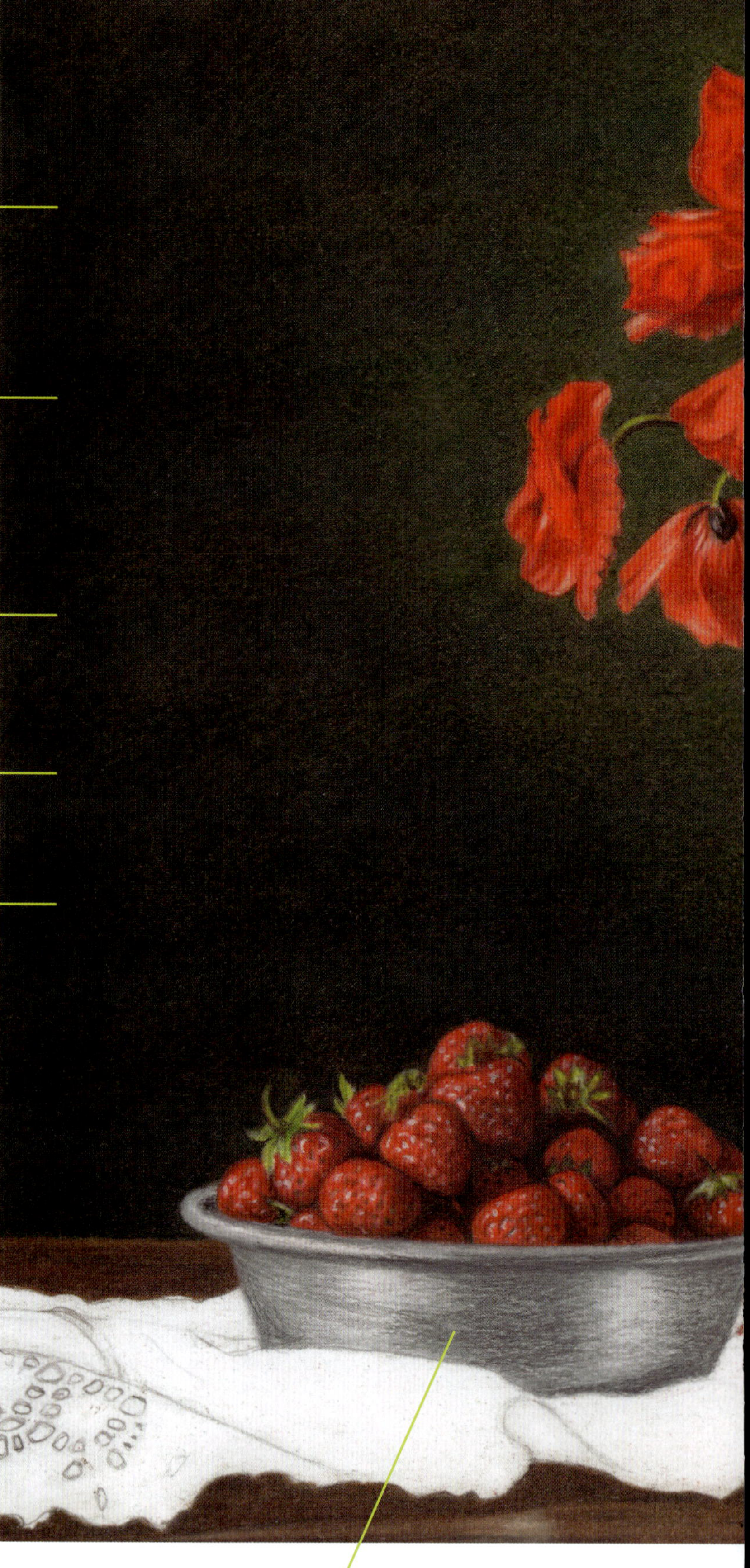

Darken the shadows with 70% and 90% Cool Grey and enhance the midtones with 50% Cool Grey. Use moderate to medium pressure (2-3) and loose strokes that crisscross and overlap in some places to convey the scratched, aging appearance of these objects.

TIP

Use a clean eraser frequently to erase the lace areas.

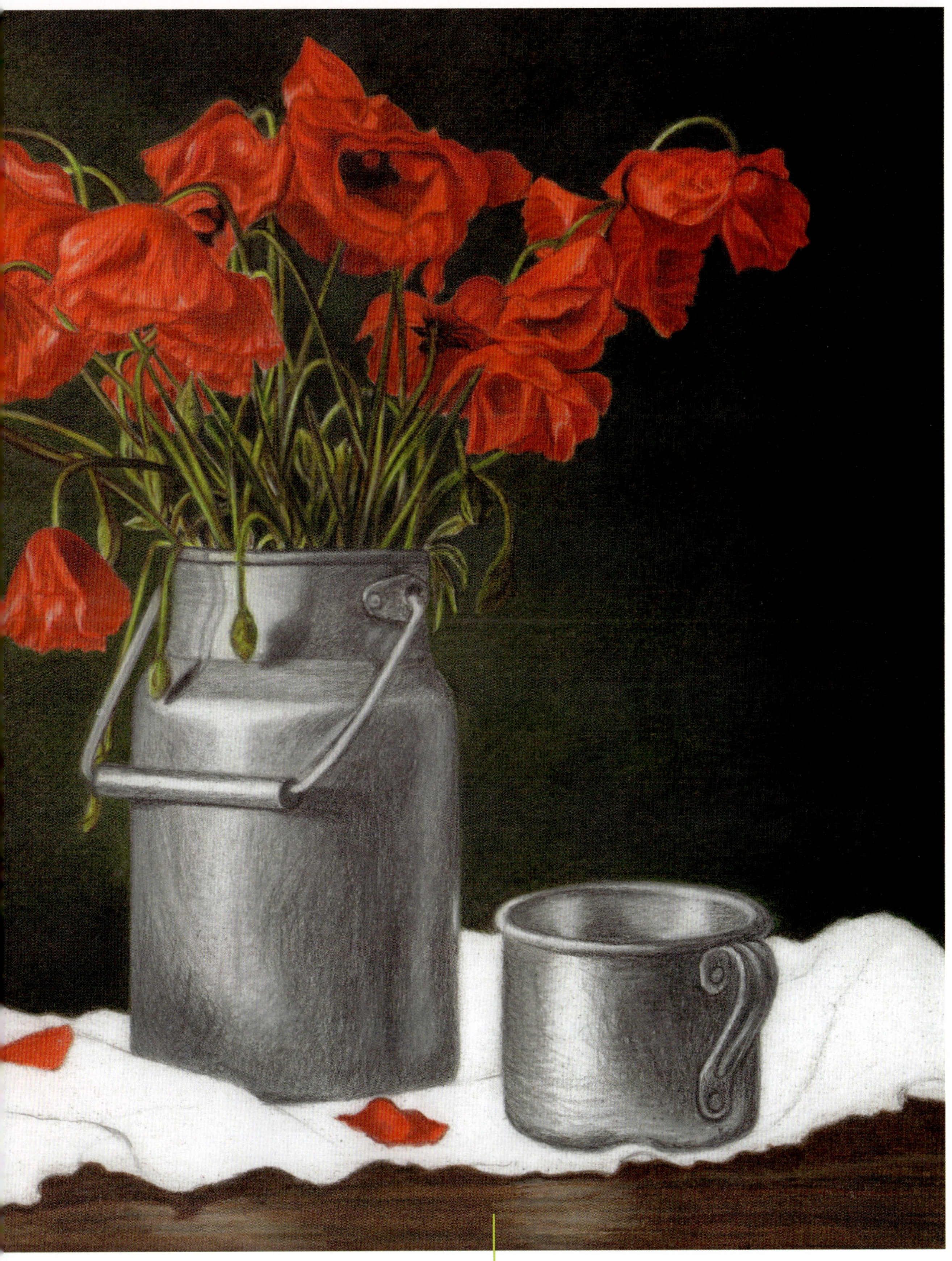

1 In the back-left corner of the table, burnish a thin streak of Light Umber just below the background. Then burnish below that and on top of the lace with Dark Umber using horizontal strokes and firm pressure (4).

2 Burnish with Dark Umber below the lace, where the shadows are, using linear strokes with firm pressure (4). Use Light Umber to burnish the remainder of the table, except the highlights. Lighten up the highlights with White if necessary.

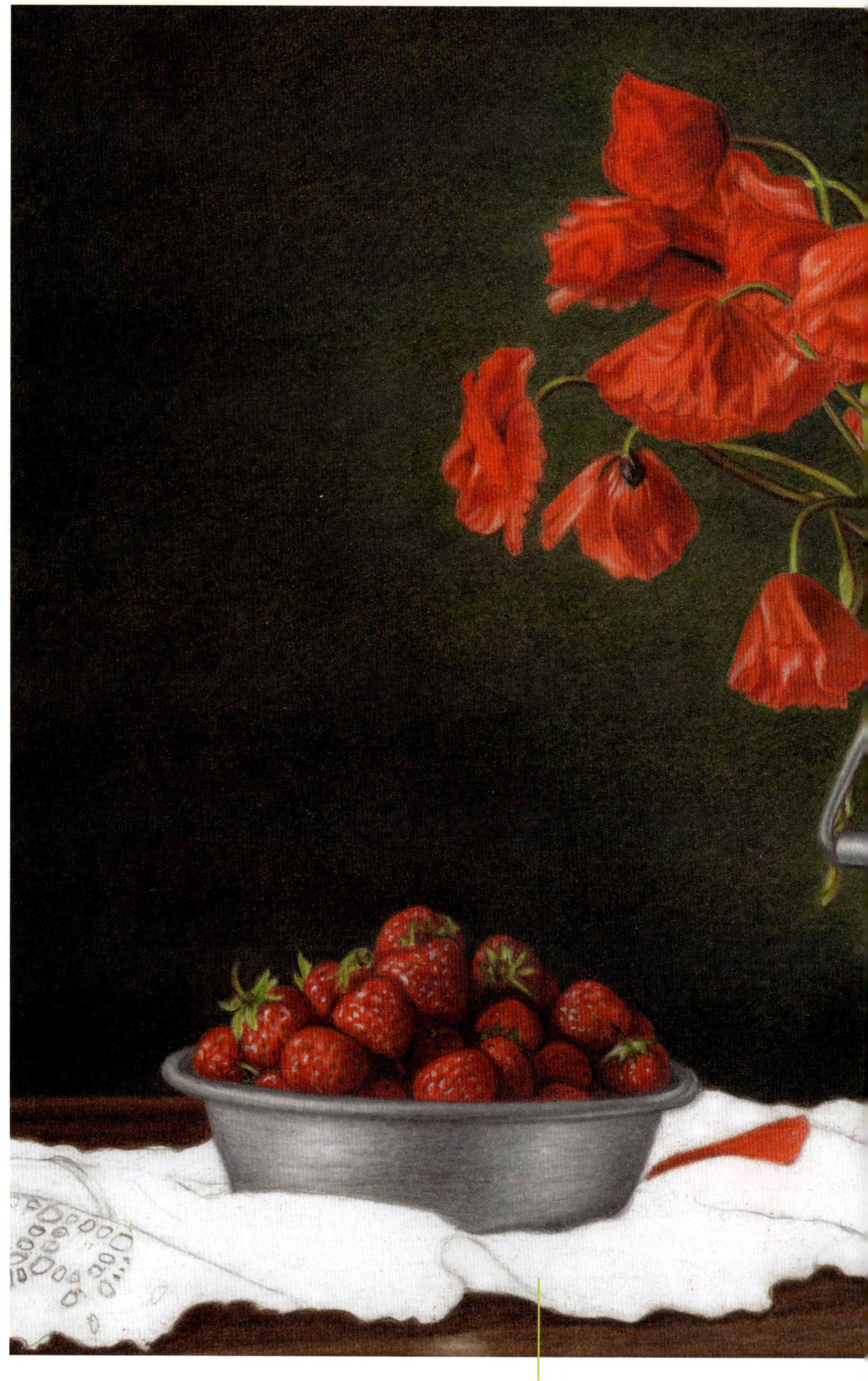

1 Darken the shadows and some grain lines in the table with Black using horizontal as well as curved strokes, plus moderate to firm pressure (3-4). Apply Dark Umber to darken the brown grain.

2 Erase smudges over the lace.

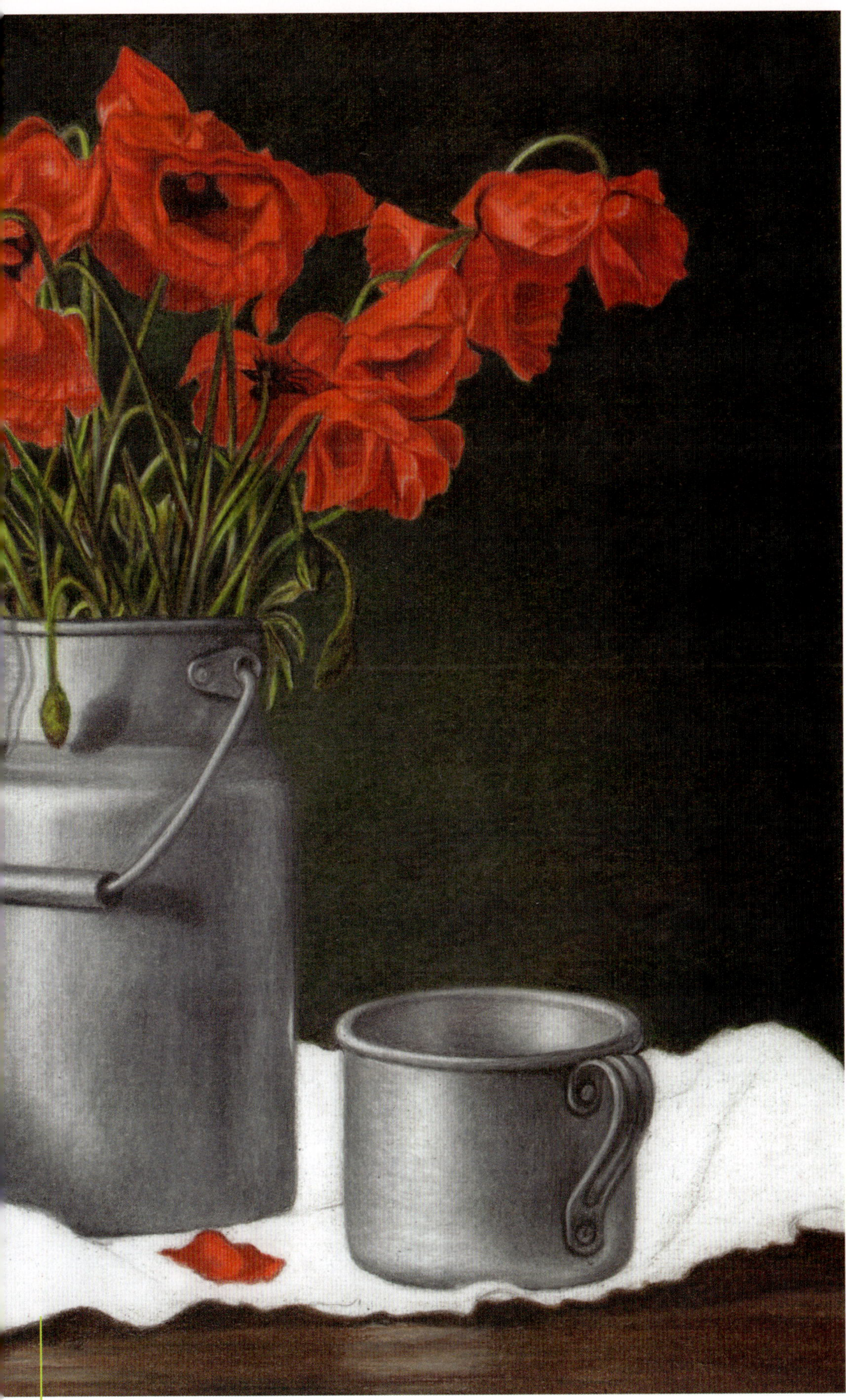

3 Soften and blend the grays in the metallic objects using White. 50% Cool Grey and White pencils work well for transitioning darker colors into lighter ones, and vice versa. The goal in this step is to achieve smooth metallic textures.

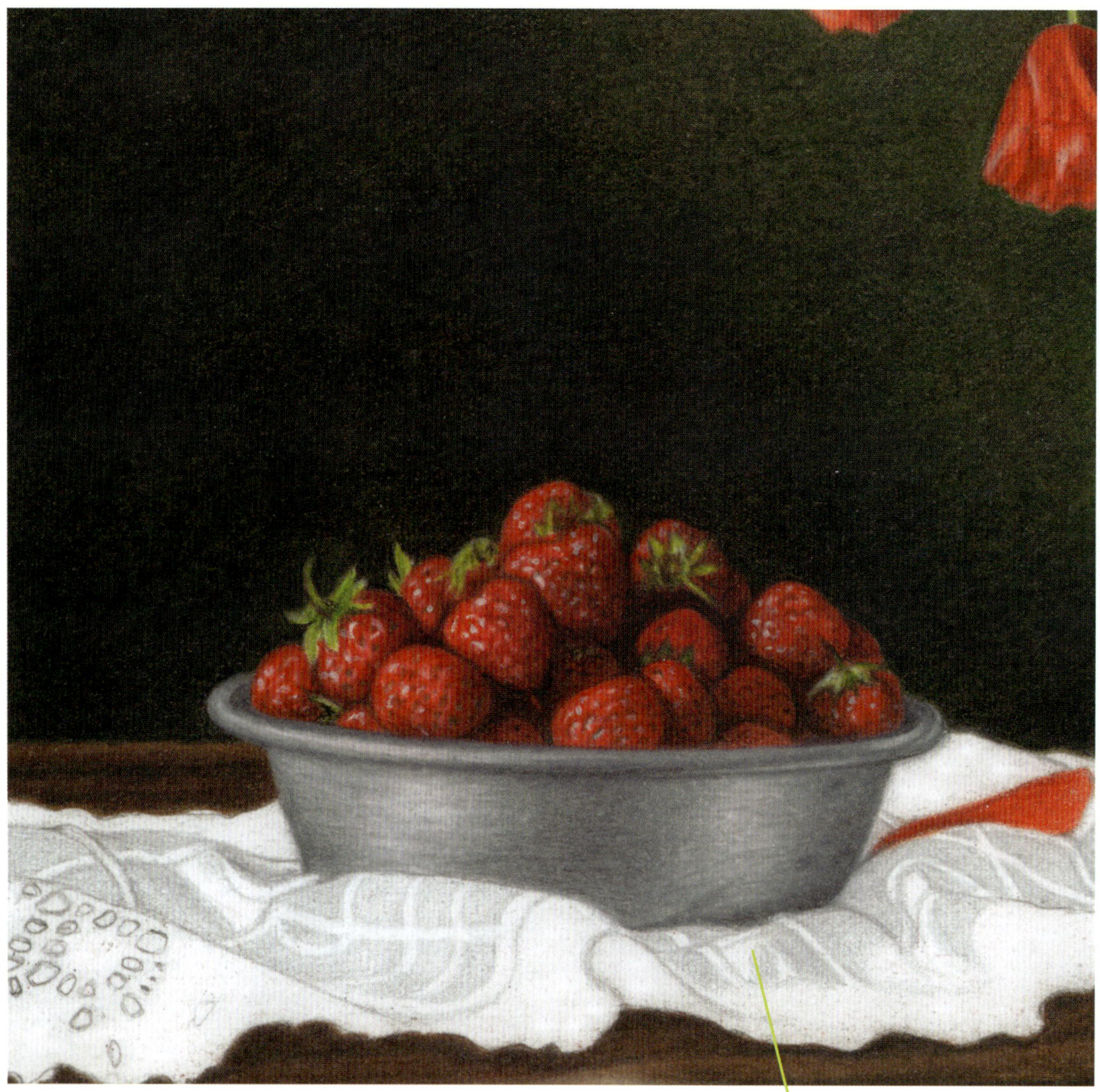

Notice the raised linear pattern throughout the fabric. Use either a graphite pencil or 30% Cool Grey to tentatively block it in.

1 Add or enhance the dark grain streaks with Black using moderate pressure (2) and horizontal strokes. Apply Chocolate over everything with medium to firm pressure (3-4) and horizontal strokes.

2 Finesse the shiny highlights with Putty Beige using horizontal strokes and medium to firm pressure (3-4). Skim a bit of Chocolate back over the dimmer sections of the highlights.

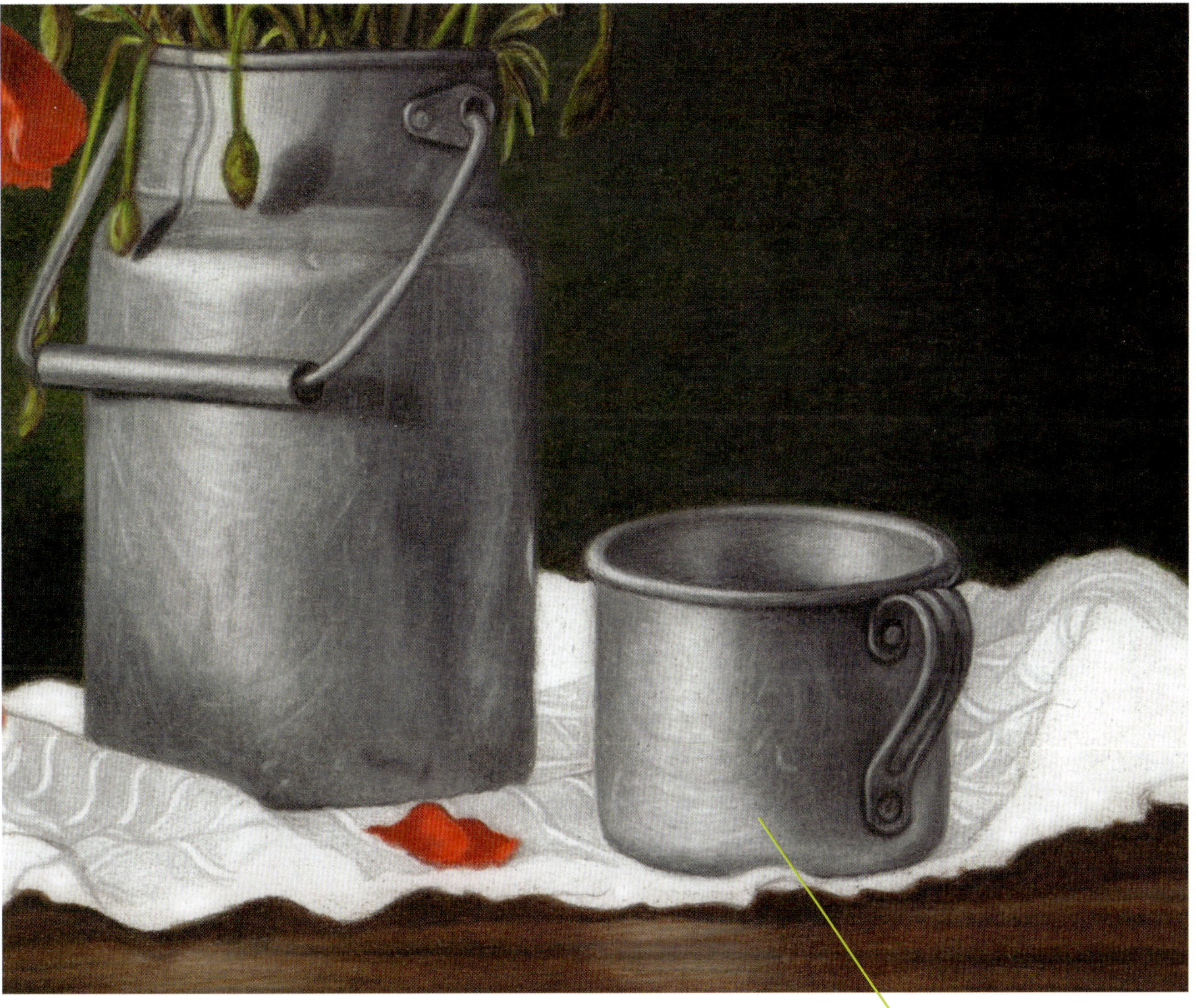

For the bowl and cup, use thin, curved, horizontal streaks with 50% Cool Grey. Soften with White.

1 Use a very sharp White with medium to firm pressure (3-4) to create random thin scratch streaks over the milk can. In some cases, lightly border one side of a thin streak with 50% Cool Grey to add depth. Soften with a skimming of White over the highlights and a skimming of 50% or 70% Cool Grey over the darker areas.

2 Create the little dent at the curved area near the milk can's handle by carving a tiny half-circle with White, bordering on the left side with 70% Cool Grey, and softening with a sharp White.

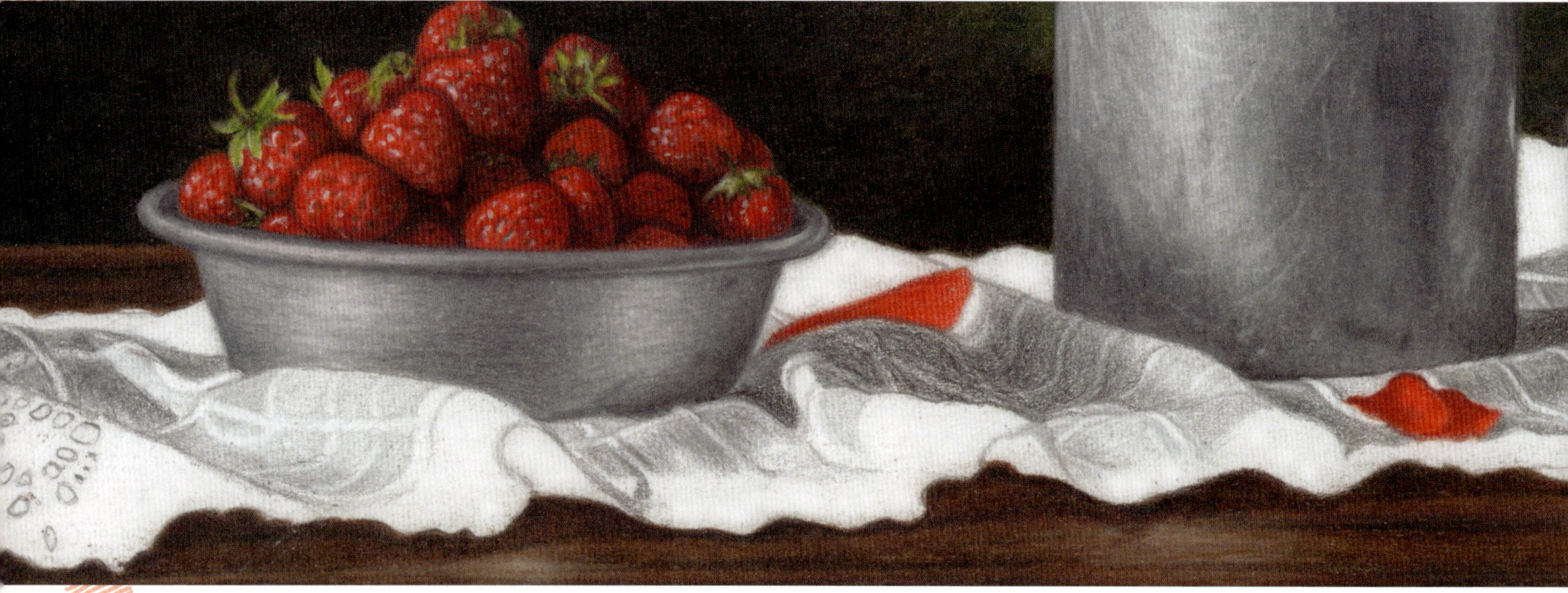

1 Develop the grays throughout the lace fabric. Work with 30% Cool Grey for the lighter areas, 50% Cool Grey and 70% Cool Grey for the midtones, and 90% Cool Grey for the deep shadows.

2 Apply color around the striped woven pattern, and then go back and lightly fill in those strips with a skimming of an appropriate gray pencil. Use tiny, overlapping strokes and moderate pressure (2).

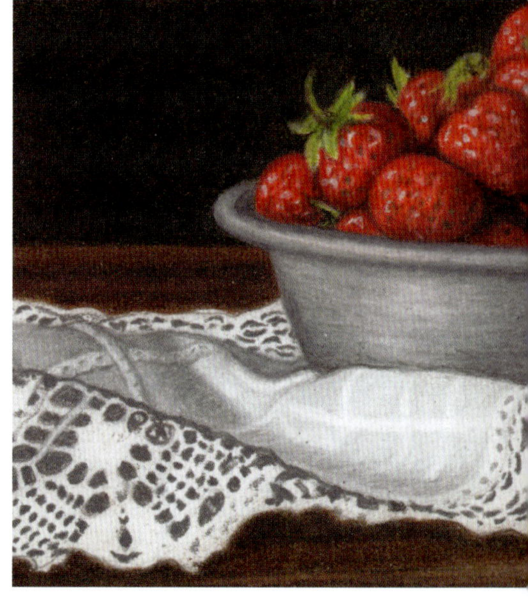

TIP

When working on the lace, tape your reference (you can use my final artwork) directly over the completed portion of your artwork so that the picture of the lace is only inches away from the lace you're drawing.

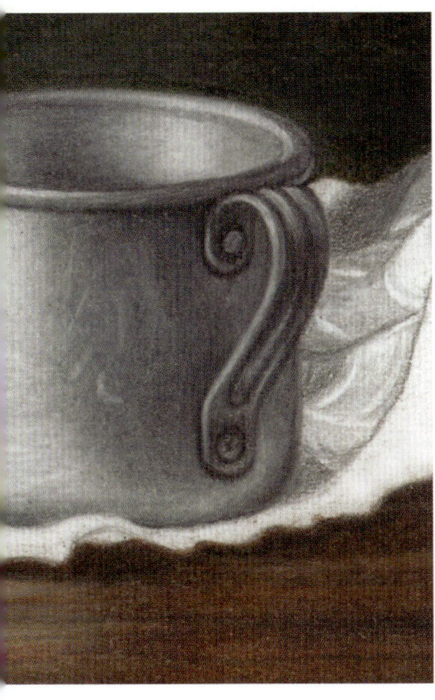

TIP

Graphite pencil smudges easily, so keep a piece of clean paper under your hand.

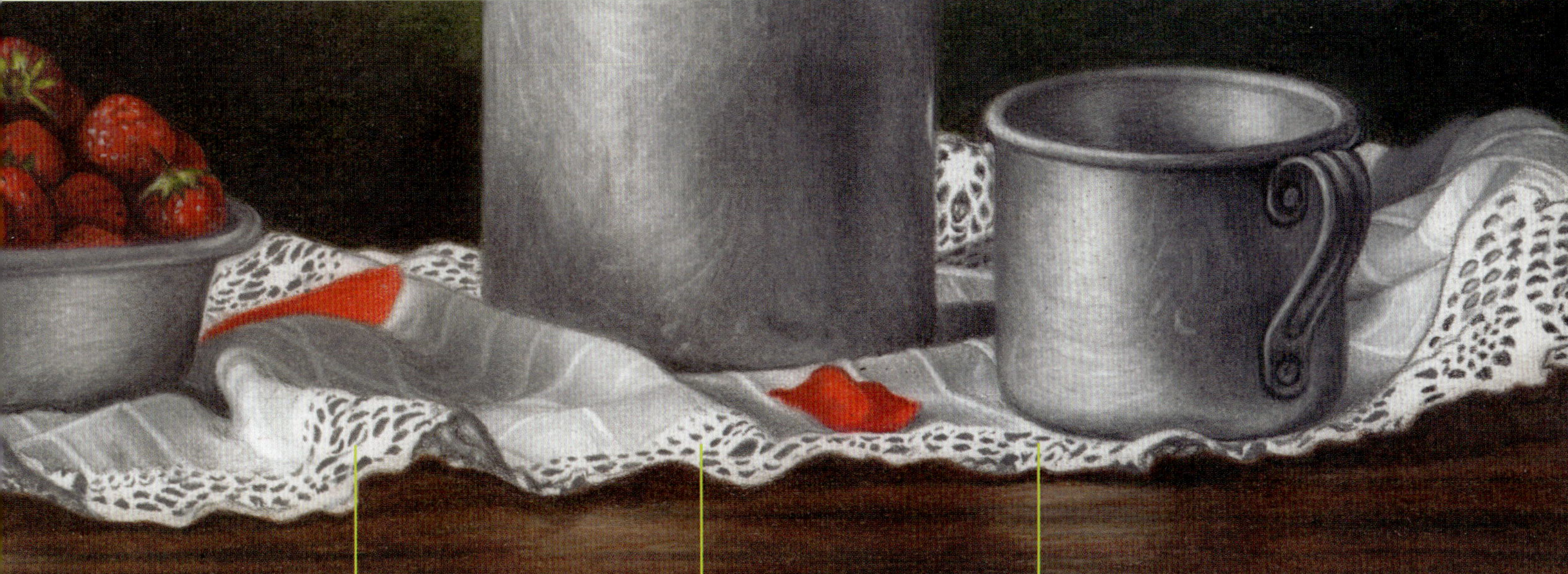

1 Blend the existing shaded areas throughout the lace, and then draw in the lace holes, working with Cool Greys, Black, and White. Use sharply pointed pencils and tiny, overlapping strokes. Vary your pressure.

2 Begin with White and blend the gray areas around the white lattice strips. Use light pressure (1). To the left of the bowl, work with 50% Cool Grey in the shaded area; then blend and soften with White, and apply more 50% Cool Grey. Use only 30% Cool Grey for the bright lace area next to it.

3 Notice the dark areas. For these, work with 50%, 70%, and even 90% Cool Grey. Squint! It's the best way to quickly determine if you need to go darker. Remember to blend!

4 Use a sharp 70% Cool Grey for all but six of the light lace holes on the far right. Then color over them with 70% Cool Grey.

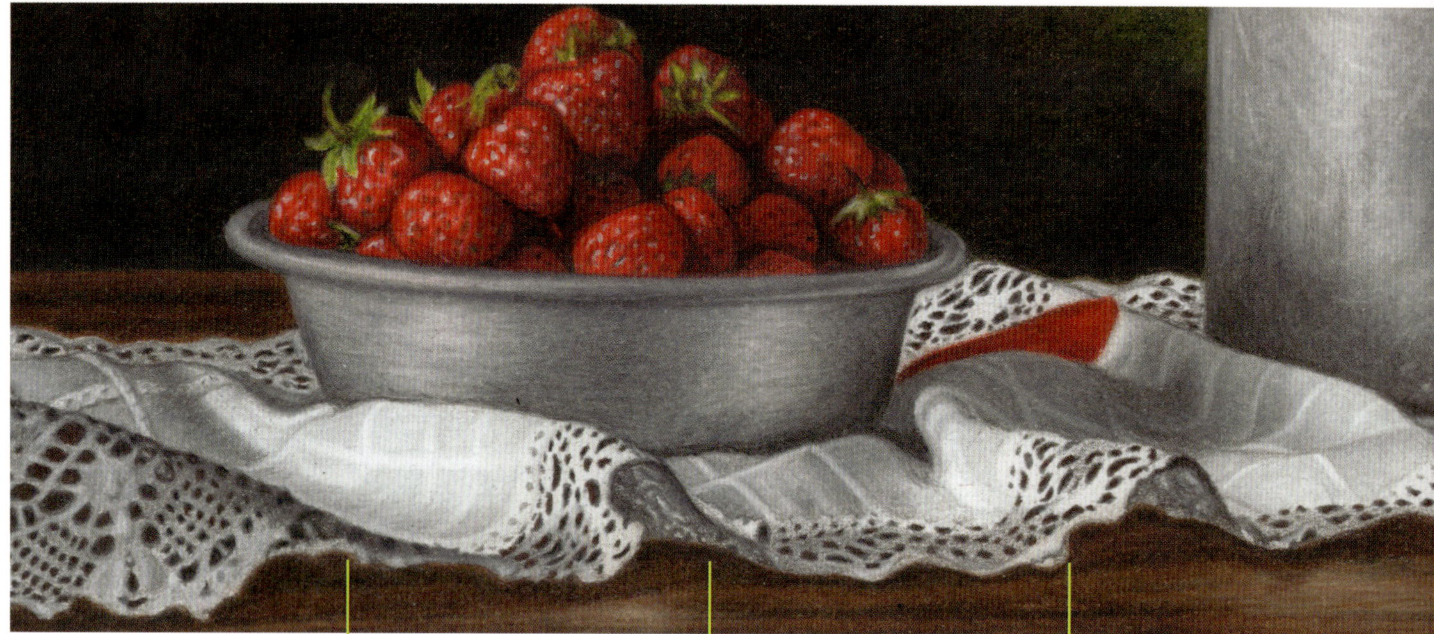

1 Color over the holes with Black using medium to firm pressure (3-4) to deepen the value. Then apply Dark Umber over the blackened holes to create the appearance of the table showing through.

2 Next use your Cool Grey pencils to shade the still-unshaded lace sections with holes. Use a very sharp 50% Cool Grey and light to moderate pressure (1-2). For darker areas and the far-right section, use 70% Cool Grey.

3 Smooth out some of those sections with a sharp White and moderate pressure (2) to create a polished, finished look.

4 For the large section on the far right, work with 50% and 70% Cool Greys, Black to accentuate the dark holes, and White to fill in those six light holes.

Review your lace from left to right. Squint! Evaluate your darks and lights, and adjust accordingly. Soften where necessary and ensure that defined edges are crisp at the creases and where the lace meets the wood table.

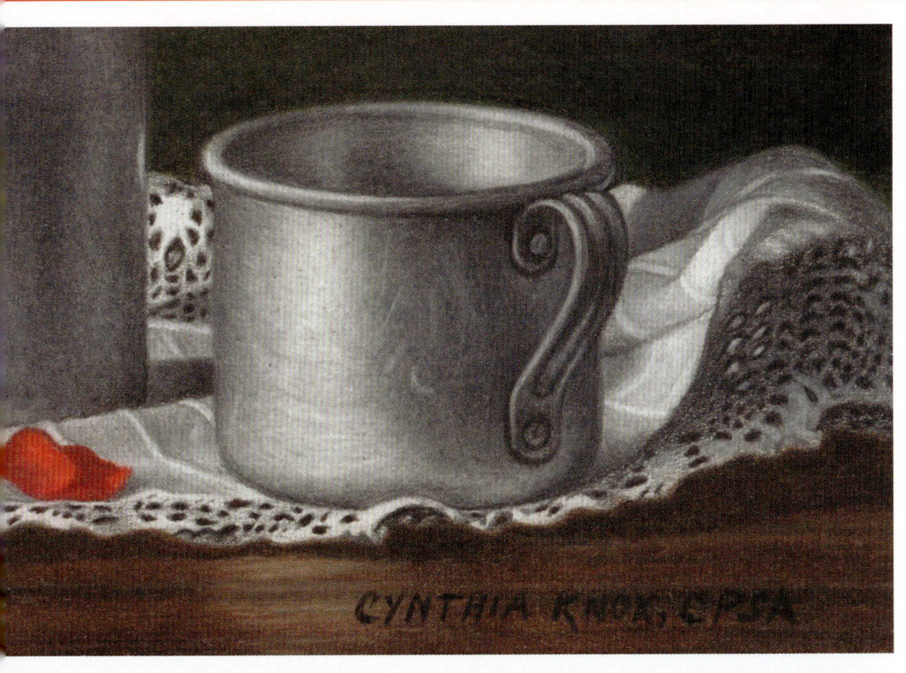
CYNTHIA KNOX, CPSA

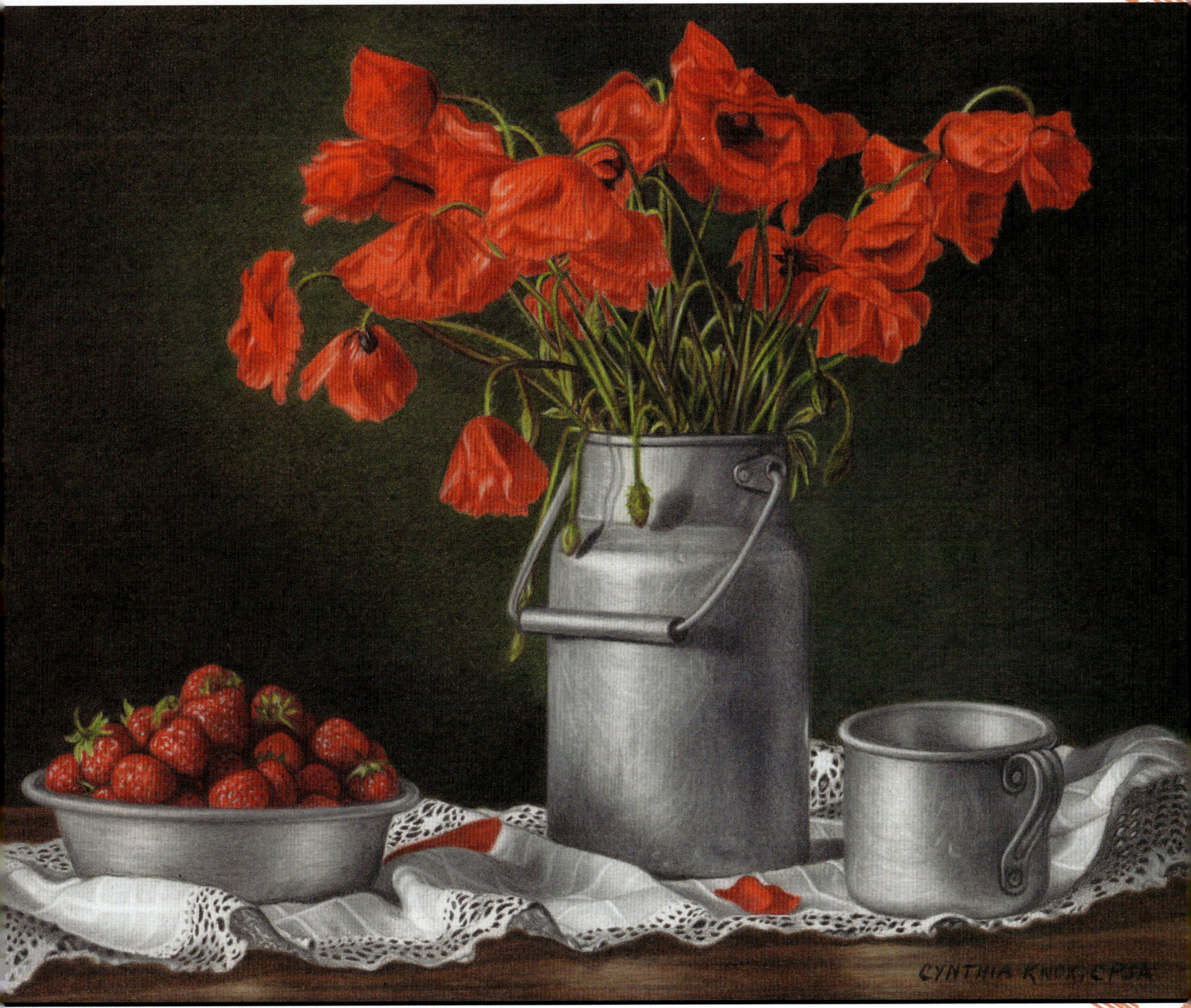

FINISHING TOUCHES

1 Darken the shadows of the two fallen petals on the lace with Tuscan Red and a bit of Black. Use light pressure (1) with Black and color over everything with Crimson Red to diffuse the darks.

2 Create random little "fuzzies" over some of the poppy stems. Use a very sharp Limepeel to carve through the waxy layers. Soften and shorten your fuzzies with Olive Green to finish.

3 Review the entire artwork. Soften any waxy blips with a sharp pencil. Look at the edges of the metallic objects, poppies, stems, strawberries, and the lace where it meets the table and background. Everything should be crisp and not blurred. If the background needs further smoothing, go ahead and do that with Black or Olive Green. Soften and blend with White. Do you need to darken the shadows over the strawberries? If so, gently use the Black STABILO pencil with a very sharp point and a light touch (1).

4 Sign your name with a sharp Black STABILO pencil. Proceed slowly and "sketch" each letter of your name due to the heavy wax buildup. Spray with a final fixative or workable fixative to seal in the wax layers and prevent filmy residue.

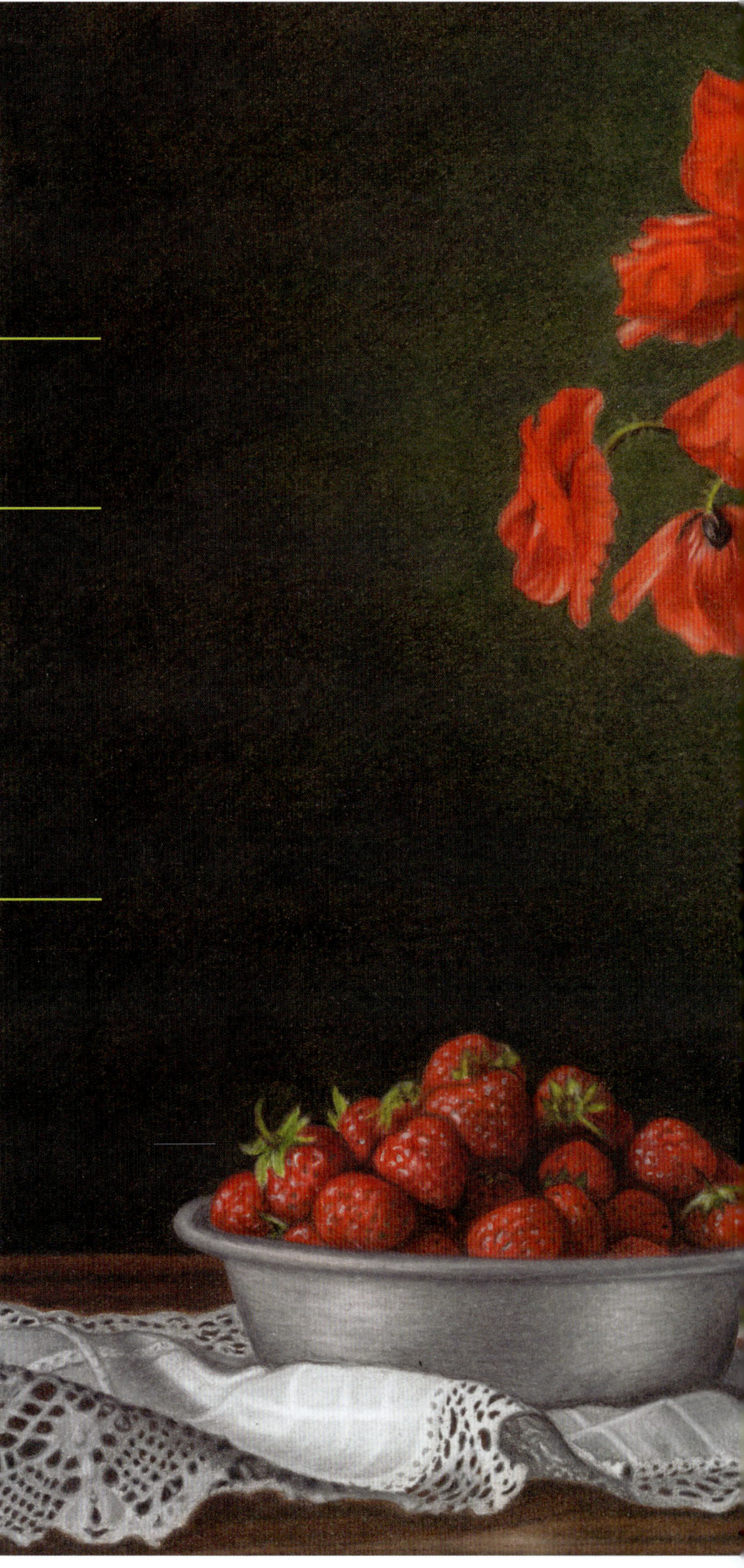

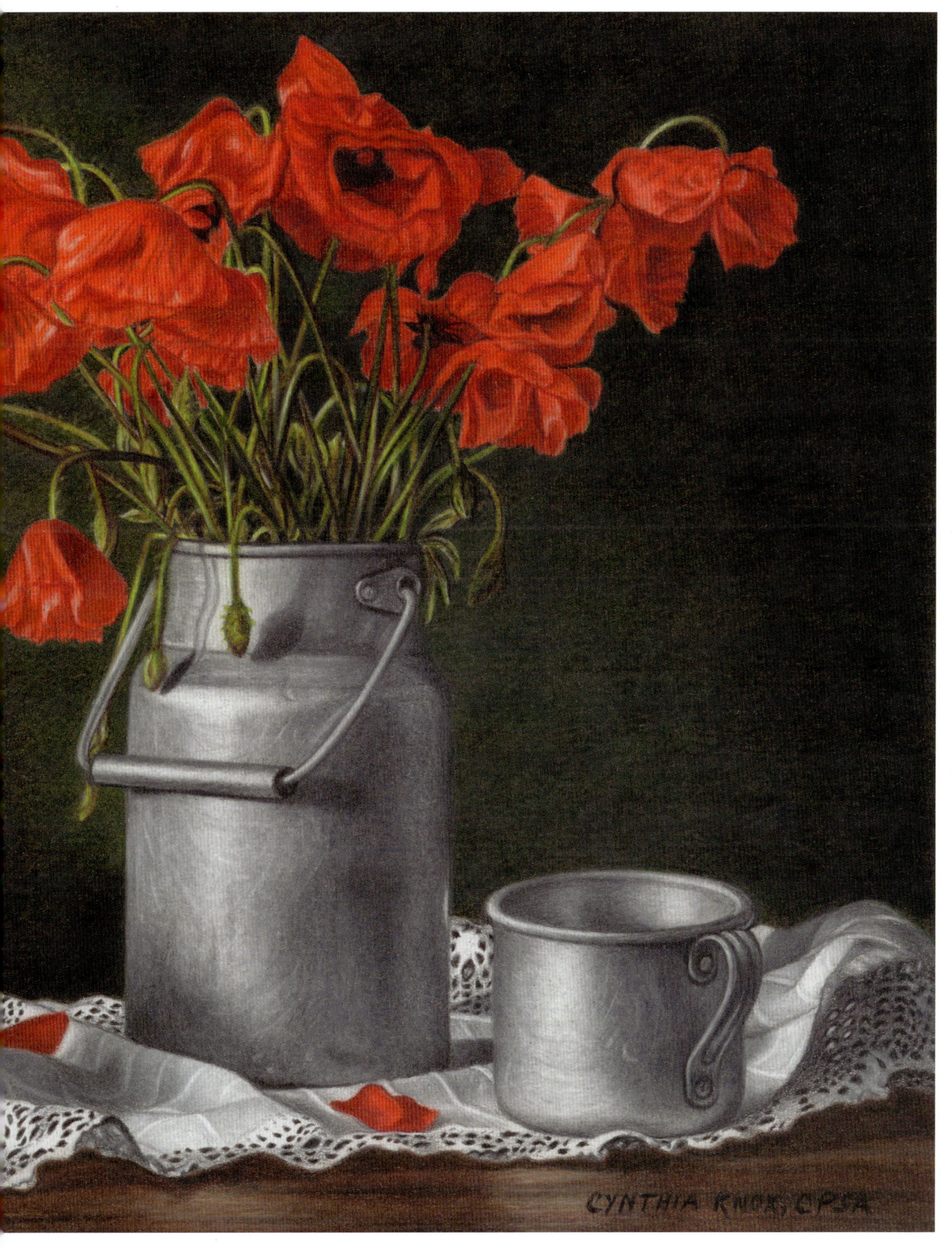
CYNTHIA KNOX, CPSA

Project 2:

Peaches

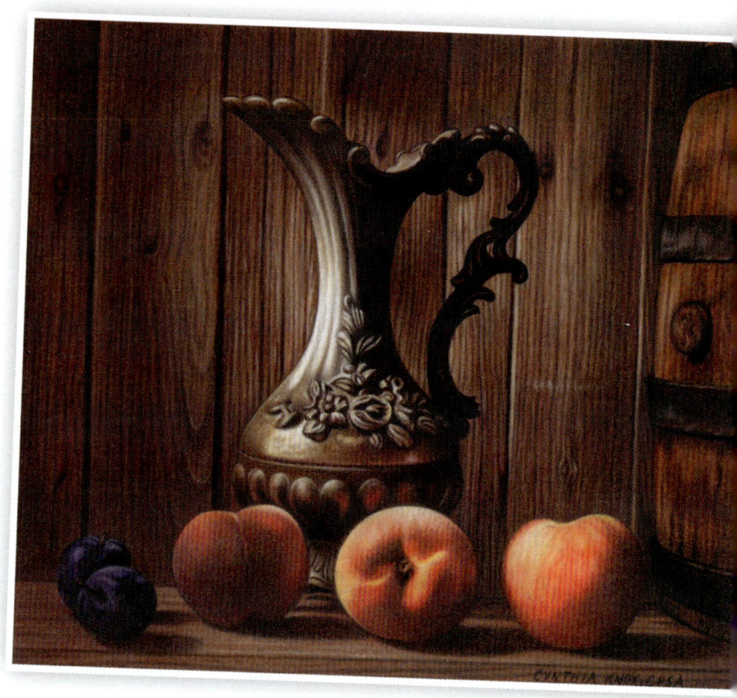

This striking still life suggests the opening of a nearby window or door that allows early morning sunlight to filter in. The lighting transforms a few ordinary objects into a captivating scene that draws the viewer in for further examination. Observe the beautiful juxtaposition of textures featured in the soft, fuzzy peach skin and antique metallic pitcher. The dimly illuminated plums rest against a grainy wood backdrop, and the aged wooden barrel complements the light wood table.

PALETTE

Prismacolor Premier:
132 Dioxazine Purple Hue
916 Canary Yellow
922 Poppy Red
924 Crimson Red
933 Violet Blue
935 Black
937 Tuscan Red
938 White (x2)
940 Sand
941 Light Umber
942 Yellow Ochre
943 Burnt Ochre
944 Terra Cotta
945 Sienna Brown
946 Dark Brown
947 Dark Umber
996 Black Grape
997 Beige
1002 Yellowed Orange
1028 Bronze
1031 Henna
1082 Chocolate
1084 Ginger Root
1085 Peach Beige

STABILO All:
8046 Black
8052 White

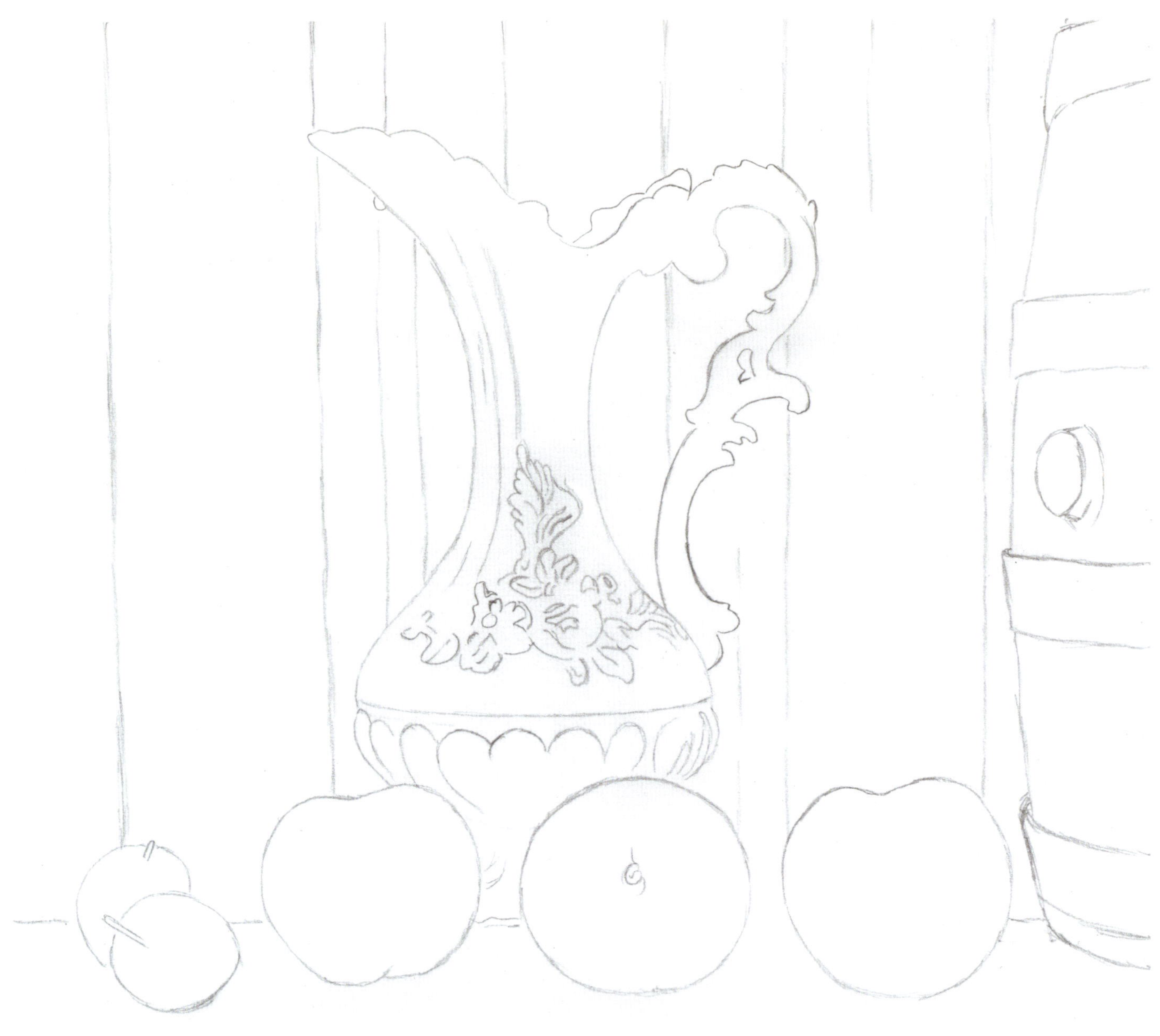

Before you begin, check the vertical wood lines of your line drawing. Ensure that they are relatively straight and correct them now using a ruler.

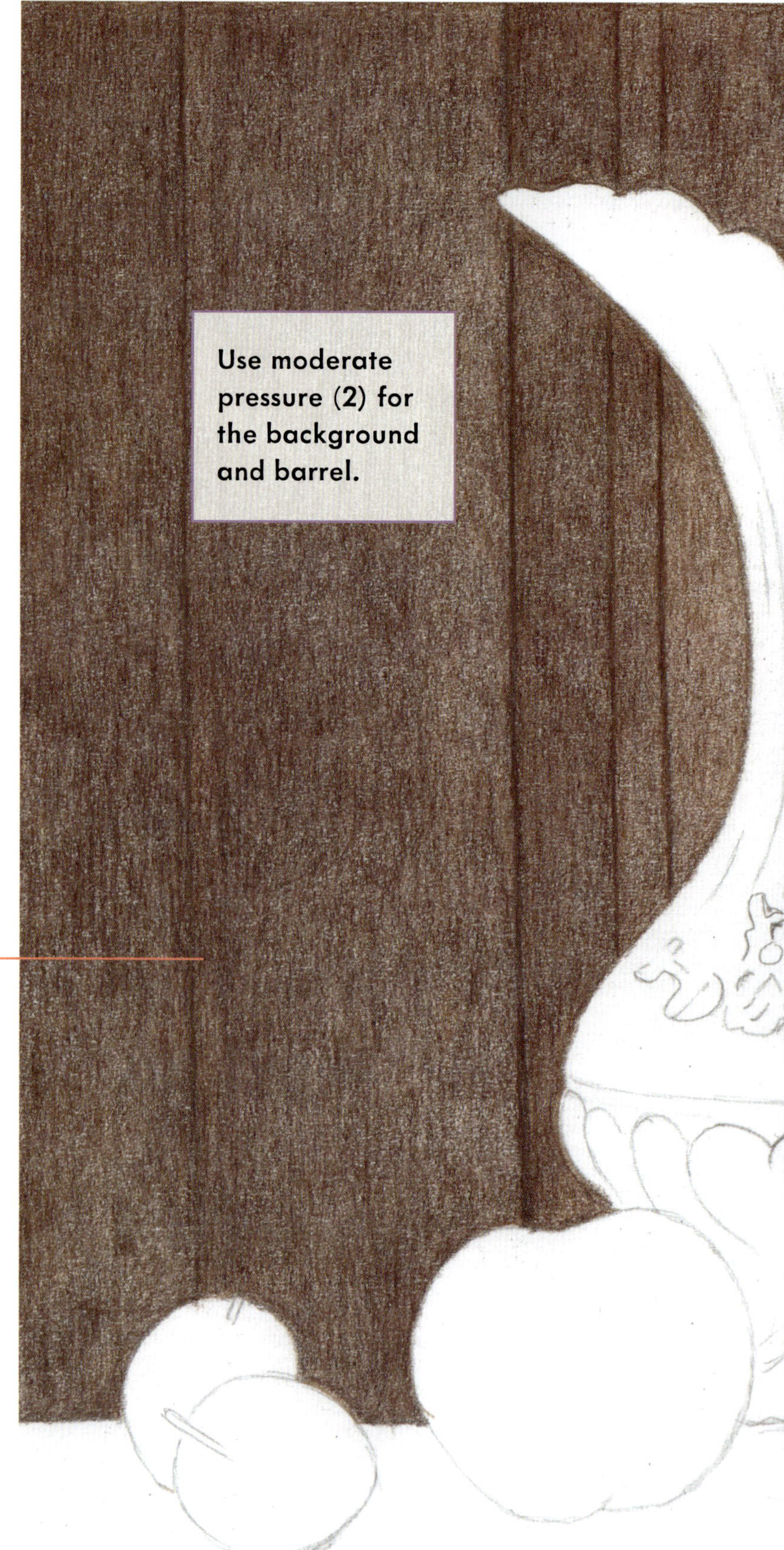

BACKGROUND

1 Begin the background with an overall application of Light Umber with vertical strokes. Darken the vertical grain lines with Dark Umber and medium pressure (3).

2 Apply Dark Brown vertically over the Light Umber.

3 Apply Dark Umber over the Dark Brown to darken the wood. Use a slightly lighter touch on the right side, where the wood is illuminated.

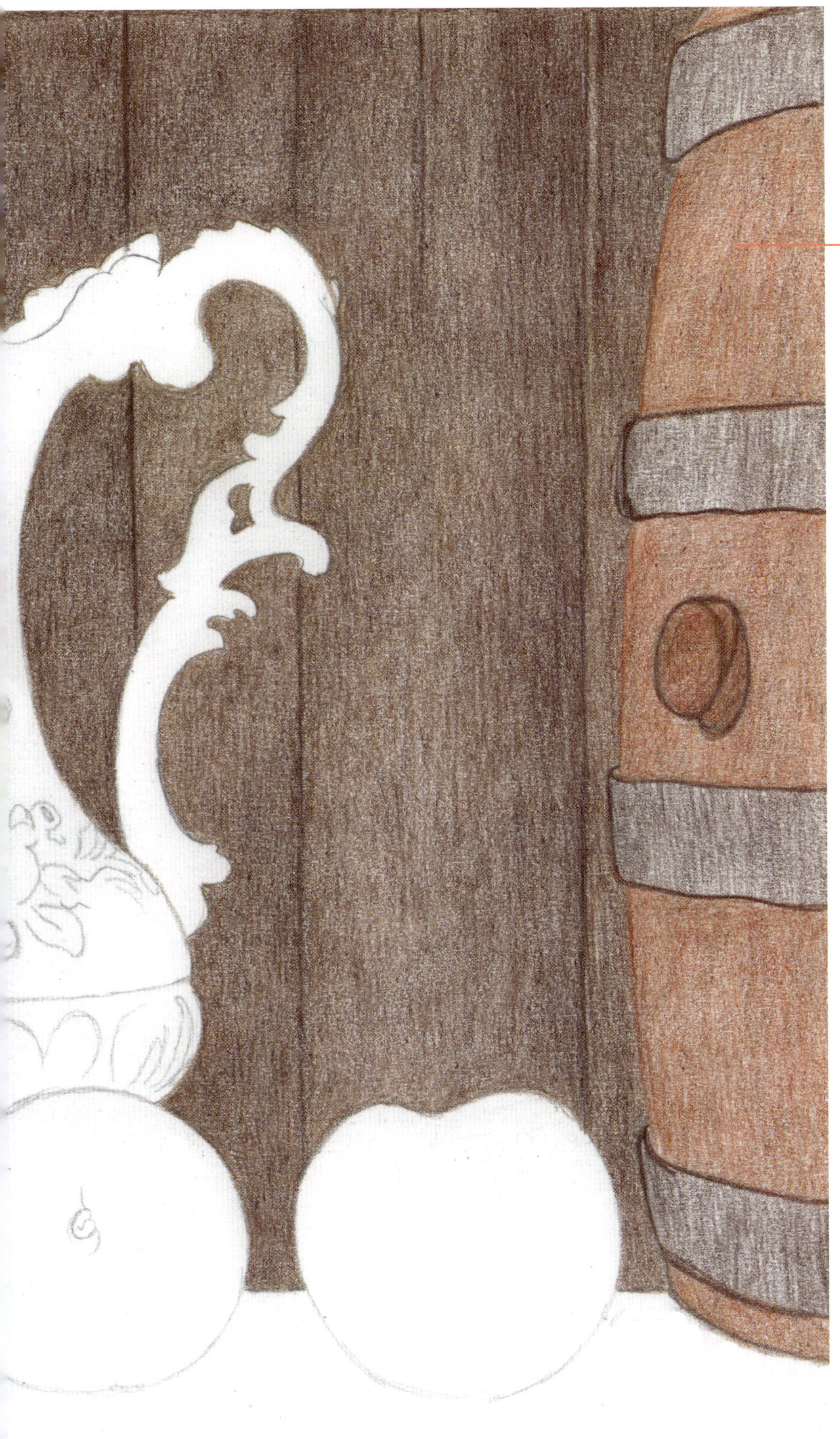

BARREL

1 Outline the horizontally curved barrel bands and bung with Dark Umber. Over everything but the curved hoops, apply Burnt Ochre with slightly curved vertical strokes in the direction of the wood grain.

2 Follow with a layer of Dark Brown and then Terra Cotta. Fill the wide horizontal bands with Dark Brown and vertical strokes.

BACKGROUND

1 Apply Dark Umber over the darkest areas of the entire background using vertical, overlapping strokes and medium pressure (3).

2 Over the Dark Umber, apply Black. Apply Light Umber with medium pressure (3) and vertical strokes over the lighter section in the middle.

3 Apply Chocolate over the entire background using vertical strokes and moderate pressure (2).

LEFT SIDE

1 Over most of the board, apply Dark Umber with medium pressure (3) in the darkest-brown areas and moderate pressure (2) in the lighter-brown areas (right side). Use vertical, overlapping strokes.

2 Over the lightest sections, burnish with Peach Beige. Use medium to firm pressure (3-4) and vertical, overlapping strokes.

3 Skim Dark Umber over all but the lighter wood using moderate to medium pressure (2-3). Use light pressure (1) to skim the lighter wood.

4 Use moderate pressure (2) and vertical strokes to skim Black over all but the lightest wood. Repeat with more Dark Umber. Deepen the long vertical grooves between the boards using Black and medium to firm pressure (3-4).

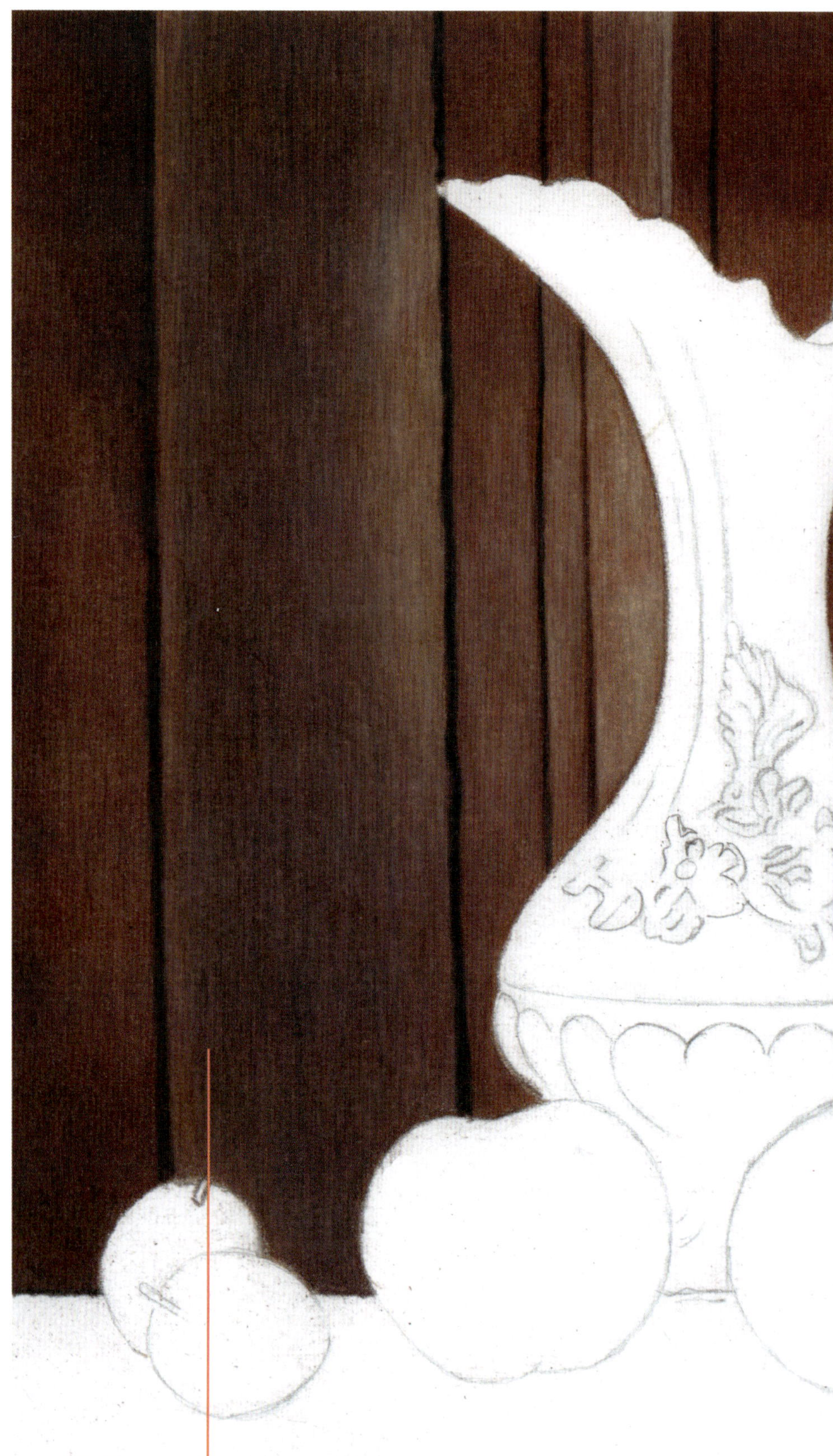

Apply Tuscan Red overall with loose, vertical strokes. Use light pressure (1) over the highlighted sections and moderate pressure (2) over the remainder. Follow with a layer of Dark Umber.

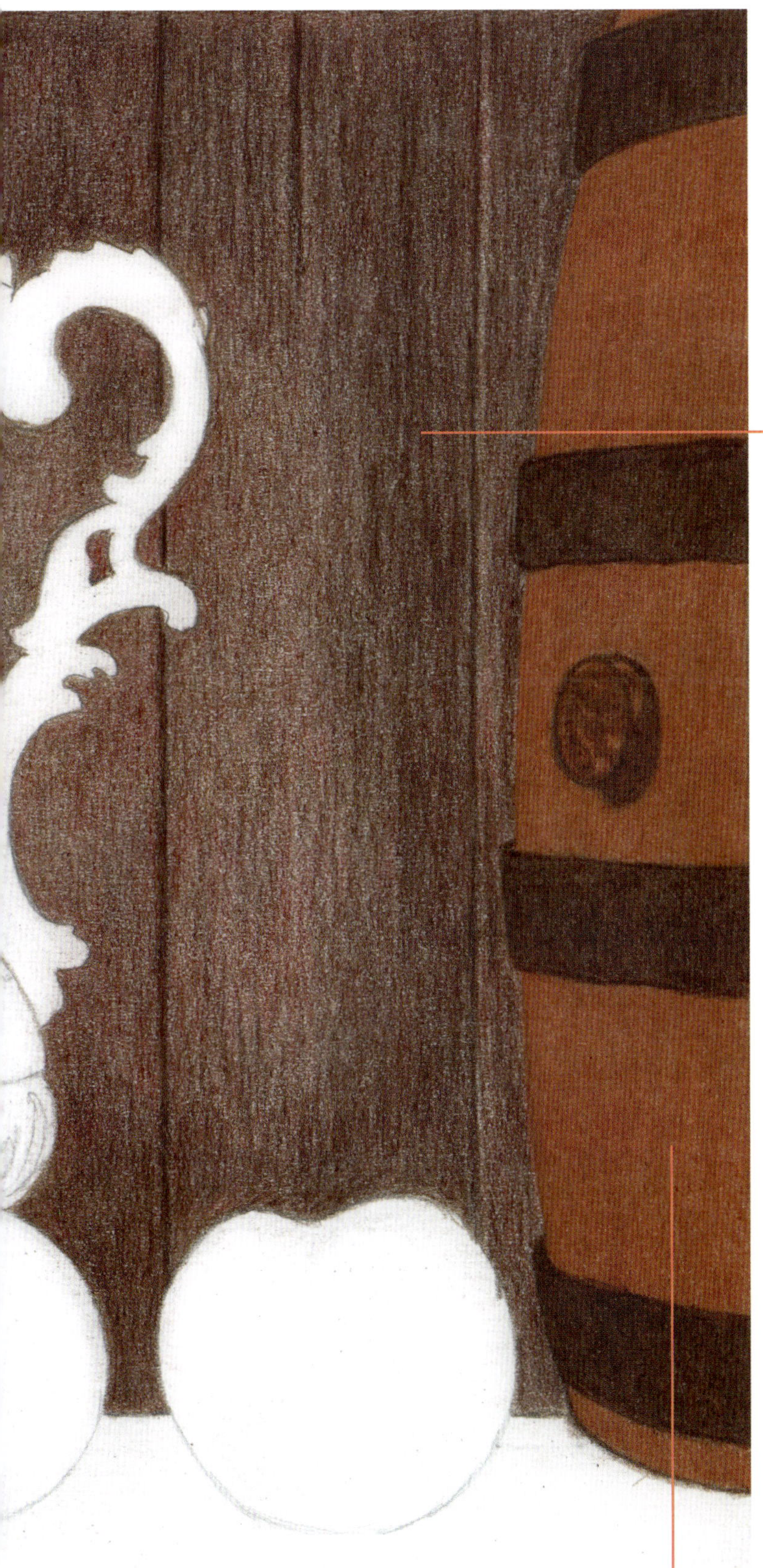

RIGHT SIDE

1 Apply Sienna Brown overall with medium to firm pressure (3-4) and overlapping vertical strokes.

2 Use Black to reinforce the long black vertical lines. Begin with moderate (2) and increase to medium pressure (3) for the darker grooves.

BARREL

Layer Sienna Brown over the entire barrel except for the four wide bands, vertically curving the strokes in the direction of the barrel's grain. Use circular, overlapping strokes around the bung and medium to firm pressure (3-4) to eliminate paper specks and achieve a polished, smooth surface. Darken the four wide bands with Dark Umber, firm pressure (4), and vertical, overlapping strokes. Apply Dark Umber over most of the bung with firm pressure (4) and overlapping circular strokes.

Develop the wood and bung with more Sienna Brown using loose, vertical strokes and moderate pressure (2). Apply more Dark Umber and then Terra Cotta over the four wide bands to intensify the color. Use loose, vertical strokes and moderate pressure (2).

BACKGROUND

1 Skim Dark Brown over all but the highlight in the middle of the right side. Use linear, overlapping, and slightly diagonal strokes for better pigment adherence, with moderate pencil pressure.

2 Apply Ginger Root in the same manner down the lighter sections. Use a sharp point, diagonal strokes, and moderate pressure (2).

3 Skim Dark Brown over the lighter wood on the right side.

4 Warm up the wood on the left side of the highlighted area with Sienna Brown and moderate pressure (2).

6 Lighten with White over the brightest area midway down and on the pitcher's left. Use moderate to medium (2-3) pressure.

7 Color over the entire dark right area with Sienna Brown. Use skimming and diagonal strokes, a sharp point, and moderate to medium pressure (2-3).

8 Drag the black upper pigment into the lower area of the panels with overlapping strokes to create a smooth transition.

9 Apply Black over the darkest sections of the panels using vertical, overlapping strokes and moderate pressure (2).

Apply Dark Brown with moderate to medium pressure (2-3) and overlapping vertical strokes.

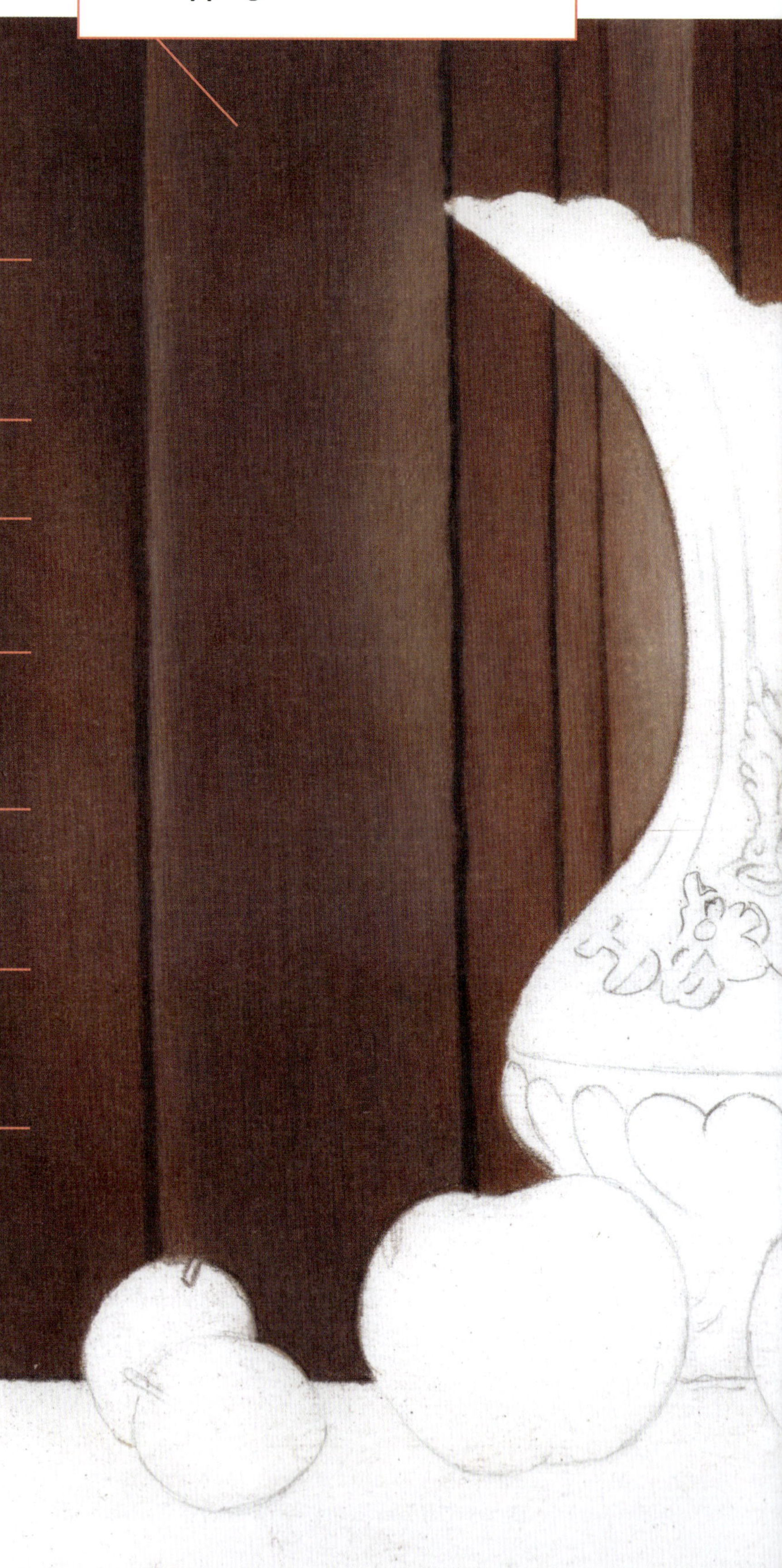

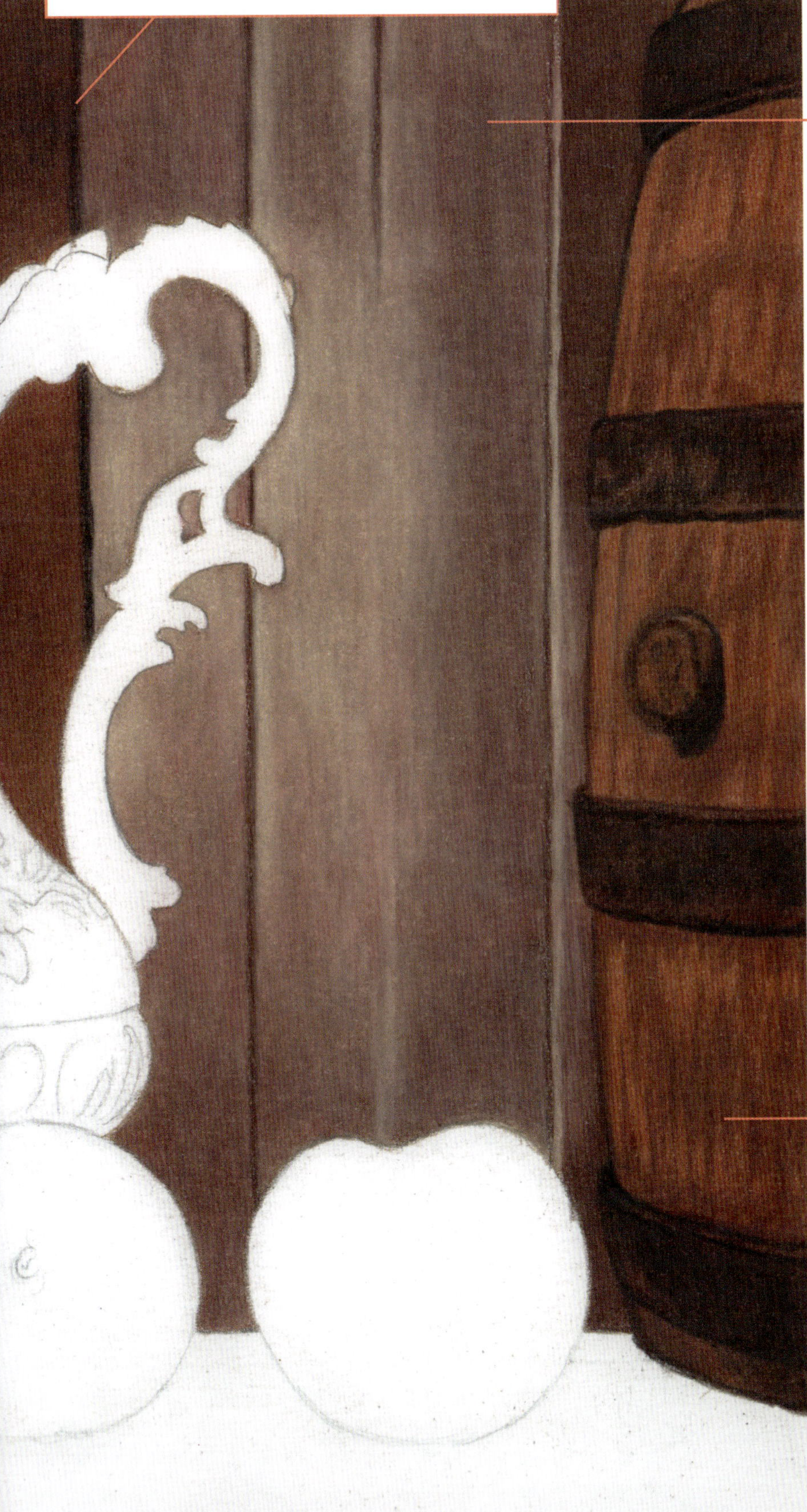

Skim a bit of Black across the middle area with a sharp point and light to moderate pressure (1-2).

1 Burnish all but the dark upper section next to the barrel with Beige using firm pressure (4) and vertical, small, overlapping strokes.

2 Burnish the very darkest sections at the top and bottom of the far-right panel next to the barrel with Dark Umber using firm pressure (4). Outline the barrel with Black.

BARREL

1 Develop the wood with Dark Umber using loose, sketchy, and vertically curved strokes, with moderate to medium pressure (2-3).

2 Use Black to intensify the dark areas of the horizontal bands and the deep shadow around the bung. Apply moderate to medium pressure (2-3) with overlapping vertical strokes and preserve the thin, lighter horizontal rims.

Use a ruler to check that the two left wood panels are mostly straight, and correct them if necessary using sharp Black and White to "erase." If you use White, color over it with Dark Umber and slightly diagonal, firm (4) strokes.

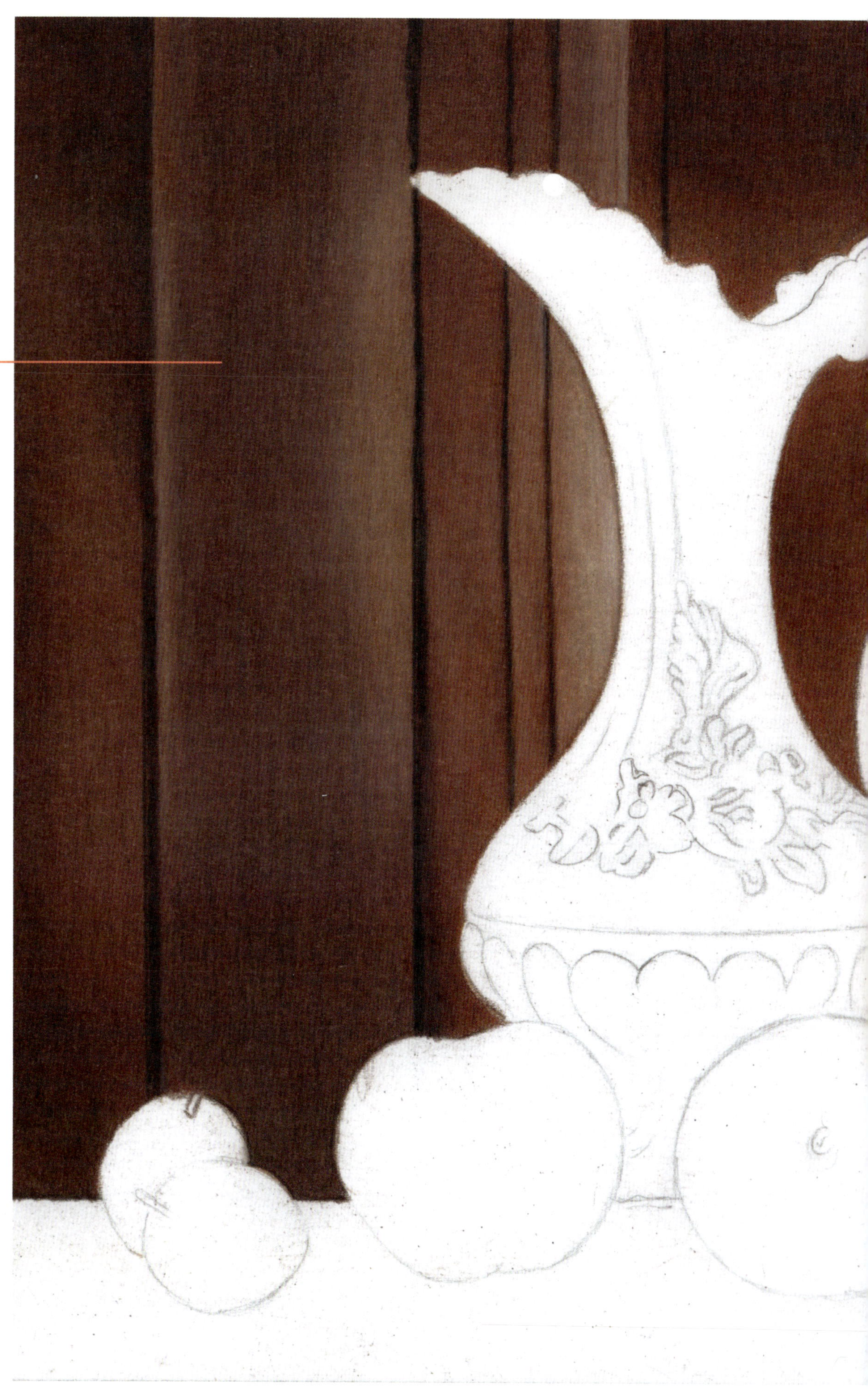

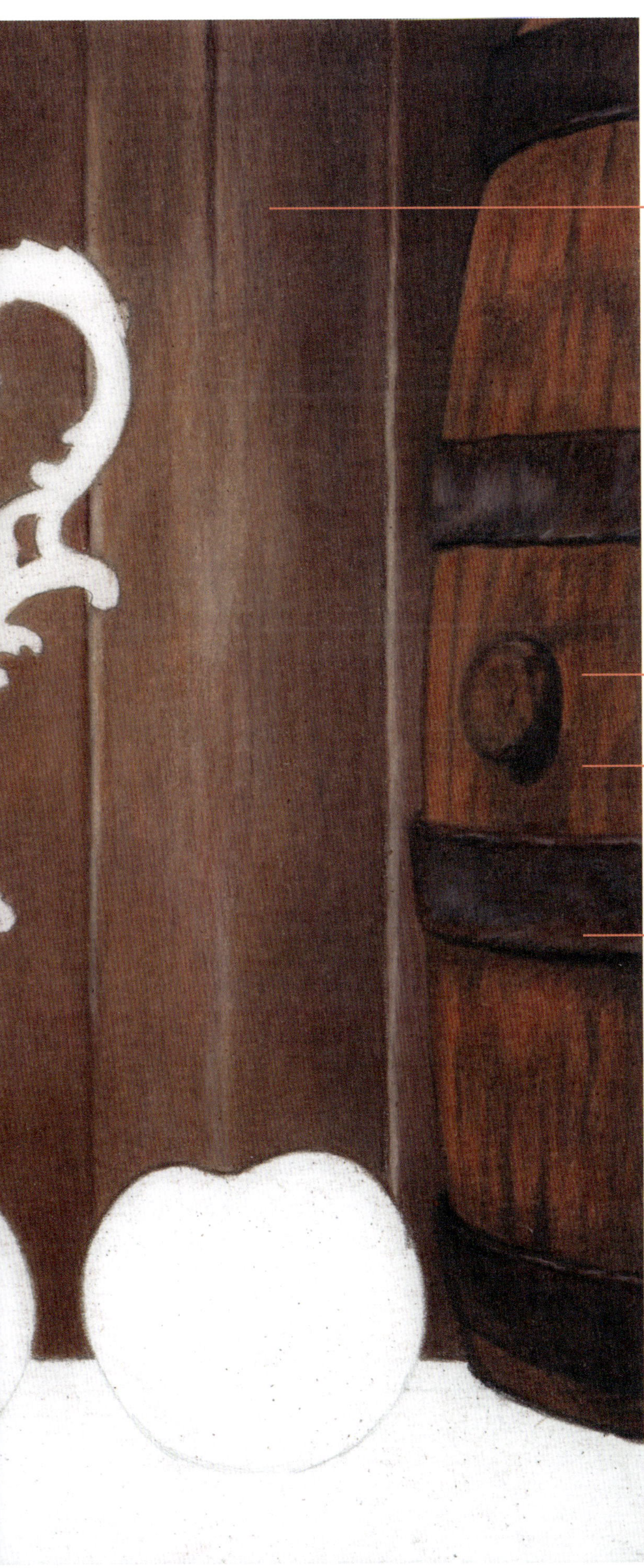

1 Darken all of the brown areas in the right side of the background, except for the lightest brown, with Dark Umber. Skim with loose, overlapping, vertical strokes and moderate pressure (2). Increase your pressure to medium (3) over the darkest sections. Skim Black over the darkest sections with moderate to medium pressure (2-3).

2 Soften and blend using more Dark Umber, Black, and Sienna Brown with varied pressure and strokes for smooth transitions.

BARREL

1 Skim Black over the darkest patches throughout the wood with loose strokes and moderate pressure (2). Apply Terra Cotta over all of the wood to blend down the Black.

2 Lightly (1-2) develop the vertical grain lines with Black.

3 Over the horizontal bands, apply White to lighten random areas. Use a sharp point, medium pressure (3), and squiggly, connected strokes. Skim Dark Brown lightly to soften the White. A touch of Sienna Brown restores warmth.

4 Use a sharp White to line some areas of the rims. Soften with Dark Brown and/or Sienna Brown.

TIP

I like to complete all of the colors and values in wood before adding the grain and knot details. This ensures that the highlights and shadows are correct.

Soften and expand the highlighted areas throughout the background with Beige and moderate to medium pressure (2-3). Use Sienna Brown to diffuse the Beige into the surrounding colors.

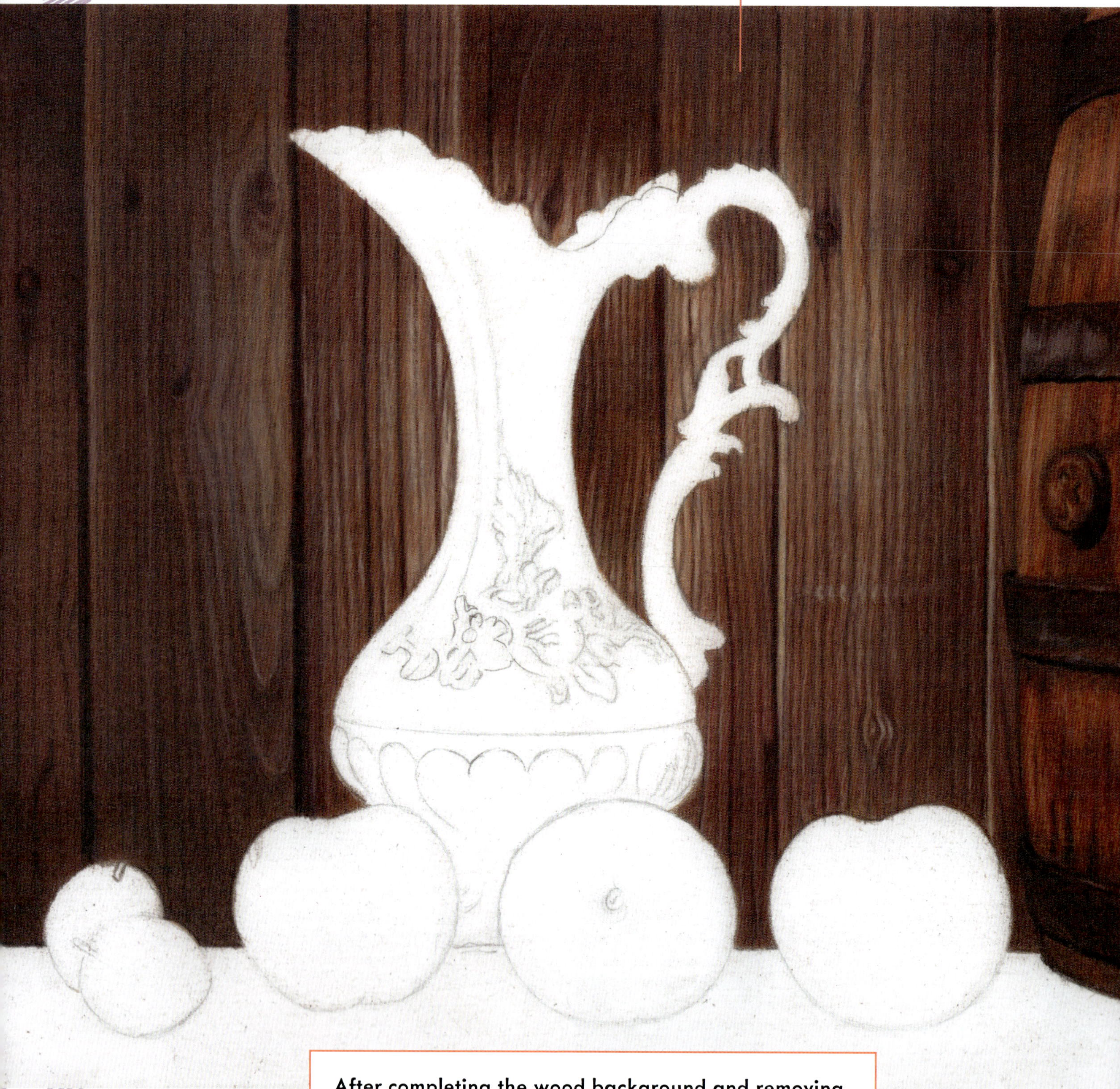

After completing the wood background and removing the wax bloom, rip up pieces of scrap paper and place them over the uncolored areas of your piece. Shake a can of workable fixative and test it in the air facing away from you and the artwork to ensure that it does not spit. Now spray about 6 inches away from your artwork several times to seal in the wax layers.

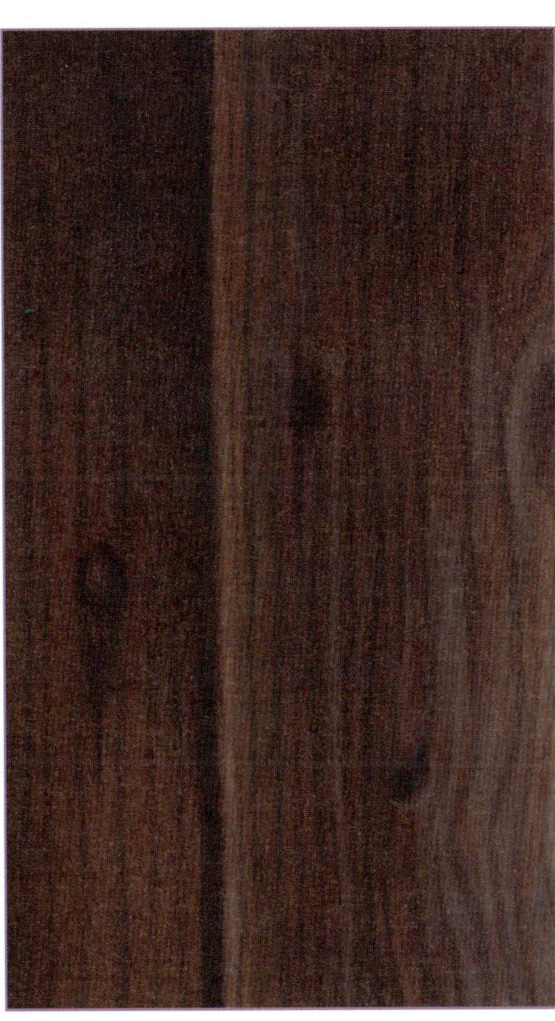

1 Over the darker wood sections, use sharp Black and increasing pressure to sketch in the grain lines.

2 Over the lighter wood sections, use sharp Dark Umber. The lines should look thin, sketchy, and slightly uneven. Adjust the lines as needed using Black or Dark Umber to darken and Sienna Brown or Terra Cotta to lighten.

3 To lighten between the grain lines in the lighter areas, use sharp Peach Beige or Beige.

4 To darken sections of color, lightly skim Dark Umber or Black with a sharp point.

5 To enhance the warmth of the wood, add Terra Cotta to the brown areas and Terra Cotta or Tuscan Red to the black areas.

6 Draw thin lines with Beige randomly throughout to create slight highlights and grain dimension, and use Sand to create the lightest streaks of grain.

7 Draw knots and nail markings with Black. Emphasize them with Terra Cotta or Tuscan Red, and lighten with Beige or Sienna Brown.

8 When you are finished, gently use a soft cloth and small circular strokes to lift any wax bloom. Then enhance the deepest black areas with Black STABILO.

BARREL

1 Complete the wood with more Dark Umber and Black over the dark areas and Terra Cotta over the reddish-brown and lower black areas. Use White to lighten, and add a touch of Sienna Brown and/or Beige. Darken the bung with Dark Umber and Black. Complete with touches of Beige and Terra Cotta.

2 Darken the horizontal bands with Dark Umber and Black. Use Terra Cotta and Tuscan Red to add warmth, and White and Beige to “carve” in the uneven highlights throughout with a sharp point. Use Black to reinforce the dark shadows.

3 Remove any additional waxy residue and apply Black STABILO over the darkest areas.

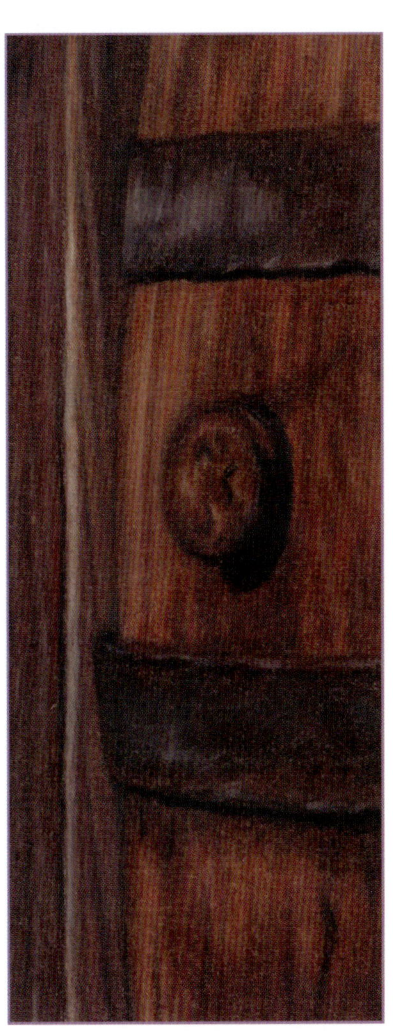

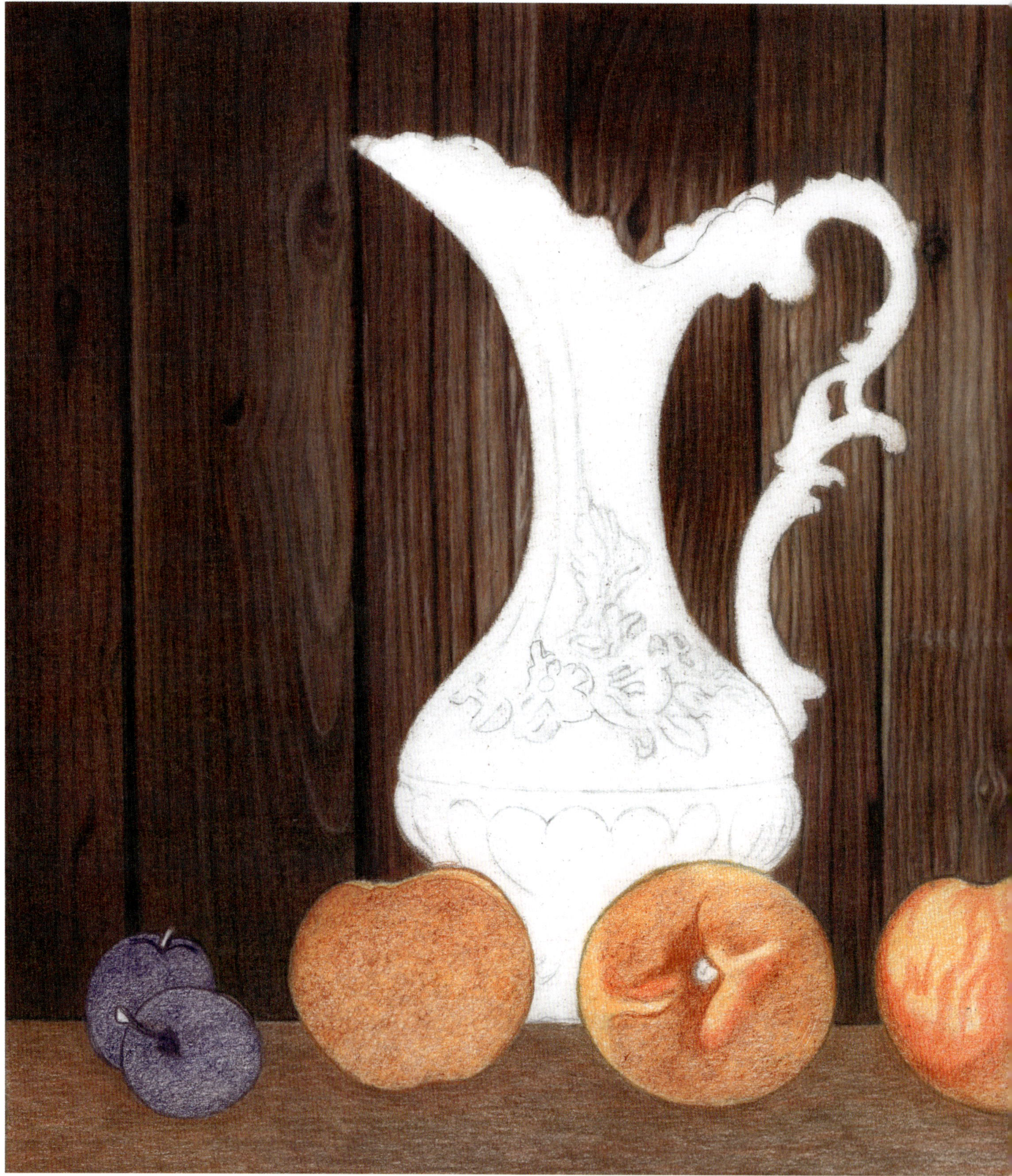

PLUMS

1 Apply Black Grape over both plums, except for the white areas, using small, rounded, and overlapping strokes and moderate pressure (2).

2 Establish the darker lines of the back plum and stem shadow of the front plum with Black Grape and medium pressure (3).

PEACHES

1 Apply Yellowed Orange over each peach with small, rounded, overlapping strokes and moderate pressure (2).

2 Add Terra Cotta over the darker areas.

3 Apply Poppy Red over the two small center areas of the middle peach and much of the far-right peach with small, rounded, overlapping strokes and moderate pressure (2).

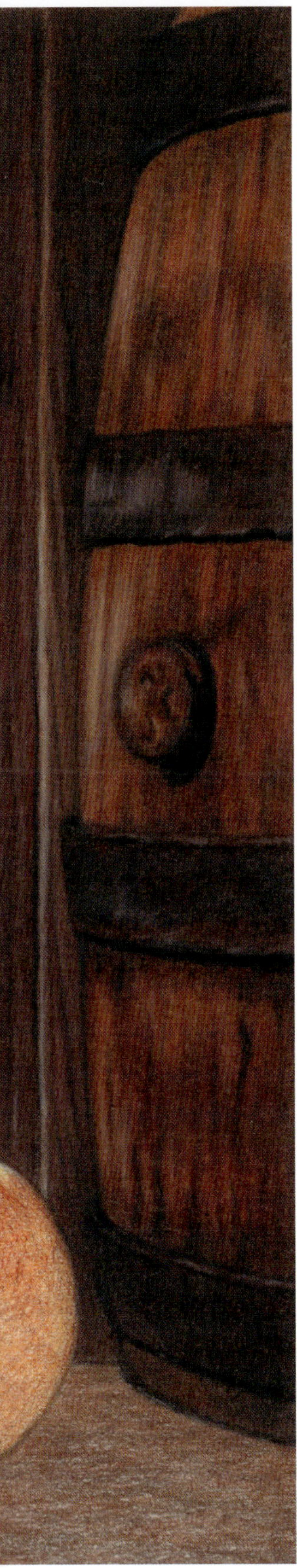

Color Violet Blue over both plums using tiny, rounded, overlapping strokes and moderate pressure (2). Block in the dark shadows with Black.

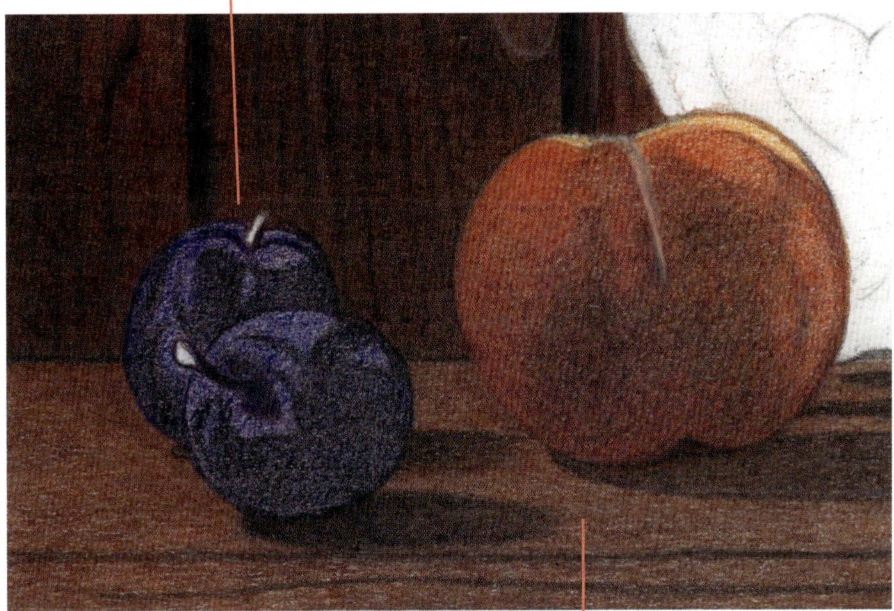

1 Deepen the color of the left peach with Henna and small, rounded, overlapping strokes applied with moderate pressure (2). Follow with a layer of Black Grape to dim the reddish hue.

2 Use Black to block in the deeper peach coloring and shadowed areas of the left peach. Begin with light to moderate pressure (1-2) and build density with a sharp point and tiny, rounded, overlapping strokes.

3 Use a sharp White to create the indentation down the center.

4 Brighten the reddish hue of the middle and right peaches with Crimson Red applied over all but the yellow areas.

Deepen the overall brown hue of the table with Dark Umber. Use small, horizontally linear, and overlapping strokes with moderate pressure (2). Block in the shadows and more prominent wood grain with Black.

TABLE

1 Begin the table with Light Umber applied horizontally using moderate pressure (2).

2 Add Burnt Ochre for warmth followed by Dark Brown to deepen the hue overall. Continue using horizontal strokes and increase your pressure to medium (3) for the Burnt Ochre and Dark Brown.

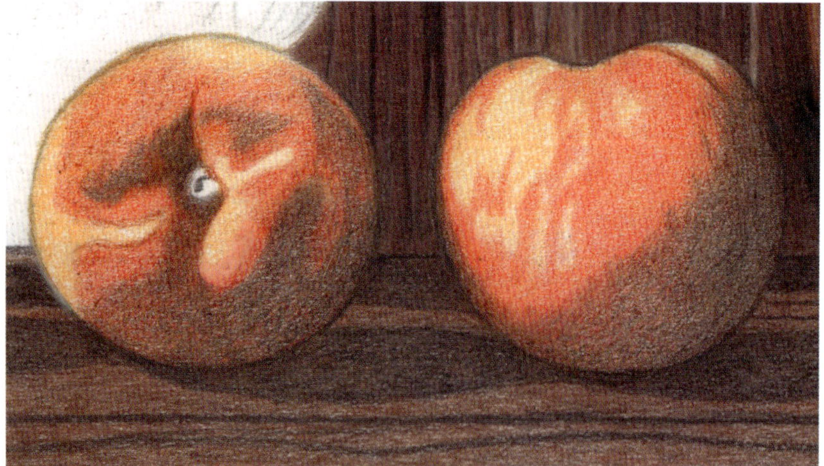

Block in the extreme darks with Black beginning with light pressure (1) and increasing to moderate (2). You may need several layers.

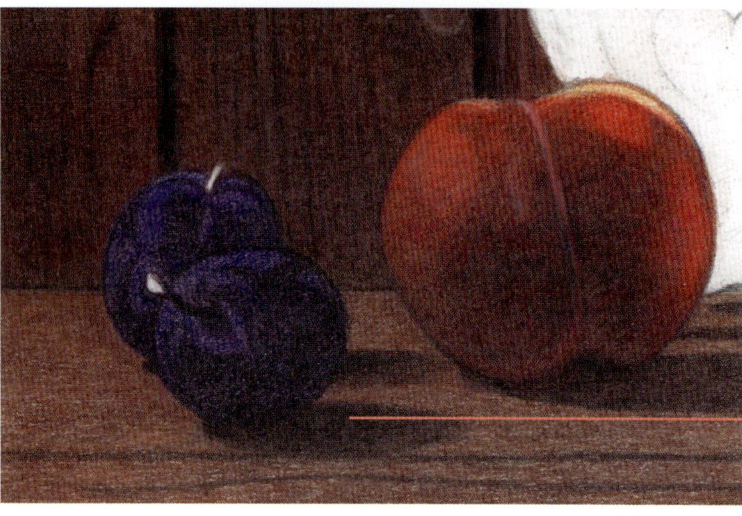

Reinforce the dark shadows on the table with Black using small, overlapping strokes and medium pressure (3).

1 Color in both plums with Dioxazine Purple Hue and small, rounded, and overlapping strokes applied with moderate pressure (2).

2 Apply another layer of Black over the dark shadows with medium pressure (3).

1 Intensify the red hue of the peach with a layer of Crimson Red applied with a very sharp point and tiny, rounded, overlapping strokes. Begin with moderate pressure (2) and increase to medium (3) over the black areas.

2 Follow with another layer of Black applied over the existing black sections. Use White to correct any mistakes.

1 Enhance the color with another layer of Crimson Red. Apply color over all but the yellow areas with tiny, rounded, and overlapping strokes and moderate to medium pressure (2-3) with a sharp point.

2 Apply another layer of Black over the dark shadows.

3 Skim Yellowed Orange over the tiny center stem end (2).

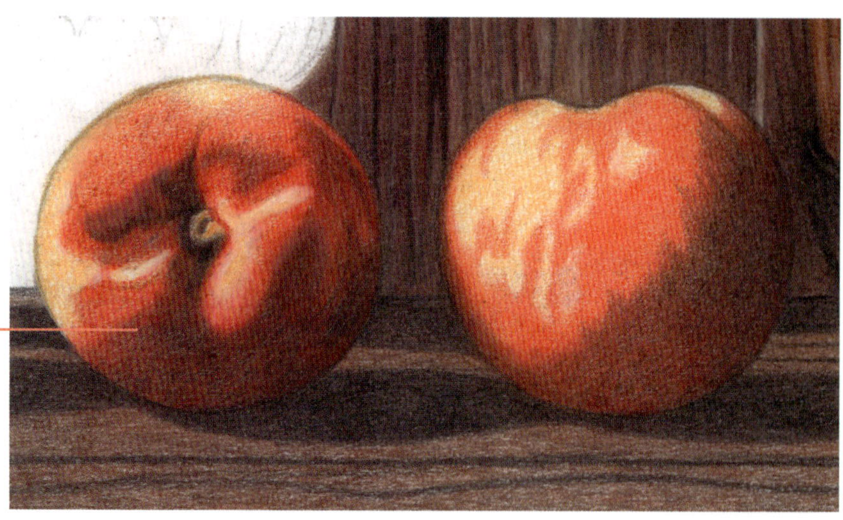

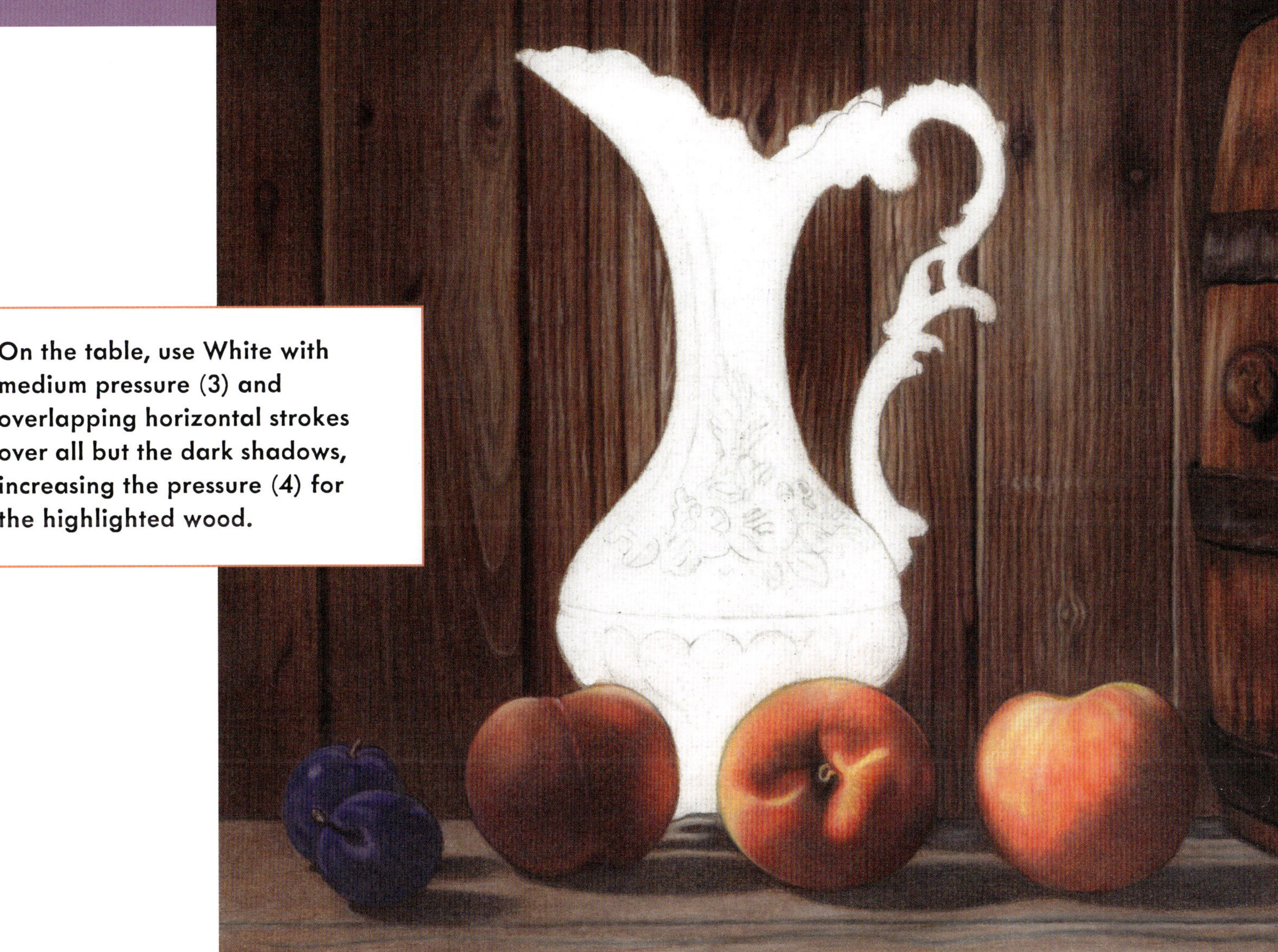

On the table, use White with medium pressure (3) and overlapping horizontal strokes over all but the dark shadows, increasing the pressure (4) for the highlighted wood.

PLUMS

1 Border the plum stems with Black and lightly (1) fill them in with Dark Brown.

2 Use White with varied pencil pressure and a sharp point to blend and burnish the very smooth skin, including the black shadows.

3 Re-outline the plums with Black as needed everywhere but the left sides.

RIGHT PEACH

1 Work with White, including over the large black shadow. Keep pencil pressure to moderate (2) and medium (3).

2 Work with White, Crimson Red, and Canary Yellow to achieve the random striations of blotchy, vivid color.

LEFT PEACH

1 Use sharp White and tiny strokes to softly blend the top-left side of the peach downward. Begin with light pressure (1) and increase to moderate (2). Use firm pressure over just the sun-kissed areas at the top and sides.

2 Correct the colors and shapes with White, Crimson Red, Black Grape, and/or Black using a sharp point and very light pressure.

MIDDLE PEACH

1 Work with sharp White and very tiny, rounded strokes. Keep your pressure moderate (2).

2 Make necessary corrections with White, Black Grape, Black, and Crimson Red.

3 Color with Canary Yellow within the bright yellow areas. If they don't brighten sufficiently, burnish with White using firm pressure (4); then apply Canary Yellow again.

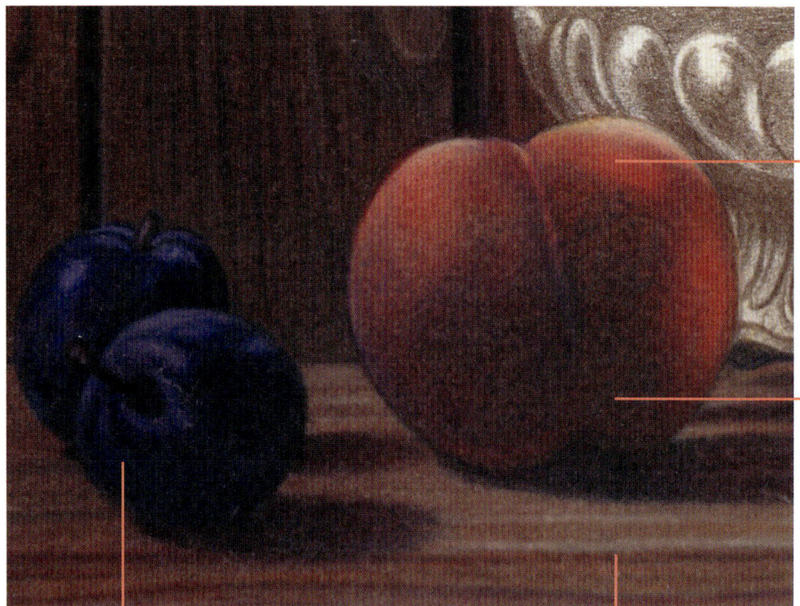

1 Add a touch more color with Henna skimmed over the upper left.

2 Slightly darken the lower-left area with Black Grape. Darken the very black areas with a bit more Black loosely stroked with small, overlapping circles.

3 Add touches of Crimson Red over the far-right side with moderate pressure (2).

1 Develop the lighter areas with White, Black Grape, and Violet Blue. Lighten, blend, and blur with White.

2 Darken the black areas with Black applied in a different direction for better pigment adherence.

3 Skim touches of Tuscan Red over some of both plums, primarily near the bottom.

4 Deepen the blacks with Black STABILO. Use a sharp point, small and rounded strokes, and moderate pressure (2). Ensure that the rounded exteriors are crisp, and bring the background up to them with Dark Umber and Black.

Create the stems with Black STABILO, a touch of Tuscan Red for the front plum, and Dark Brown for the back plum. Soften and blur with a sharp White and light pressure (1).

1 Apply Light Umber over all but the existing shadows with horizontal strokes and moderate to medium pressure (2-3). Follow with Sienna Brown.

2 Layer Black STABILO pencil over the existing peach and plum shadows. Warm up the back shadows with Tuscan Red using medium to firm pressure (3-4) so that the underlying white paper specks are colored over.

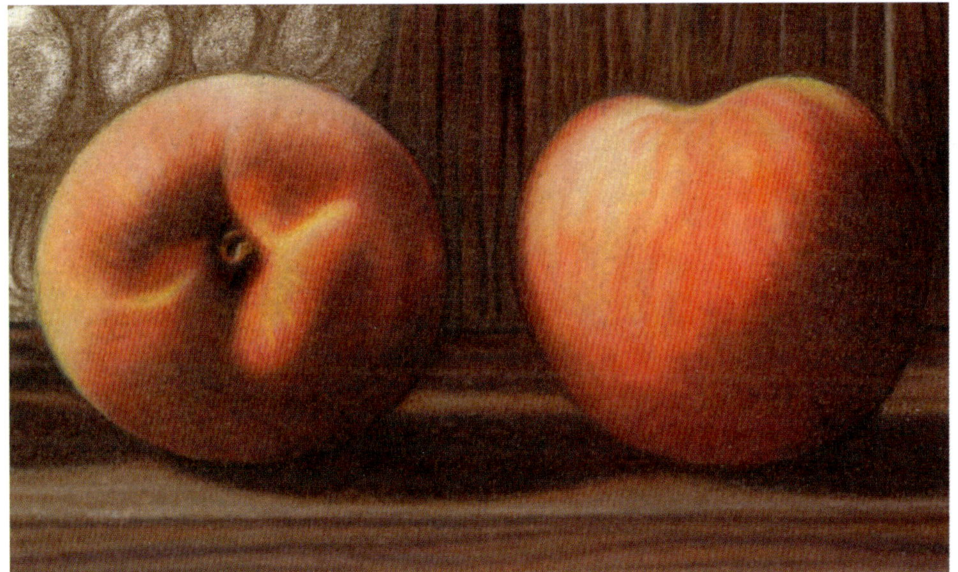

1 Burnish the top sunlit portion of the middle peach with White using tiny, overlapping strokes and firm to very firm pressure (4-5).

2 Work with Crimson Red and Yellowed Orange to develop the reddish-orange hue, alternating between slightly curved streaks and tiny circles to blend and blur the area. Vary the pressure.

3 Touch Black Grape to the dark sections above the center stem end. Use White followed by Canary Yellow to brighten the yellow areas midway down. Color Crimson Red over the far-right side.

4 If necessary, correct the curved, elliptical black shapes with a sharp White point, and then fill in the entire area with Crimson Red. Touch up with Black as needed.

5 Finish by applying more Black over the lower-right side of the deep shadow and Crimson Red over the lower-left side.

6 Complete the center stem end with Black. Use Dark Umber to separate the little ledge from the curved "U" shape. Color over that "U" shape with Crimson Red.

7 To finish the far-right side, "carve" the curve with White and fill in with Canary Yellow. Color the right side with Yellowed Orange. Draw a tiny line with Dark Brown. Color over that with Yellowed Orange.

1 Develop the yellowish-red pattern in the right peach with Crimson Red, Yellowed Orange, and Canary Yellow.

2 To achieve a lustrous glow, burnish the upper-left side with White using firm to very firm pressure (4-5) and small, overlapping strokes.

3 For the shadowed portion on the right half, skim a sharp Black from top to bottom and go in the opposite direction with your strokes.

4 Over the bottom and curving up the left side, color with Tuscan Red. Soften and transition with Crimson Red.

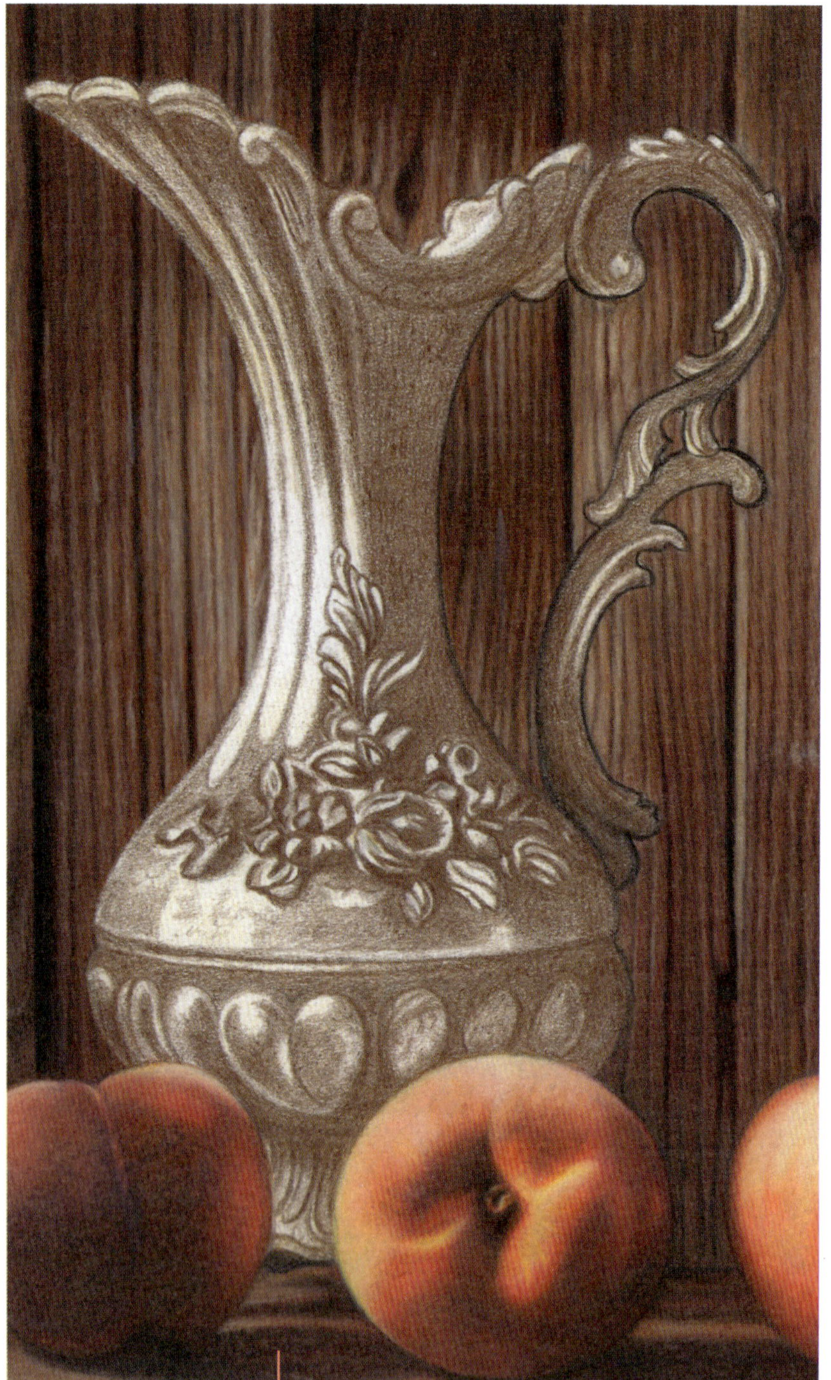

PITCHER

1 Color Sand over all but the bright highlights using small, overlapping, and rounded strokes at the top and bottom, and linear ones down the neck and handle.

2 Outline the raised patterns with Dark Brown. Use small, overlapping strokes and moderate pressure (2) to block in the dark areas of the entire pitcher.

3 Reinforce the darkest darks at the top left and down the right side with Black. Use moderate pressure (2).

TABLE

1 Apply Dark Umber over all of the shadowed areas in the table with moderate to medium pressure (2-3). Create grain streaks with a sharp Dark Umber. Emphasize some with Tuscan Red and others lightly with Black. Use Terra Cotta to soften and blur the edges.

2 Burnish light streaks into the wood with sharp White. Softly apply White behind the two front peaches and more Tuscan Red and Dark Umber behind the other peach if desired.

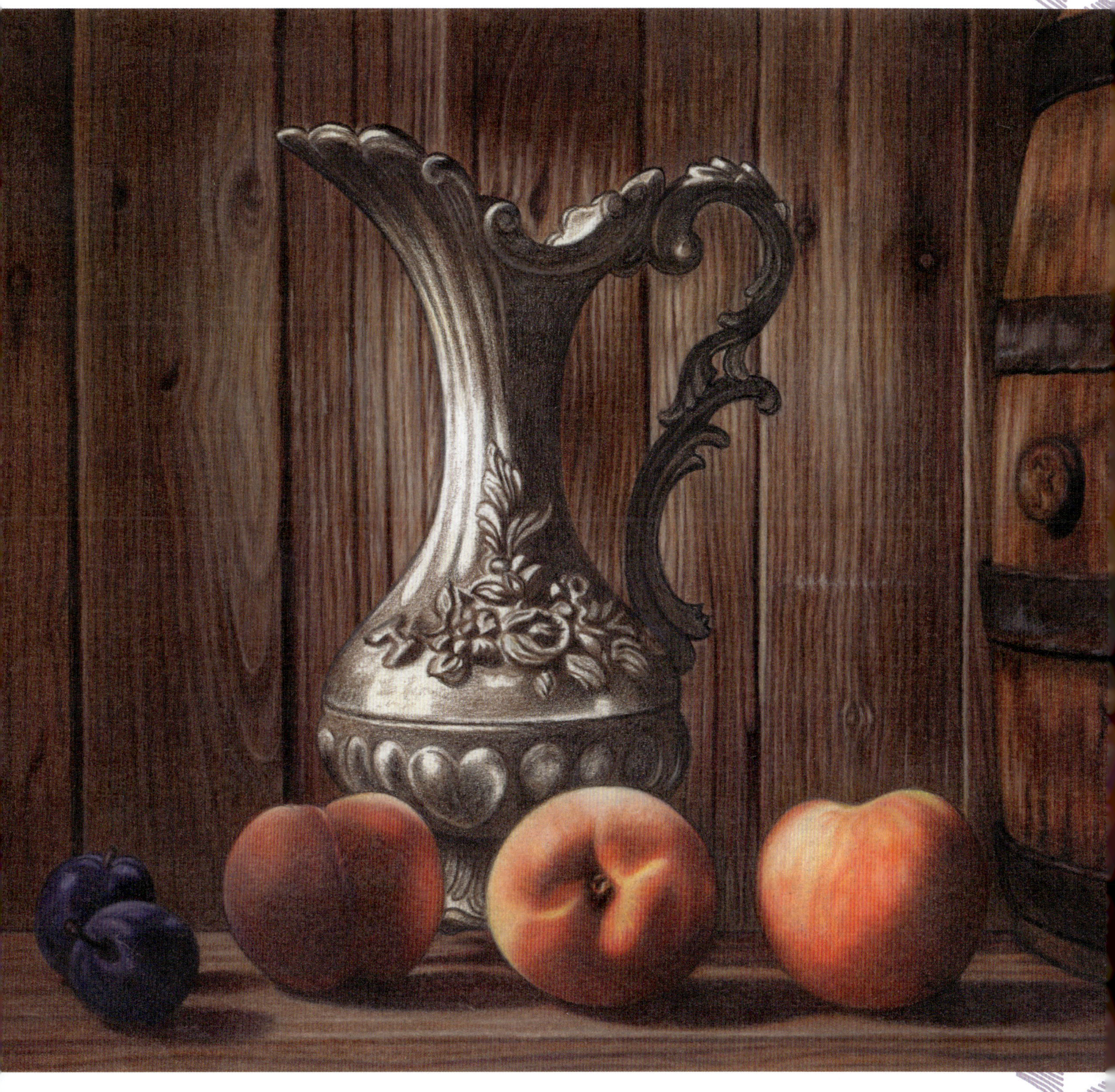

1 On the pitcher, begin with a sharp Black point and moderate pressure (2). Apply pigment with small, rounded, and overlapping strokes at the top, vertically linear down the neck/handle/base, and rounded throughout the raised detail.

2 Add a bit more Dark Brown over the brown areas on the left side, center, and base with moderate pressure (2). Use White to lighten and correct where needed.

1 Use sharp White to blend and blur the areas around the tiny white highlights. Work with Terra Cotta, Black, and Tuscan Red to transition from dark reddish-black into lighter reddish-brown. Use medium to firm pressure (3-4).

2 Preserve the white highlights at the top with sharp White. Use Dark Umber for the dark brown vertically curved grooves. Lighten the curved left border with sharp White and sharp Terra Cotta using only moderate pressure (2).

1 Use Dark Umber with light pressure (1) to create the bleached suggestion of grooves. Burnish with White using vertically curved strokes and firm pressure (4) to soften, lighten, and blend the entire section.

2 Apply a bit of Terra Cotta over the light brown streaks extending up into the bright area and just below it. Soften with White using small, rounded strokes and medium pressure (3). Apply Yellow Ochre over the small area above the raised detail to brighten it.

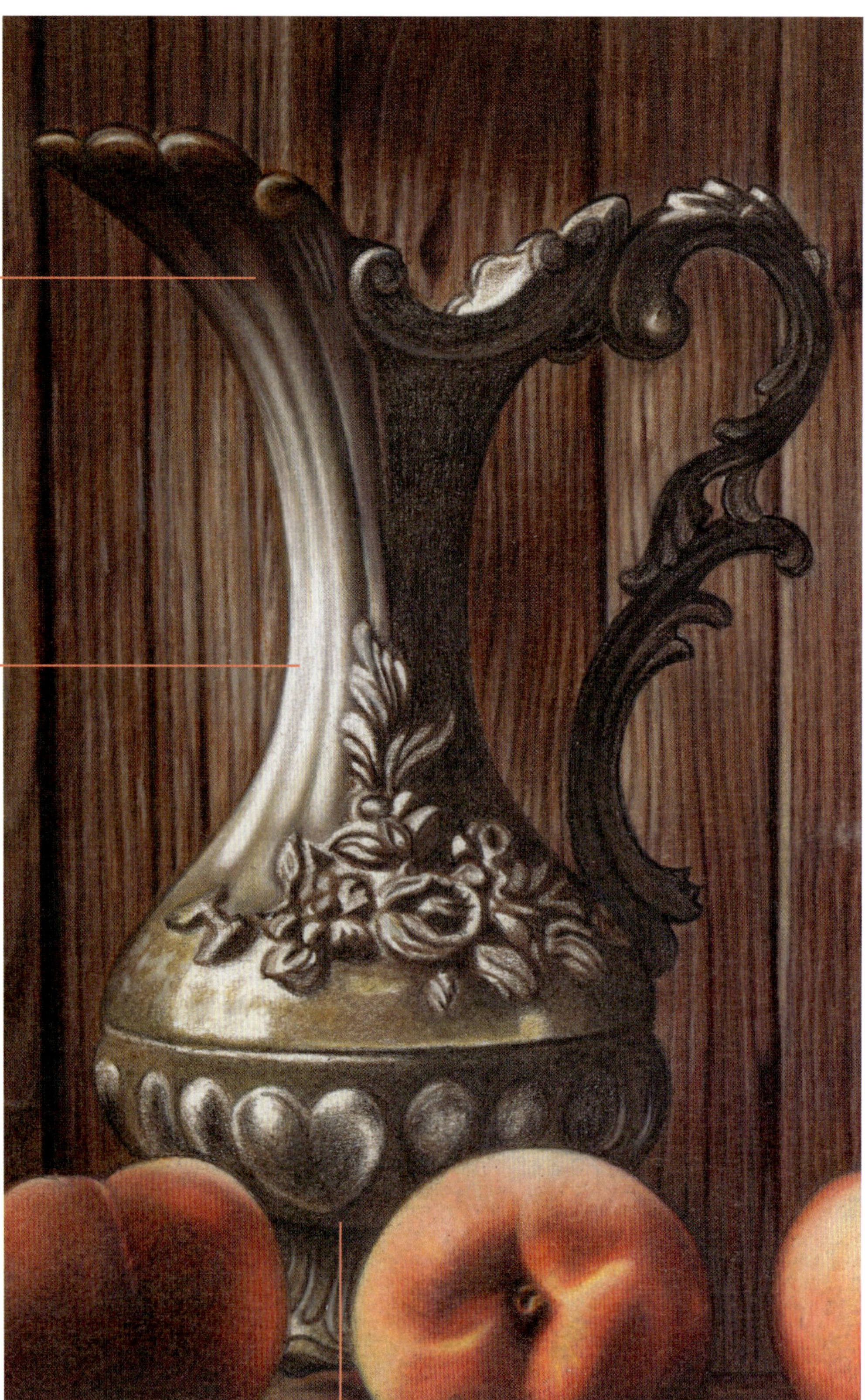

Apply Bronze over the remaining lower portion of the pitcher except for the raised detail and highlights. Use medium pressure and tiny, rounded strokes. Follow with Yellow Ochre to convey a warm bronze appearance.

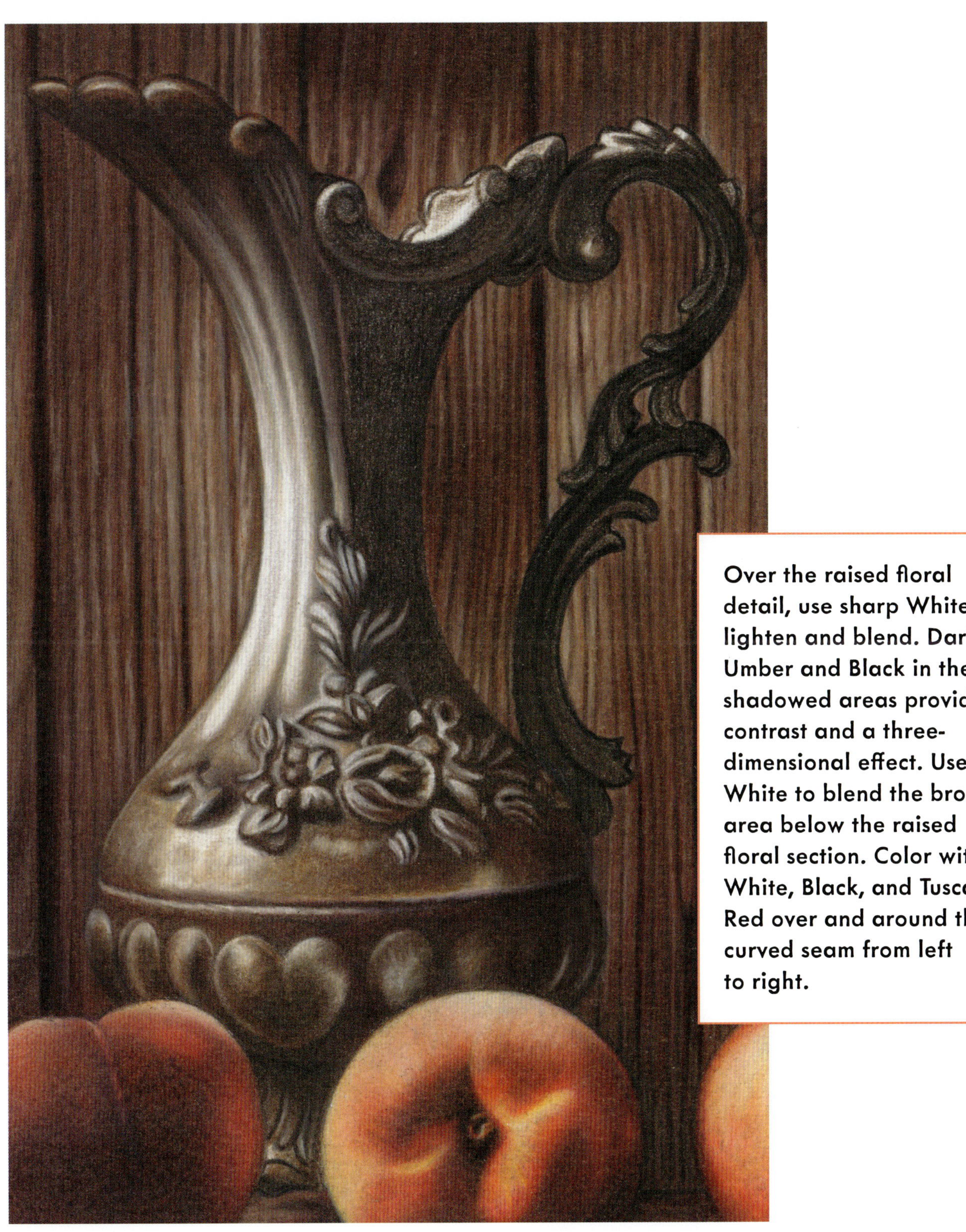

Over the raised floral detail, use sharp White to lighten and blend. Dark Umber and Black in the shadowed areas provide contrast and a three-dimensional effect. Use White to blend the bronze area below the raised floral section. Color with White, Black, and Tuscan Red over and around the curved seam from left to right.

1 Darken the bronze lower portion (excluding the highlights) with Chocolate using tiny, rounded strokes and medium to firm pressure (3-4). Proceed all the way down to the base where the pitcher rests on the wood table.

2 Develop the raised-heart detail areas with White. Use Chocolate to blend and blur the bronzed browns. Work with Dark Umber over the darkest brown areas. Apply Black to the black areas.

3 Around the raised heart detail, work with Black and Tuscan Red to darken. Apply pigment diagonally to improve adherence.

1 Develop the bronzed area below the raised floral detail and above the curved seam with Bronze, Chocolate, and Dark Umber in the dark areas.

2 Use White with firm pressure (4) to reinforce the large front-left highlight, and then lightly (1-2) add a few small random markings with Chocolate. Soften and blur with Yellow Ochre and White.

3 Work with Yellow Ochre, Chocolate, and Bronze to transition color into the right area above the seam. Bring in Dark Umber and Black to deepen the values on the far right.

4 For the reddish areas, lightly apply Crimson Red and brighten with Poppy Red. Soften with Yellow Ochre. Need to brighten more? Apply Yellowed Orange. Darken just above and below the thin horizontal highlight with Dark Umber and Black. Use Tuscan Red over the Black to warm it up.

5 For the dark bronze base and raised heart-shaped detail, use sharp White to soften and blur the lighter areas. Reinforce the darks with Dark Umber, Black, and Tuscan Red.

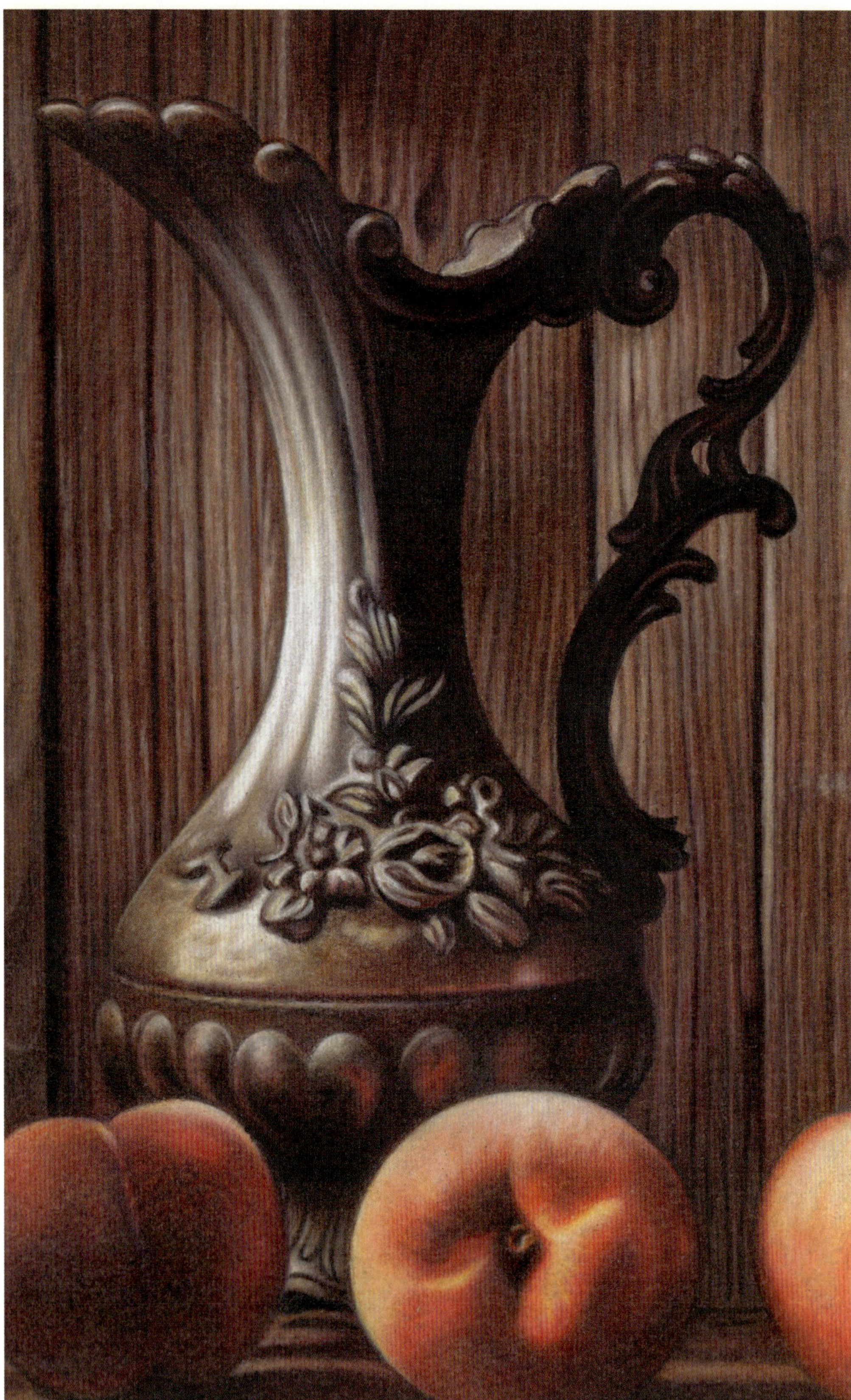

6 Create red reflections with Crimson Red, Poppy Red, and Yellowed Orange. Softly blur and blend the darks into them. Use sharp White to soften and to create the thin curved streaks on the far right. Lightly skim Dark Umber over them.

7 At the very base, work with Chocolate, Dark Umber, Black, and White to complete the raised detail.

8 Use a sharp Black STABILO and very small, overlapping strokes to deepen the black shadows on the right side of the pitcher, the handle, and the very blackest areas around and within the raised detail.

9 Follow with a burnish of Tuscan Red to warm up the overall hue using medium to firm pressure (3-4). Work with Black STABILO and Tuscan Red to create lighter and darker black areas.

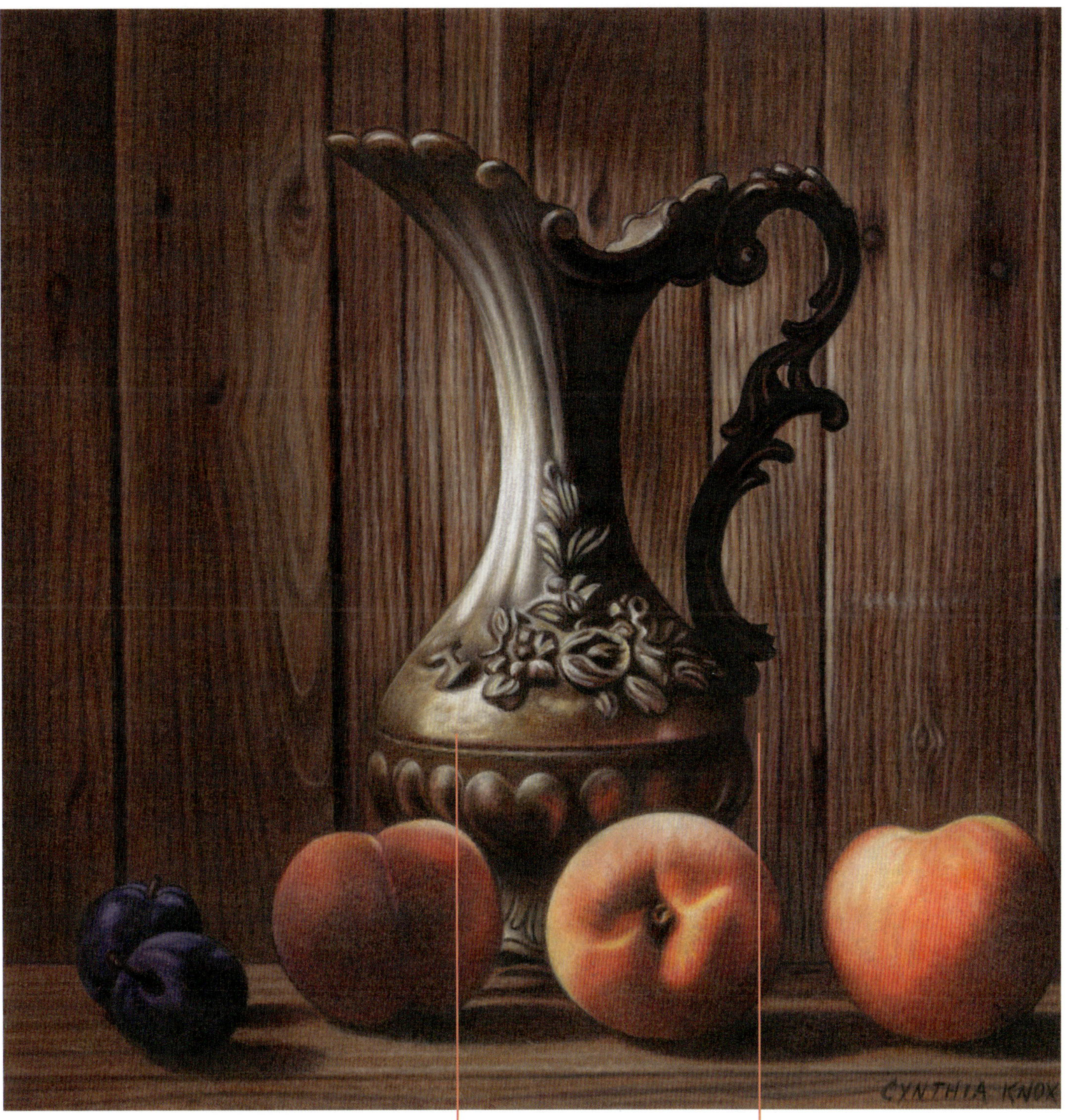

1 Carve out thinly curved lines around and down the handle with sharp White (4). Skim Tuscan Red over those lines to deepen the color using moderate pressure (2) and a sharp point.

2 At the very top, touch a bit of Dark Umber to the bronze areas within the highlights, and then blend down with White to soften (3-4).

3 To brighten highlights throughout the pitcher, use a 000 round paintbrush dipped in water. Sweep the paintbrush tip across the point of a sharp White STABILO pencil several times, and gently dot the white pigment onto the areas that you want to brighten.

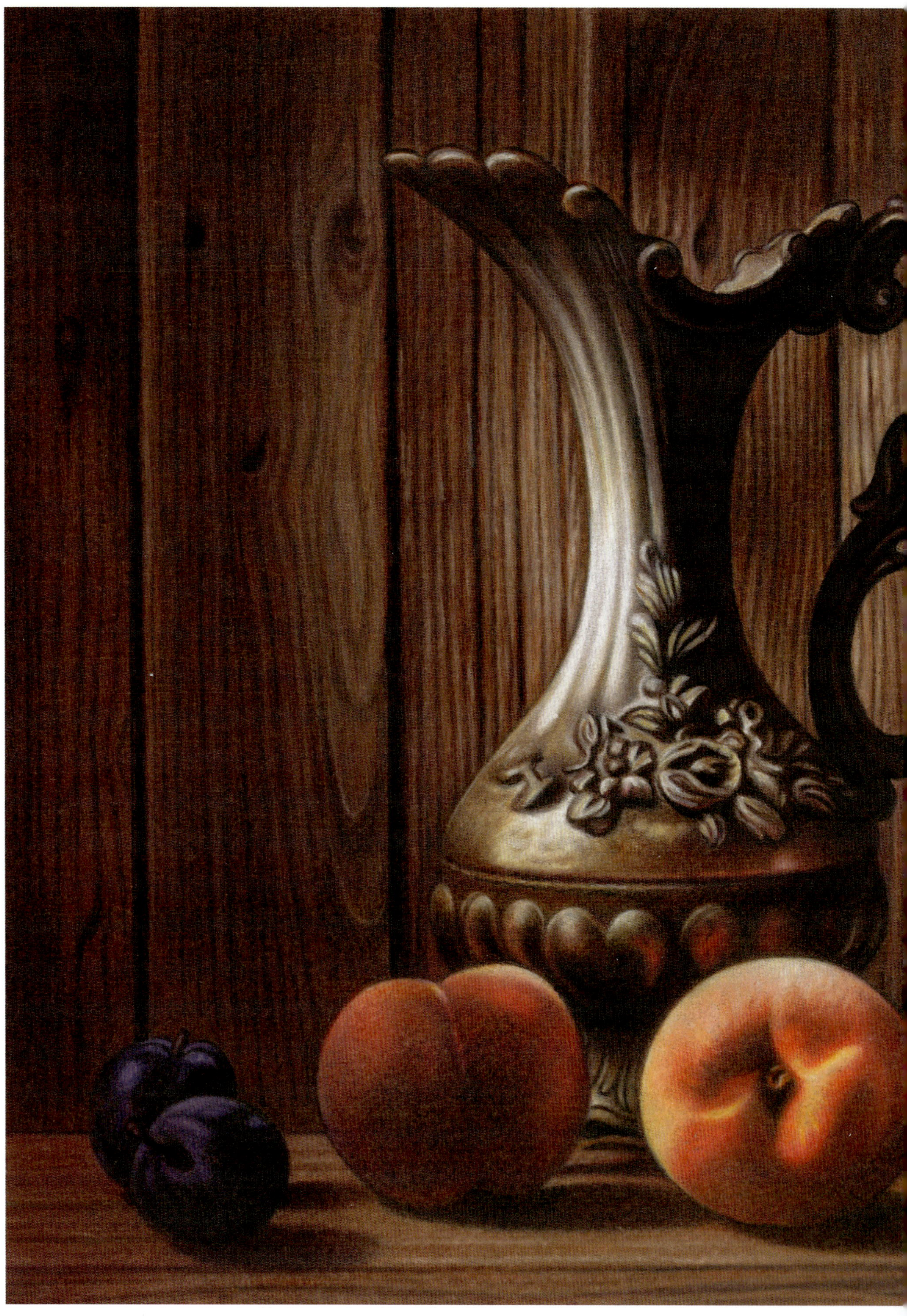

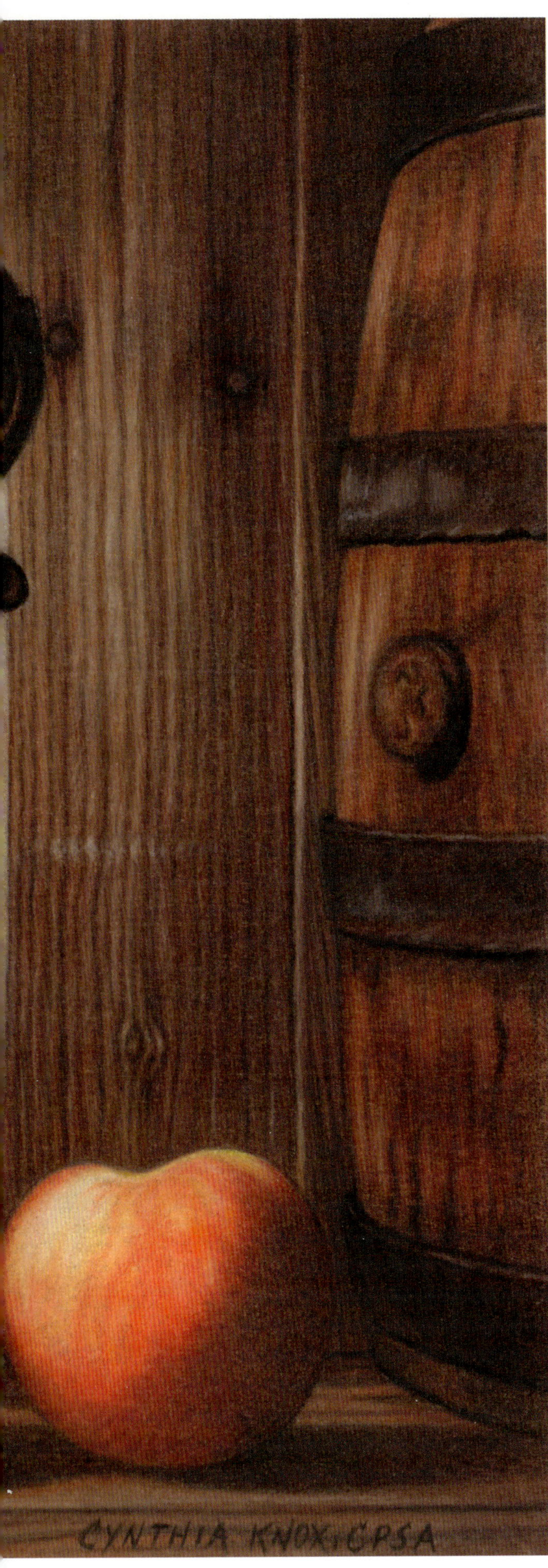

FINISHING TOUCHES

1 Check to make sure that the wood grain extends to the edges of the still-life objects. Use Dark Umber to close the gaps and sharp White to clean up any smudged areas and to lift pencil debris off the artwork.

2 Review the entire artwork. Soften any waxy blips with a sharp pencil. Look at the edges of the pitcher, plums, peaches, and barrel. Everything should be crisp and not blurred. If the background needs further smoothing, use Dark Umber, Black, or Beige. Need to deepen and enhance the black areas? Use the Black STABILO pencil for that. Start with light pressure (1) and build gently.

3 Sign your name with a sharp Black STABILO pencil. Proceed slowly and "sketch" each letter of your name due to the heavy wax buildup and fragile pencil point. Spray with a final fixative or workable fixative to seal in the wax layers and prevent a filmy residue.

Project 3:

Macarons

A bright collection of delicious pastry treats in an attractive glass dish appeals to nearly everyone, and this still life set against a simple backdrop will surely impress your viewers. Join me as I create the macaron textures with their creamy fillings, the uniquely formed glass dish, and the smooth wood background. I'll lead you step by step through this project and demonstrate how to achieve realistic results with just a handful of pencils, a piece of paper, and a few additional drawing supplies.

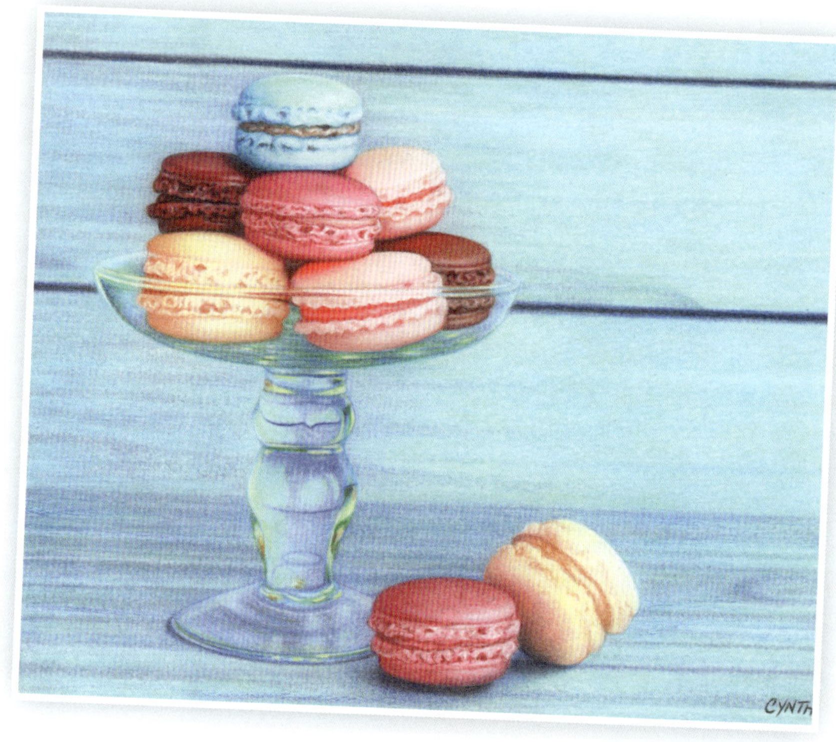

PALETTE

Prismacolor Premier:
902 Ultramarine
903 True Blue
905 Aquamarine
908 Dark Green
914 Cream
919 Non-Photo Blue
920 Light Green
924 Crimson Red
929 Pink
930 Magenta
933 Violet Blue
935 Black
937 Tuscan Red
938 White (x2)
939 Peach
943 Burnt Ochre
944 Terra Cotta
945 Sienna Brown
947 Dark Umber
992 Light Aqua
1011 Deco Yellow
1014 Deco Pink
1024 Blue Slate
1025 Periwinkle
1029 Mahogany Red
1031 Henna
1040 Electric Blue
1065 70% Cool Grey
1086 Sky Blue Light
1092 Nectar

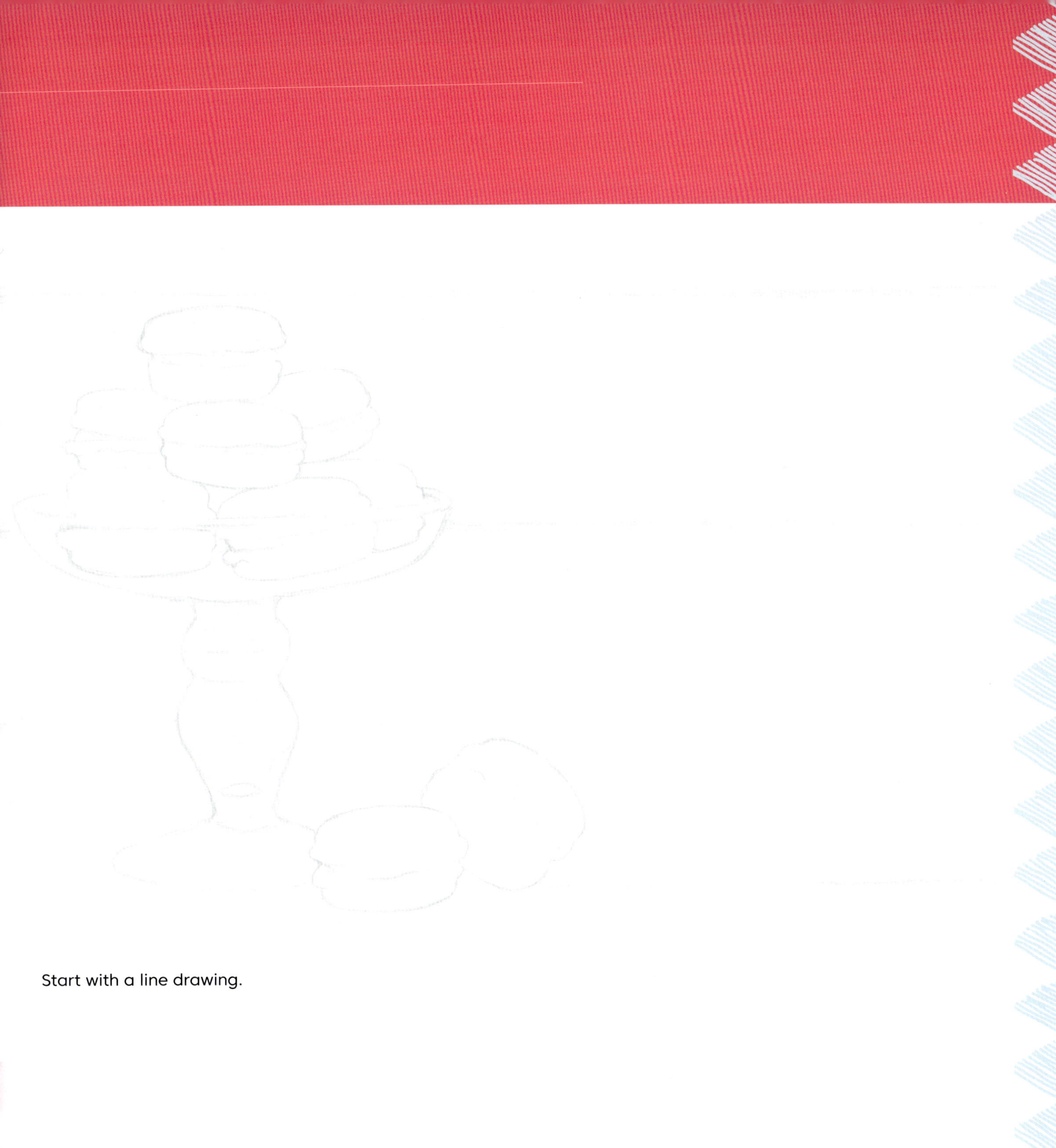

Start with a line drawing.

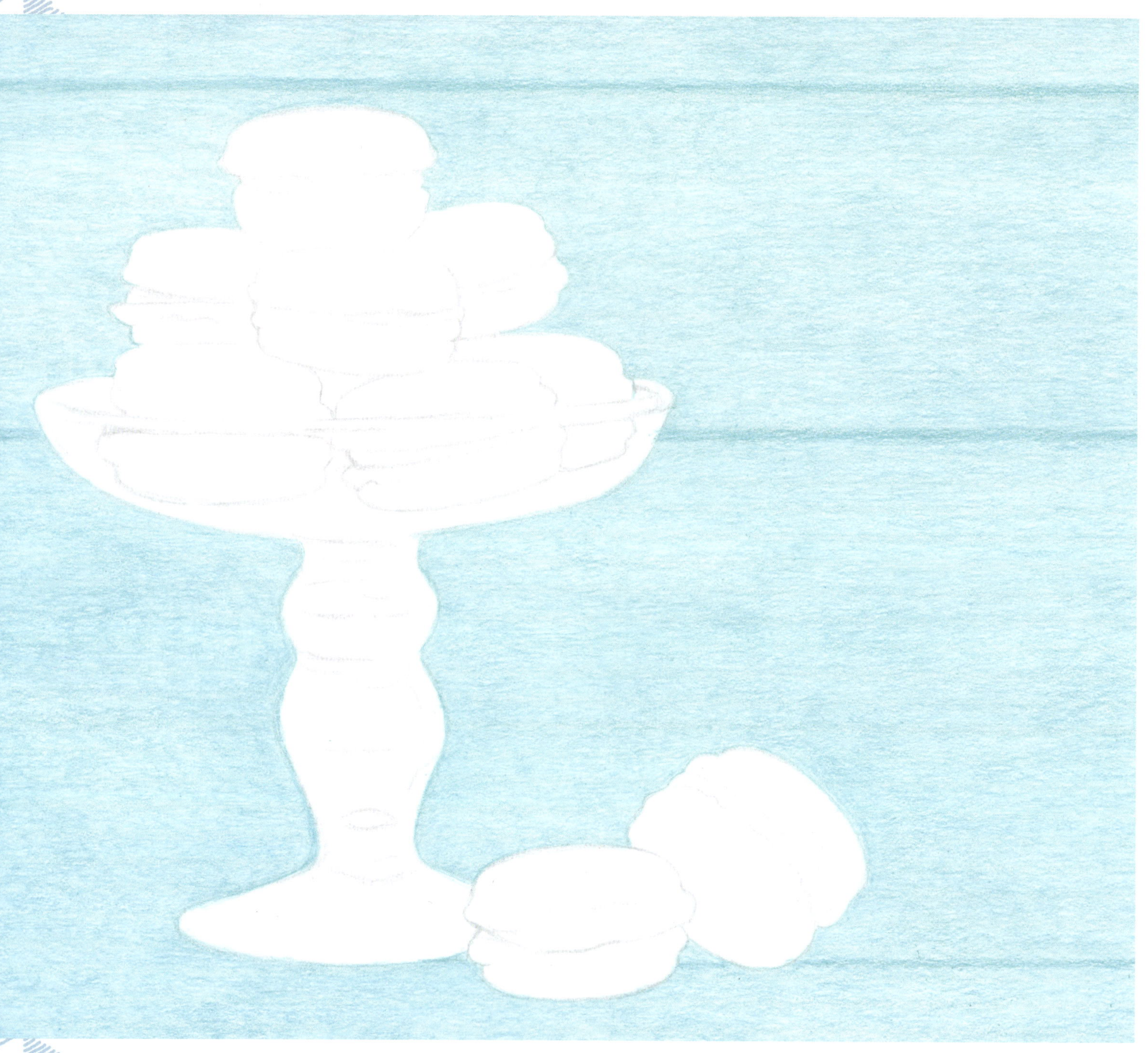

1 Begin with an overall "wash" of Sky Blue Light using horizontal strokes and medium pressure (3). Follow with an application of Light Aqua using horizontal strokes and moderate pressure (2) for a pastel aqua hue.

2 Refine the outlines of the macaron and glass shapes with sharp Light Aqua and light to moderate pressure (1-2). Slightly darken the wood grooves with Light Aqua using medium pressure (3).

Begin the top macaron with a layer of Light Aqua followed by a layer of Non-Photo Blue. Use a very light touch (1), a sharp point, and small, rounded, and overlapping strokes to avoid a linear appearance.

For the red undertones in the chocolate macarons, apply two layers of Henna with light pressure (1) and small, rounded, and overlapping strokes.

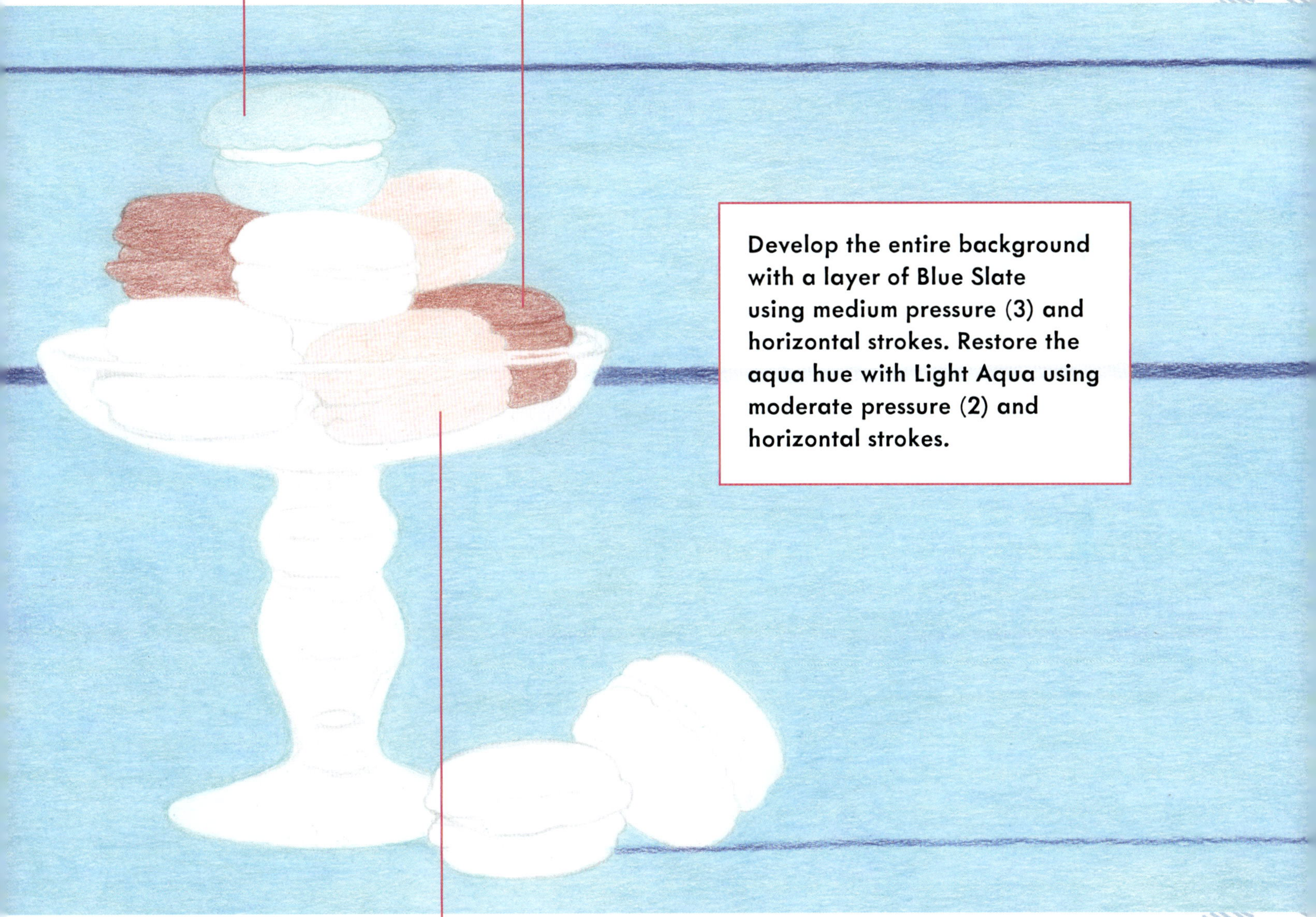

Develop the entire background with a layer of Blue Slate using medium pressure (3) and horizontal strokes. Restore the aqua hue with Light Aqua using moderate pressure (2) and horizontal strokes.

Apply a layer of Deco Pink and then a layer of Peach over the light pink macarons. Use light pressure (1) and small, rounded, and overlapping strokes.

BLUE MACARON

Lightly (1) color in the darker blue areas of the macaron with Electric Blue. Skim Light Green overall with light pressure (1) and darken the shadows with Ultramarine (1). Follow with a layer of Aquamarine (1). Next, block in the small craters with Ultramarine followed by Aquamarine.

PINK MACARONS

Apply Peach overall with light pressure (1). Increase pressure in the shadowed areas. Apply Magenta over the bright pink areas with moderate pressure (2). Use White to lighten and correct.

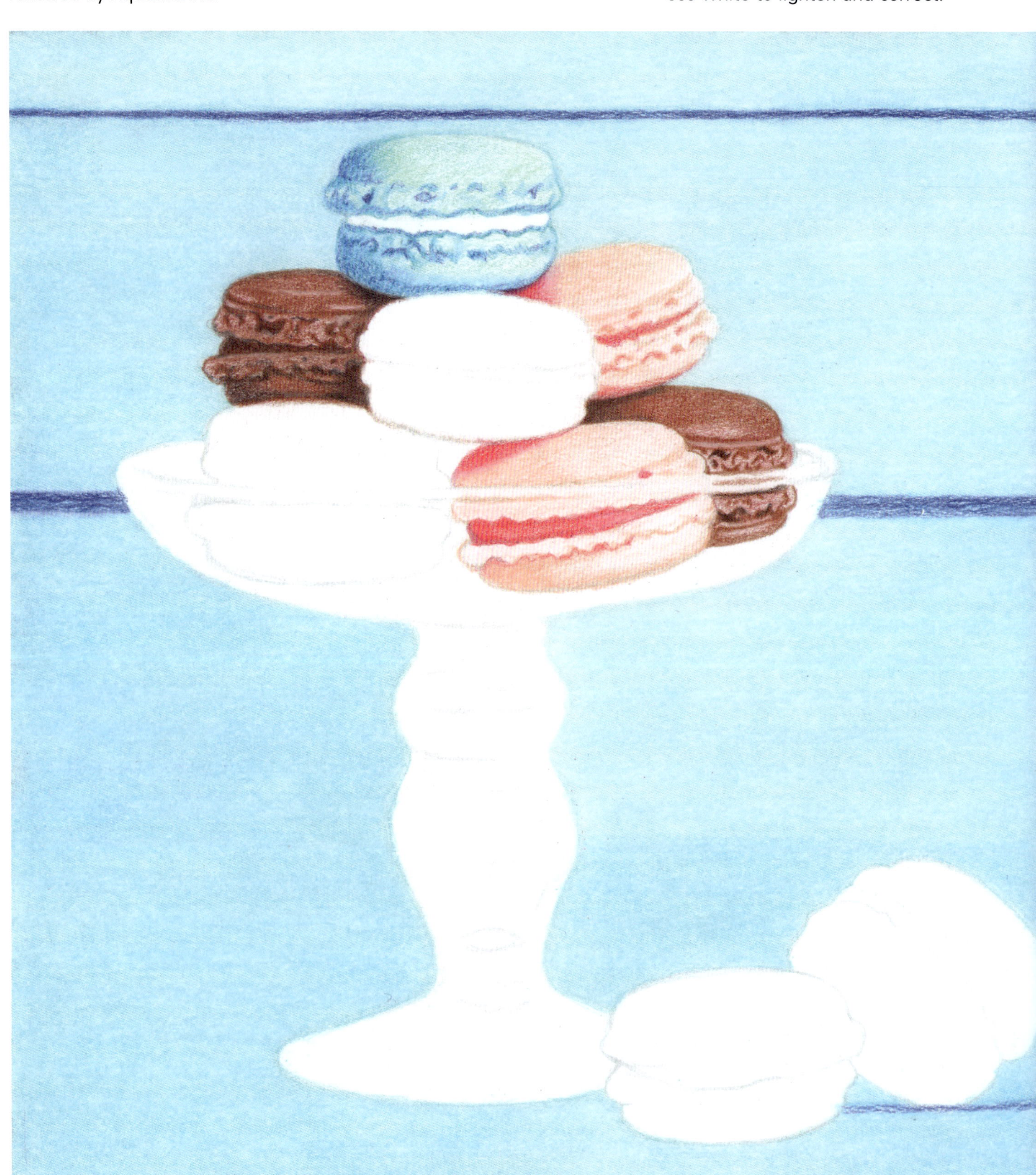

CHOCOLATE MACARONS

Use Sienna Brown to deepen the hue and introduce detail. Begin with moderate pressure (2) and increase over the darker areas. Use White to correct mistakes. Darken the shadows with Black using moderate pressure (2).

BACKGROUND

1 Blend the layers of pigment with White by applying medium to firm pressure (3-4) over the entire background except for the dark blue linear grooves. This is the burnishing process. Use very small, rounded, and overlapping strokes to create a smoothly blended surface, and move from left to right across the paper.

2 Once you have burnished the entire background and foreground with White, repeat the process over just the thin, top, horizontal area and the right side down to slightly above the lower angled macaron. Use very firm pressure (5) to lighten the aqua-colored wood.

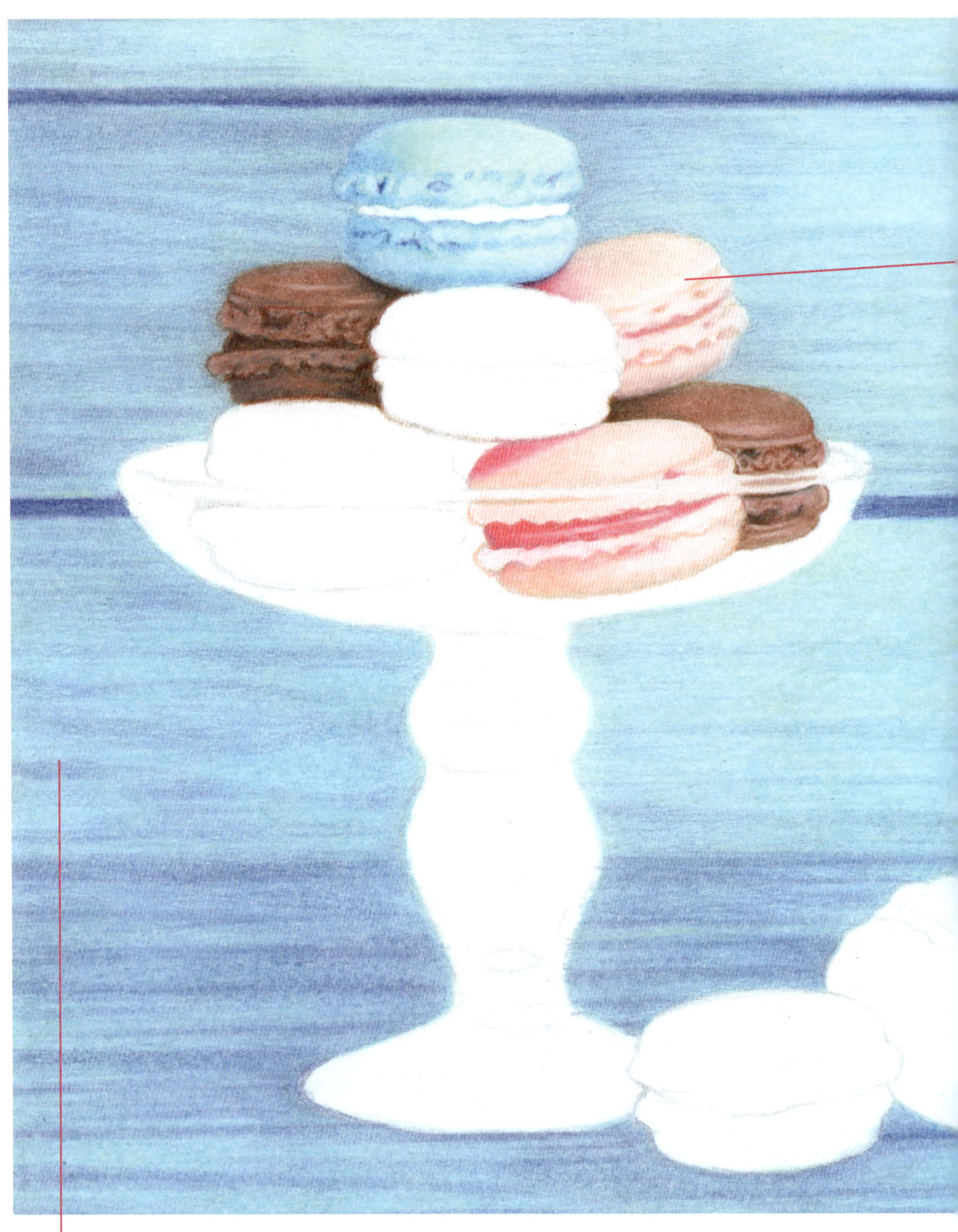

1 Restore color in the background with a layer of Light Green applied using a sharp point and moderate pressure (2) over all but the deep blue grooves. Use small, rounded, and overlapping strokes to create a beautiful mint hue.

2 To introduce the blue grain over the shiplap wood, start at the top right with a sharp Periwinkle. Use moderate pressure (2) and horizontal strokes to establish the linear grain texture throughout. Increase your pressure over the darker areas.

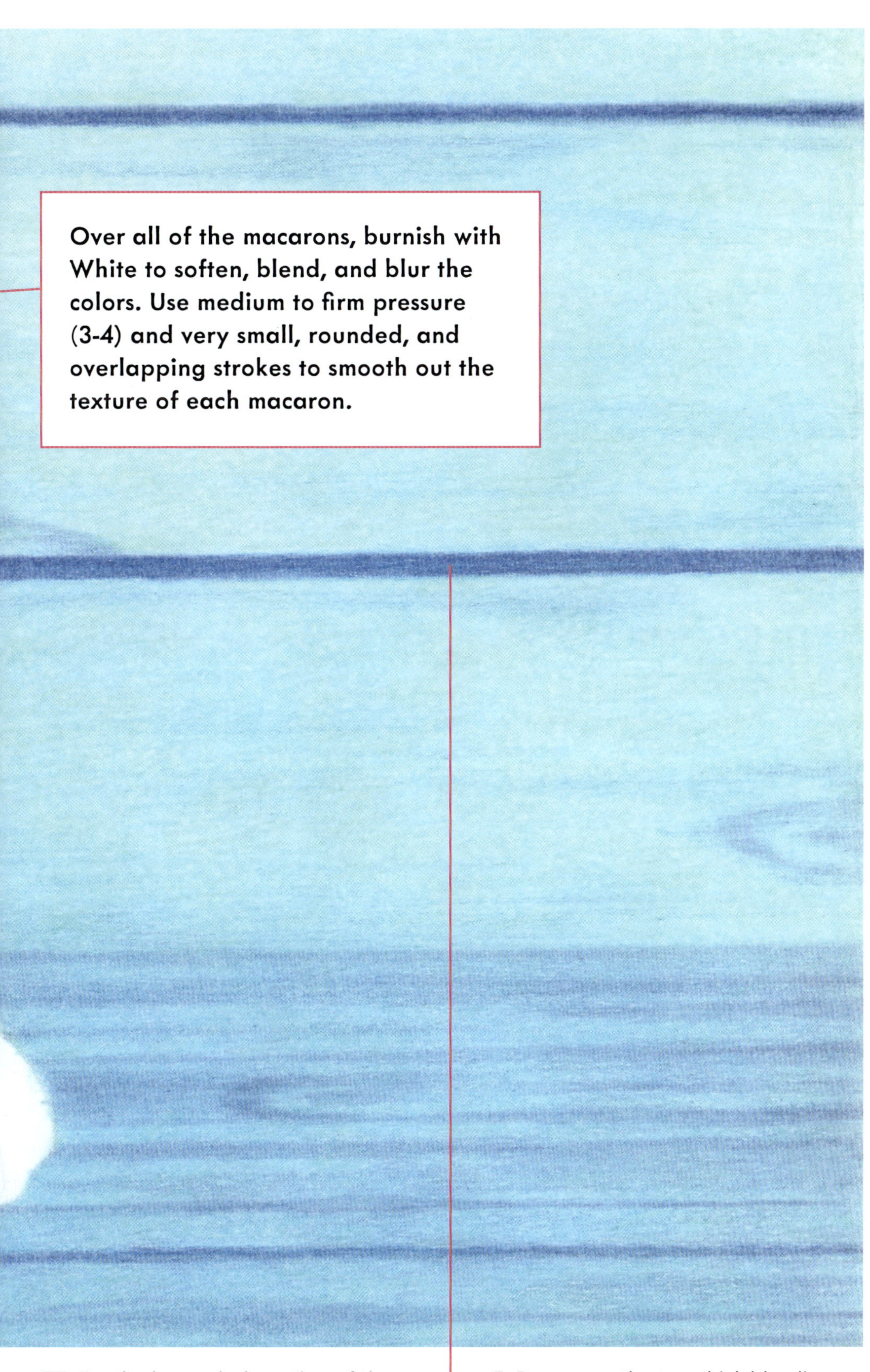

Over all of the macarons, burnish with White to soften, blend, and blur the colors. Use medium to firm pressure (3-4) and very small, rounded, and overlapping strokes to smooth out the texture of each macaron.

3 For the lower dark section of the background, establish an initial layer of Periwinkle with moderate pressure (2), followed by the grain streaks using firmer pressure (3-4). Then darken the left side of the image to emphasize the main subject.

4 Draw over the two thick blue lines with Periwinkle using medium to firm pressure (3-4) and horizontal, linear strokes.

BLUE MACARON

1 Darken the deeply shadowed areas with sharp Ultramarine and light to moderate pressure (1-2). Color Aquamarine (dark) or Light Aqua (light) over that, depending on the darkness of the shadows. Soften with White.

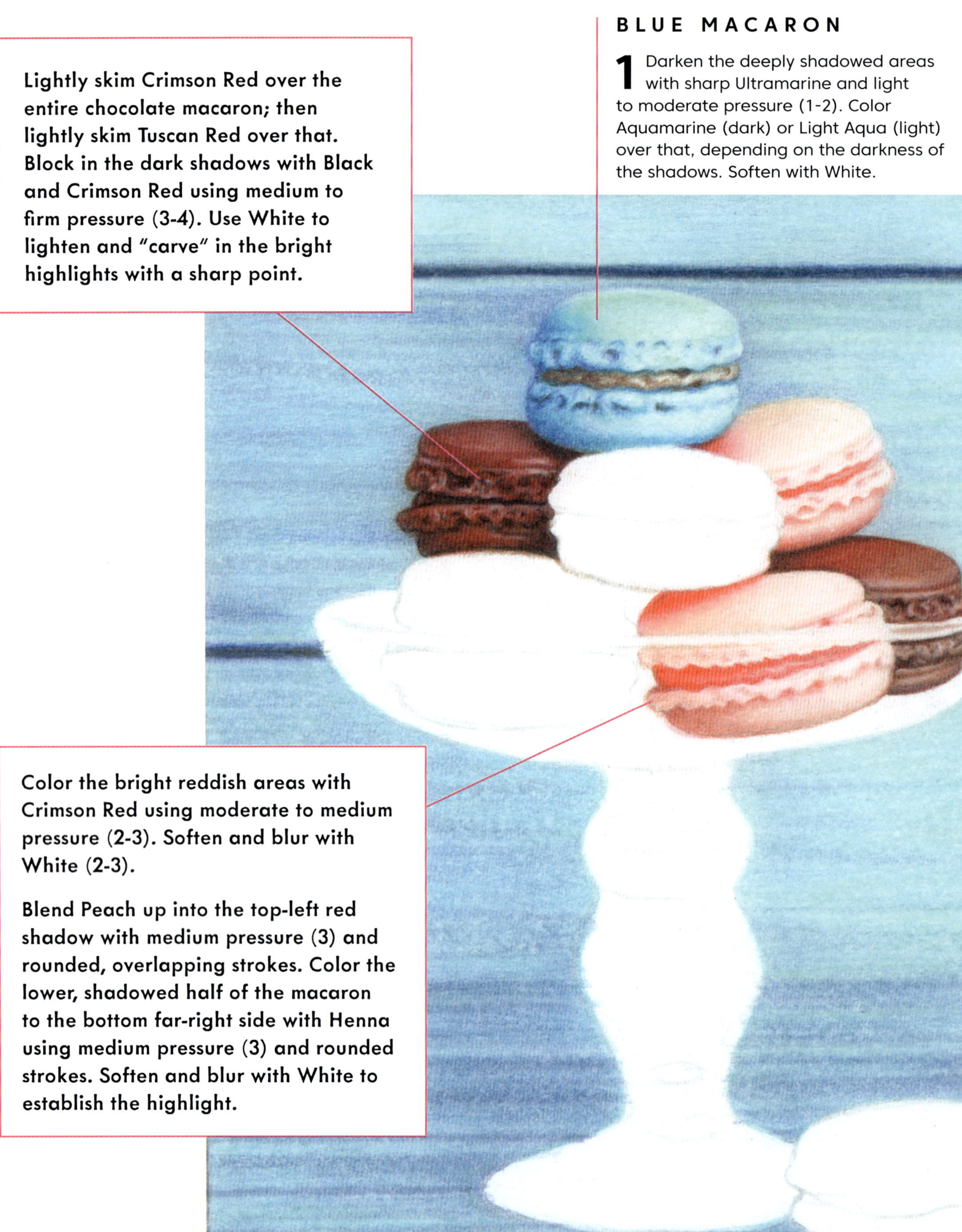

Lightly skim Crimson Red over the entire chocolate macaron; then lightly skim Tuscan Red over that. Block in the dark shadows with Black and Crimson Red using medium to firm pressure (3-4). Use White to lighten and "carve" in the bright highlights with a sharp point.

Color the bright reddish areas with Crimson Red using moderate to medium pressure (2-3). Soften and blur with White (2-3).

Blend Peach up into the top-left red shadow with medium pressure (3) and rounded, overlapping strokes. Color the lower, shadowed half of the macaron to the bottom far-right side with Henna using medium pressure (3) and rounded strokes. Soften and blur with White to establish the highlight.

2 Use Light Aqua and Light Green for the midtones and soften and blur with White. Create the highlights with White and medium to firm pressure (3-4). Add tiny accents of Black to the darkest indentations with a sharp point and light pressure (1).

3 Fill in the cream center with an initial layer of Cream followed by Burnt Ochre using tiny, rounded strokes and medium pressure (3). Deepen the darks with Dark Umber and lighten the highlights with White. Add more Burnt Ochre for warmth, and touch up with White as needed.

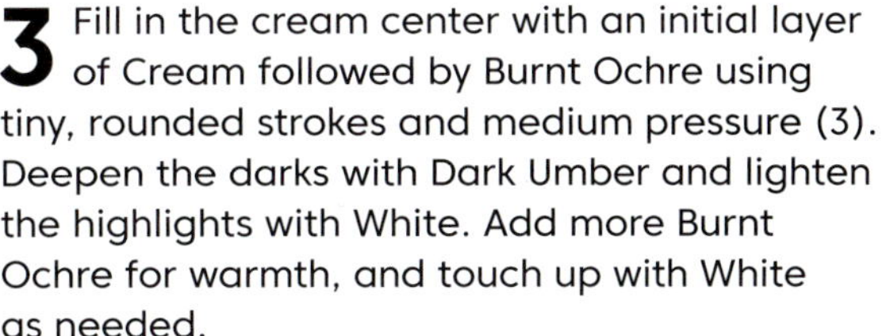

TOP PINK MACARON

1 Brighten the reddish shadows and cream filling with Crimson Red using medium pressure (3) over the reddish hues and lighter pressure (2) over the pinkish hues.

2 Soften and blur the edges with White and create a very thin white line in the middle of the filling. Add a touch of Peach over the top half of the macaron and burnish with White just below that.

RIGHT CHOCOLATE MACARON

1 Darken all shadowed areas with Tuscan Red using moderate pressure (2). Brighten up the reddish areas with Crimson Red using moderate to medium pressure (2-3).

2 Darken the black shadows with Black. Color the midtone brown areas with Burnt Ochre using medium pressure (3). Darken the lower brown areas with Dark Umber (2-3). Work back and forth with these colors and White to soften, blur, and brighten.

BACKGROUND

1 Soften and blur the light blue wood grain with White and slightly diagonal strokes to “stretch” and blur the horizontal lines. Begin with moderate pressure (2) and increase as needed to yield a smoothly blurred effect. Work back and forth with White, Periwinkle, and Light Green to create subtle striping throughout.

2 Sketch a center line through the dark blue horizontal grooves with Black using moderate pressure (2) and loose, sketchy strokes. Over the entire area of both grooves, color Ultramarine with moderate pressure (2). Soften and blur with White.

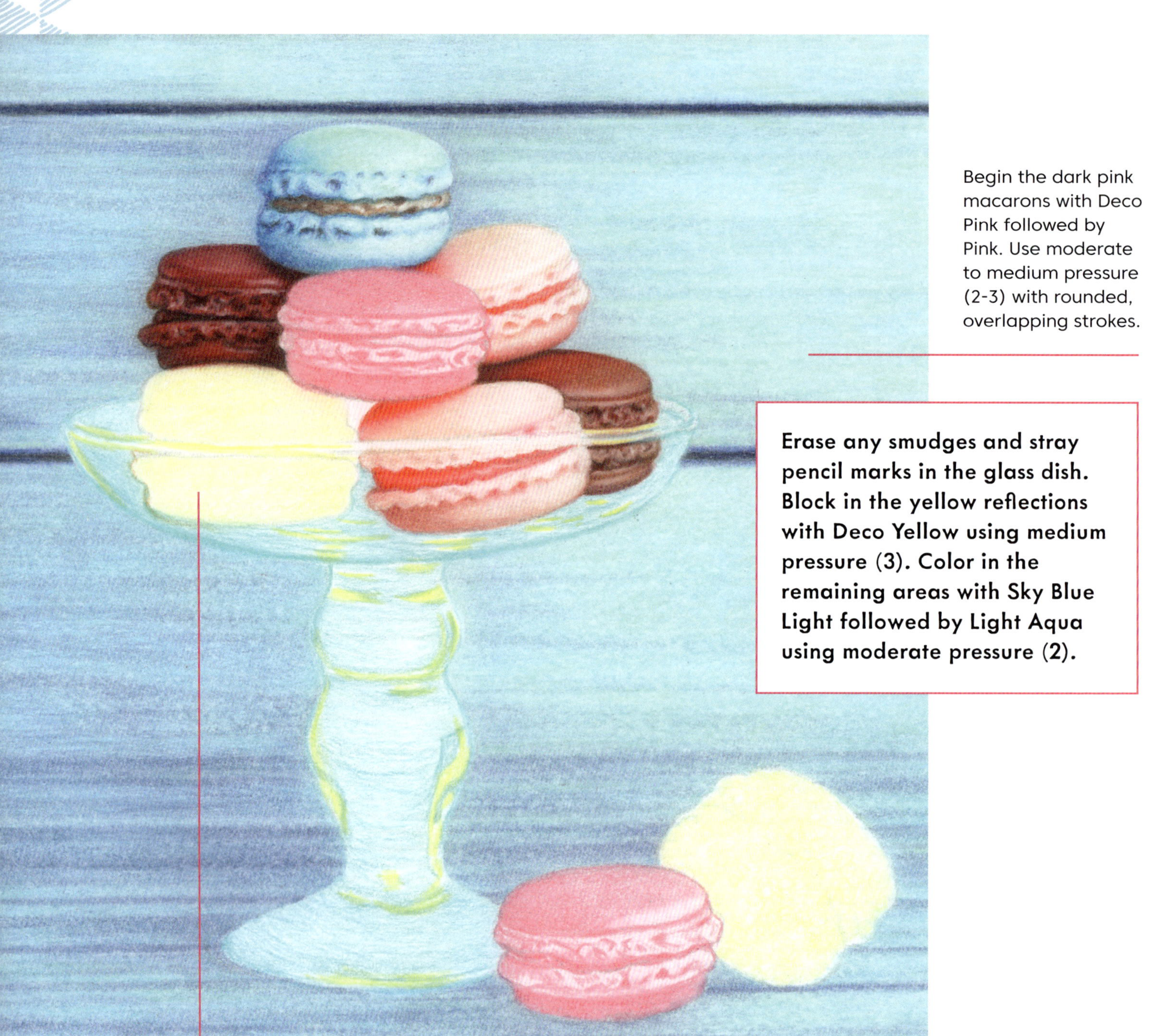

Begin the dark pink macarons with Deco Pink followed by Pink. Use moderate to medium pressure (2-3) with rounded, overlapping strokes.

Erase any smudges and stray pencil marks in the glass dish. Block in the yellow reflections with Deco Yellow using medium pressure (3). Color in the remaining areas with Sky Blue Light followed by Light Aqua using moderate pressure (2).

Color the yellow macarons with Cream followed by Deco Yellow, using moderate to medium pressure (2-3) and rounded, overlapping strokes.

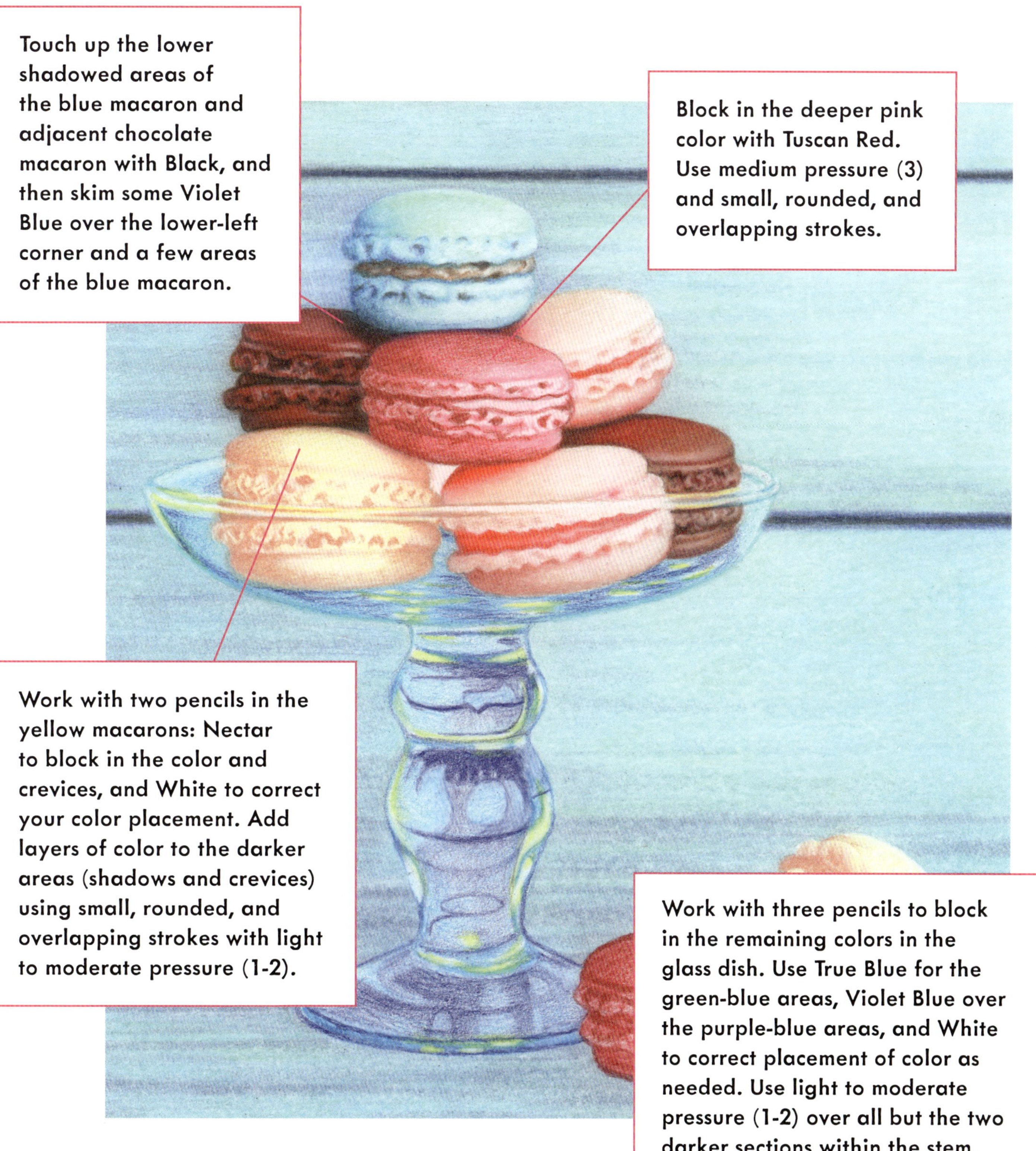

Touch up the lower shadowed areas of the blue macaron and adjacent chocolate macaron with Black, and then skim some Violet Blue over the lower-left corner and a few areas of the blue macaron.

Block in the deeper pink color with Tuscan Red. Use medium pressure (3) and small, rounded, and overlapping strokes.

Work with two pencils in the yellow macarons: Nectar to block in the color and crevices, and White to correct your color placement. Add layers of color to the darker areas (shadows and crevices) using small, rounded, and overlapping strokes with light to moderate pressure (1-2).

Work with three pencils to block in the remaining colors in the glass dish. Use True Blue for the green-blue areas, Violet Blue over the purple-blue areas, and White to correct placement of color as needed. Use light to moderate pressure (1-2) over all but the two darker sections within the stem. Increase to medium pressure (3).

TIP

If you choose to reshape the left side of the blue macaron, as I did, you can carve through with a White pencil. The point may break, but the resulting jagged edge will enable you to use even more pressure and eliminate the section that you want to "erase." Then you can restore color to the affected background with light applications of Non-Photo Blue and Violet Blue. Soften and blur with White using horizontal strokes.

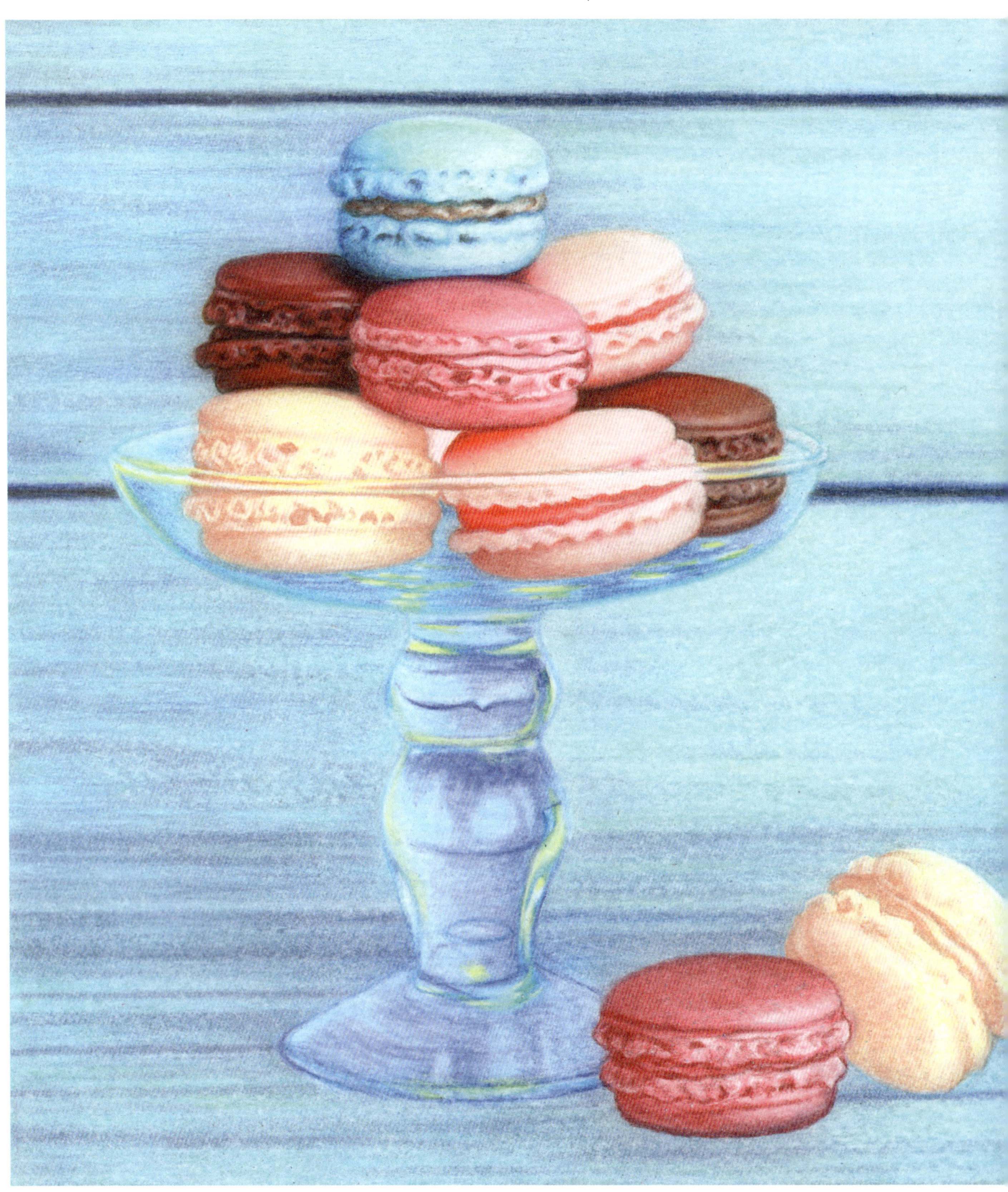

Now you will burnish what you have just done with White to meld the layers of color together over the pink and yellow macarons, as well as within the glass dish. Begin with a sharp point and moderate pressure (2). Increase your pressure to medium (3) or even firm (4) to blend and lighten the existing layers of color. Use sharp White to lighten the outline of the stem and base.

TIP

Symmetry in the shape of the glass dish is important. It helps to occasionally squint to match up the left to the right side. Use a sharp White pencil to easily correct and re-carve the glass borders.

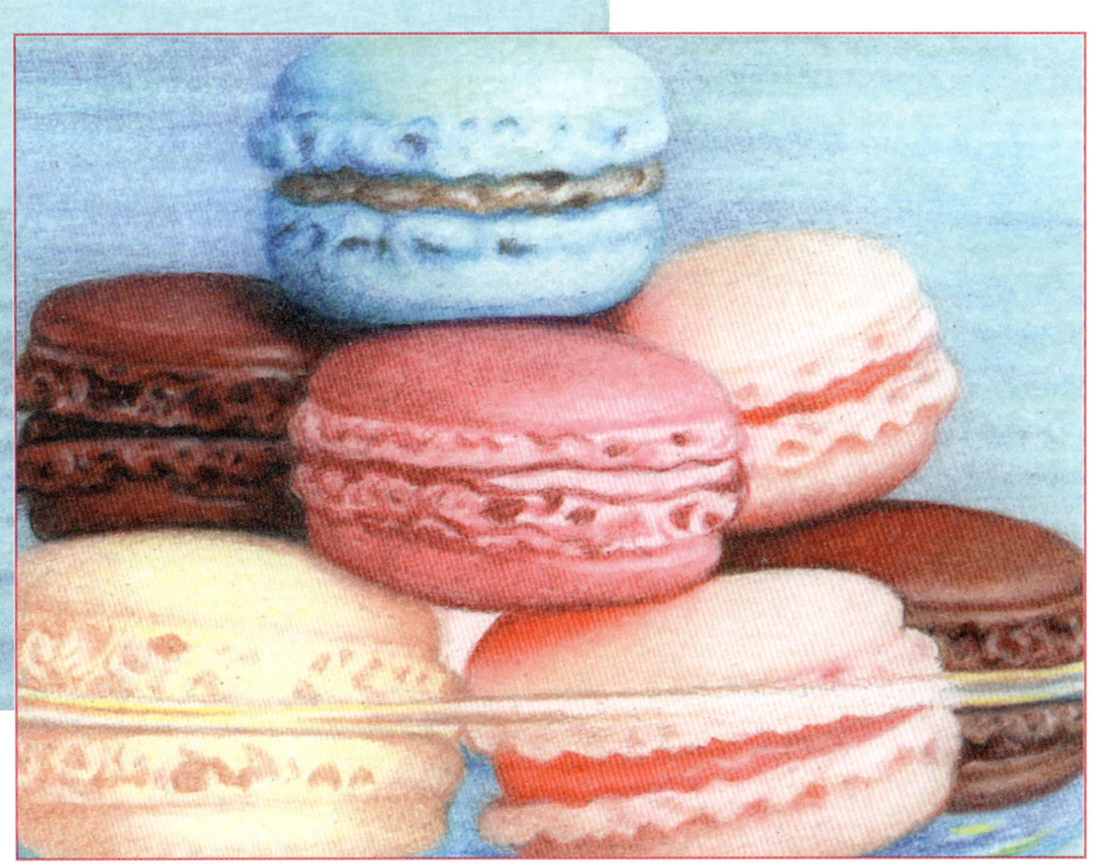

DARK PINK MACARONS

1 Darken the shadowed areas with Mahogany Red using tiny, rounded, overlapping strokes. Sweep a bit of Tuscan Red over the left top and bottom. Use White to soften and blend.

2 Color in the filling of the top macaron with Nectar and draw a thin center highlight with White. Apply a light touch of Black to the left side of the lower macaron's filling.

3 In the small shadowed space beneath the center pink macaron, apply Dark Umber with moderate pressure (2) and tiny, rounded strokes. Darken the "V" base with Black and add Tuscan Red for a reddish reflection. Soften and create a small curved area with White.

YELLOW MACARONS

1 Brighten up the top macaron with Deco Yellow. Deepen the shadows and darker crevices with light Terra Cotta and soften with White. Complete the filling with Terra Cotta, a blending of White, and touches of Tuscan Red.

2 For the bottom yellow macaron, deepen the shadow with Mahogany Red using tiny, rounded, and overlapping strokes and light to moderate pressure (1-2). Very lightly (1) add Black with a sharp point to the darkest area of the shadow. Blend the layers with Burnt Ochre and use Mahogany Red to transition the darkest area into the midtone.

3 Finish with a light application of Dark Umber over the darkest area. Work with White to transition into the lightest area. Skim Deco Yellow over the entire macaron except for the very bright top. Use small, rounded strokes and light to moderate pressure (1-2). Complete the filling with a light application of Terra Cotta over the reddish-brown area and touches of Dark Umber at both ends. Tweak with White and Deco Yellow.

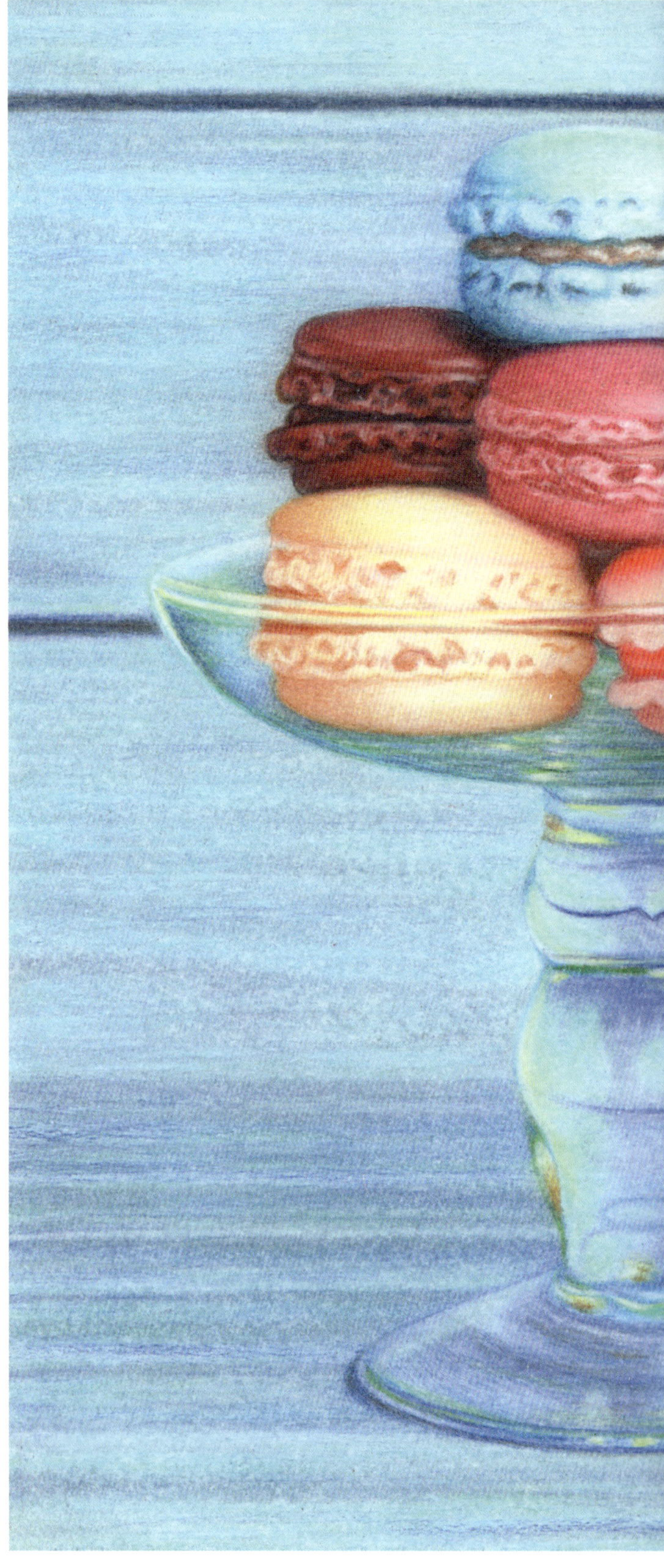

GLASS DISH

1 Darken the interior of the bowl and preserve and shorten the reflections with Dark Green and Violet Blue. Blend and smooth overall with a sharp White and light to moderate pressure (1-2). Add thin, light streaks with White using firm pressure (4).

2 Complete the rim with Deco Yellow and Terra Cotta across the yellow macaron, Mahogany Red and Tuscan Red over a portion of the light pink macaron, and Sienna Brown and True Blue over the chocolate macaron. Work with White, True Blue, and Violet Blue to complete.

3 For the stem and base, move from top to bottom using these same pencils, and then soften and blur with White. Follow the curved patterns throughout. Use 70% Cool Grey over the Violet Blue to deepen the hue. Create the bright yellow and orange areas with Deco Yellow and Terra Cotta. Light Green colors the lighter aqua areas, and True Blue colors the lighter blue areas.

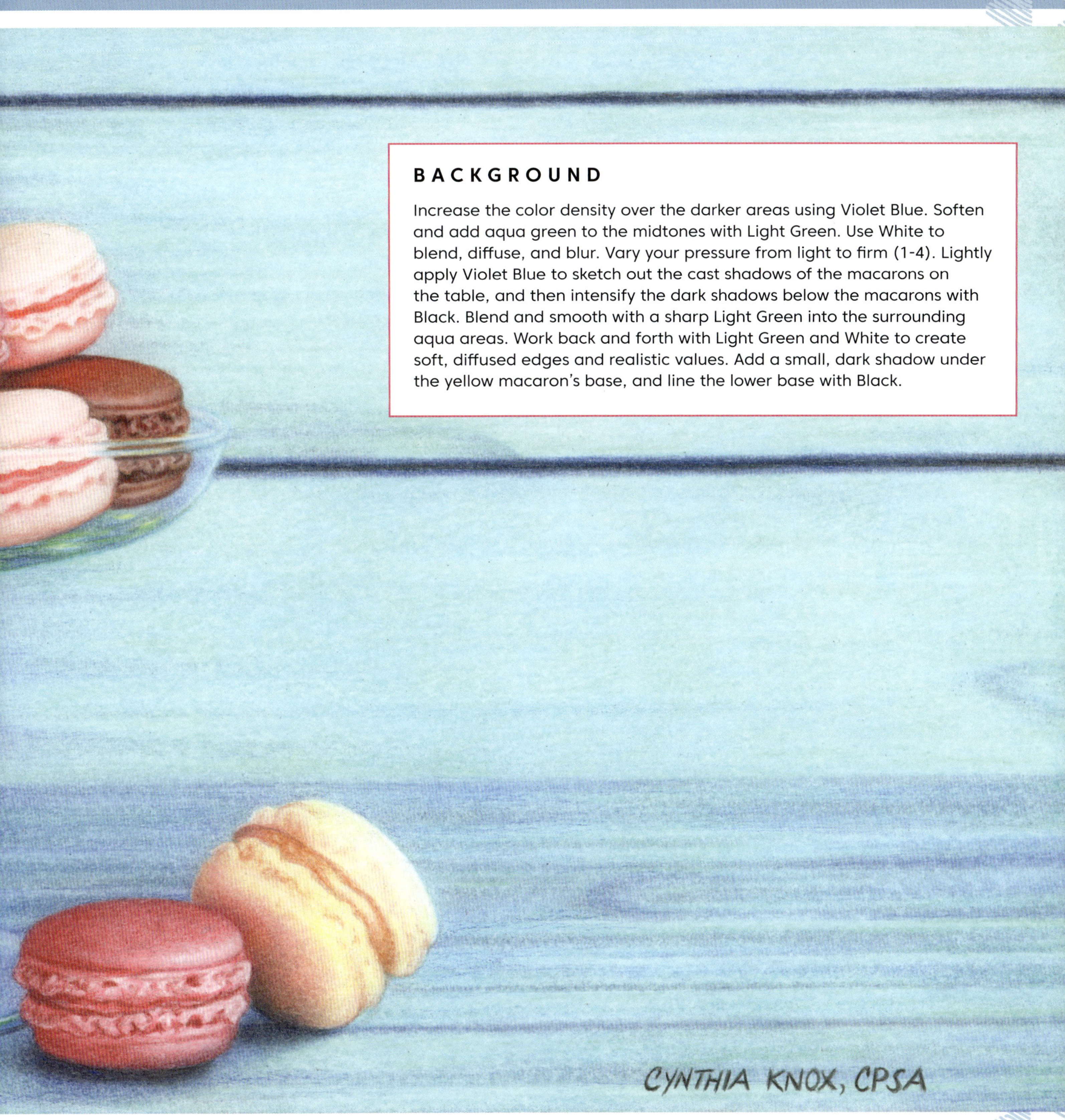

BACKGROUND

Increase the color density over the darker areas using Violet Blue. Soften and add aqua green to the midtones with Light Green. Use White to blend, diffuse, and blur. Vary your pressure from light to firm (1-4). Lightly apply Violet Blue to sketch out the cast shadows of the macarons on the table, and then intensify the dark shadows below the macarons with Black. Blend and smooth with a sharp Light Green into the surrounding aqua areas. Work back and forth with Light Green and White to create soft, diffused edges and realistic values. Add a small, dark shadow under the yellow macaron's base, and line the lower base with Black.

TIP

If the pigment no longer adheres, apply color with a sharp point, lighter pressure, and diagonal strokes. Diagonal strokes are also good for diffusing areas of color and "stretching" them for a blurred effect.

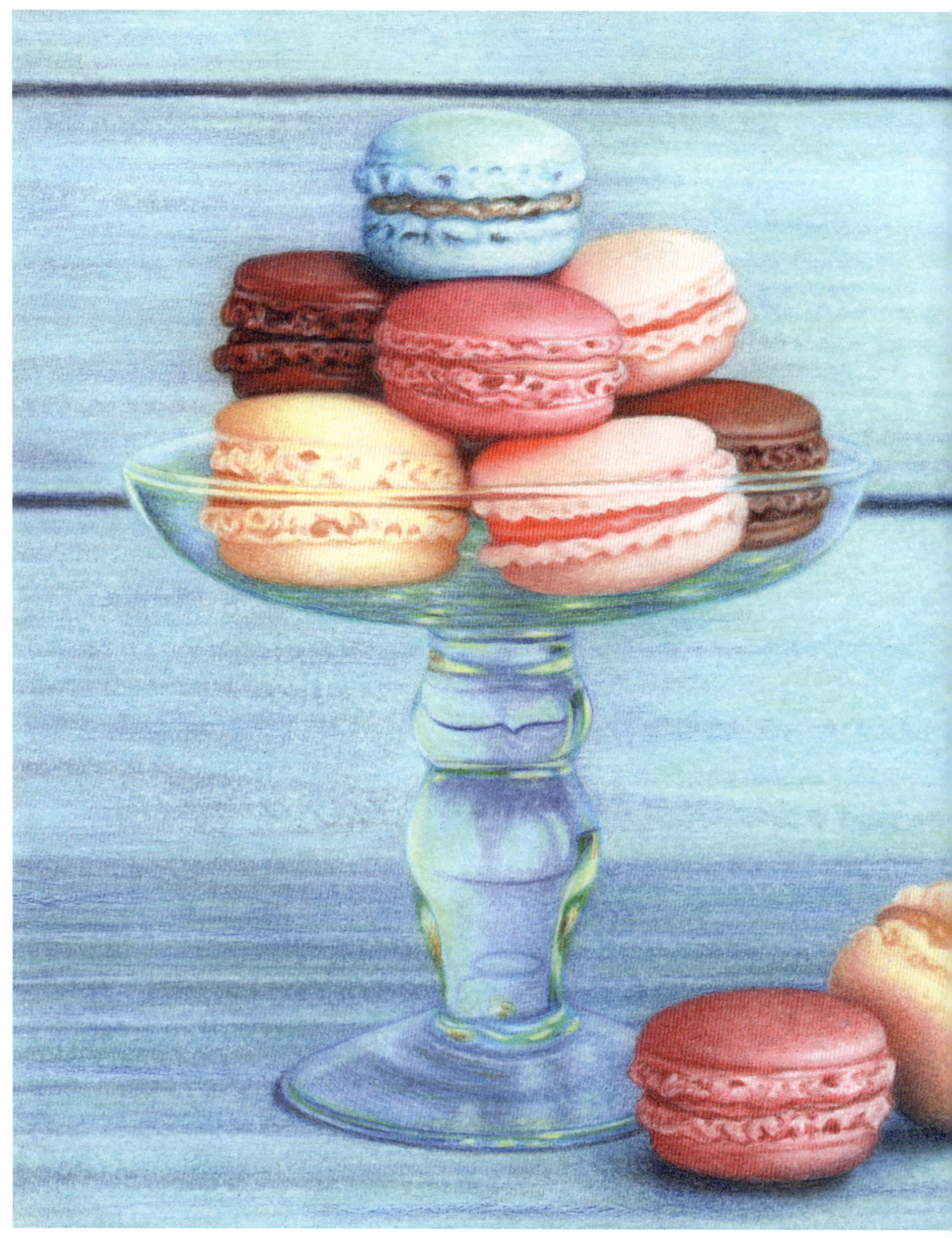

FINISHING TOUCHES

Review the entire project to ensure that it features a subject with crisp edges, as well as a smoothly blurred background and foreground. The White pencil helps to accomplish both. Sign your name with a sharp Black and spray with workable or final fixative to seal in the waxy layers of pigment and prevent them from rising to the surface.

CYNTHIA KNOX, CPSA

Project 4:
Sunflowers

Late summer offers up glorious sunflowers, and they fade as we look forward to fall with its crisp, delicious apples. This composition embraces both seasons and suggests a pensive mood with its softly diffuse lighting. Here we'll render a variety of textures, including velvety petals and leaves, copper earthenware, ripe fruit, and variegated wood grain.

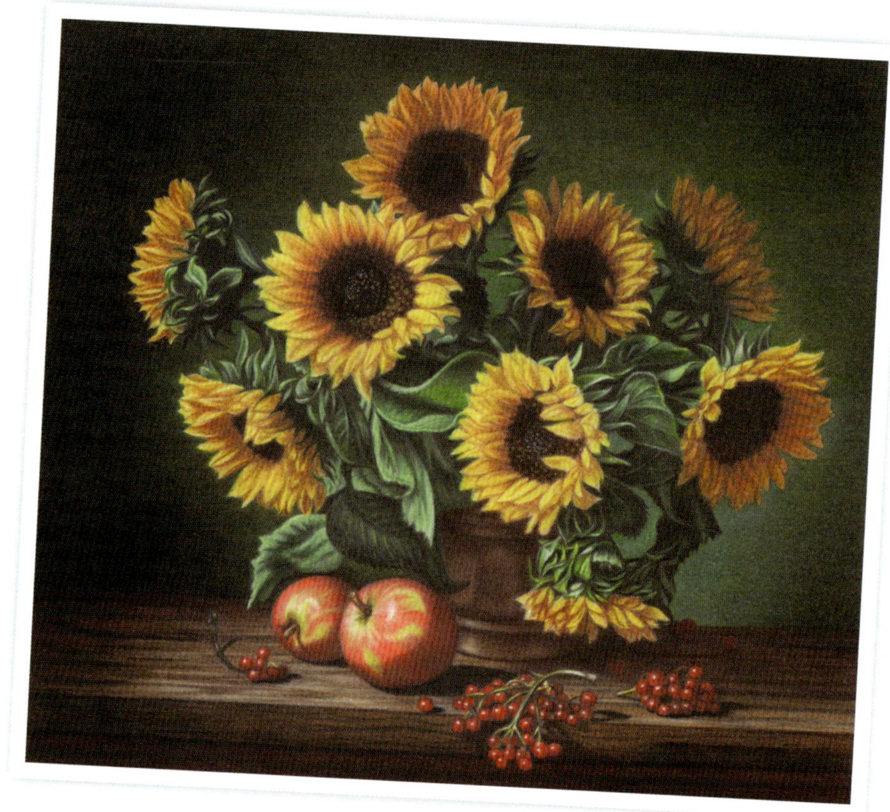

PALETTE

Prismacolor Premier:
901 Indigo Blue
908 Dark Green
911 Olive Green
912 Apple Green
915 Lemon Yellow
916 Canary Yellow
917 Sunburst Yellow
918 Orange
922 Poppy Red
923 Scarlet Lake
935 Black
937 Tuscan Red
938 White
941 Light Umber
944 Terra Cotta

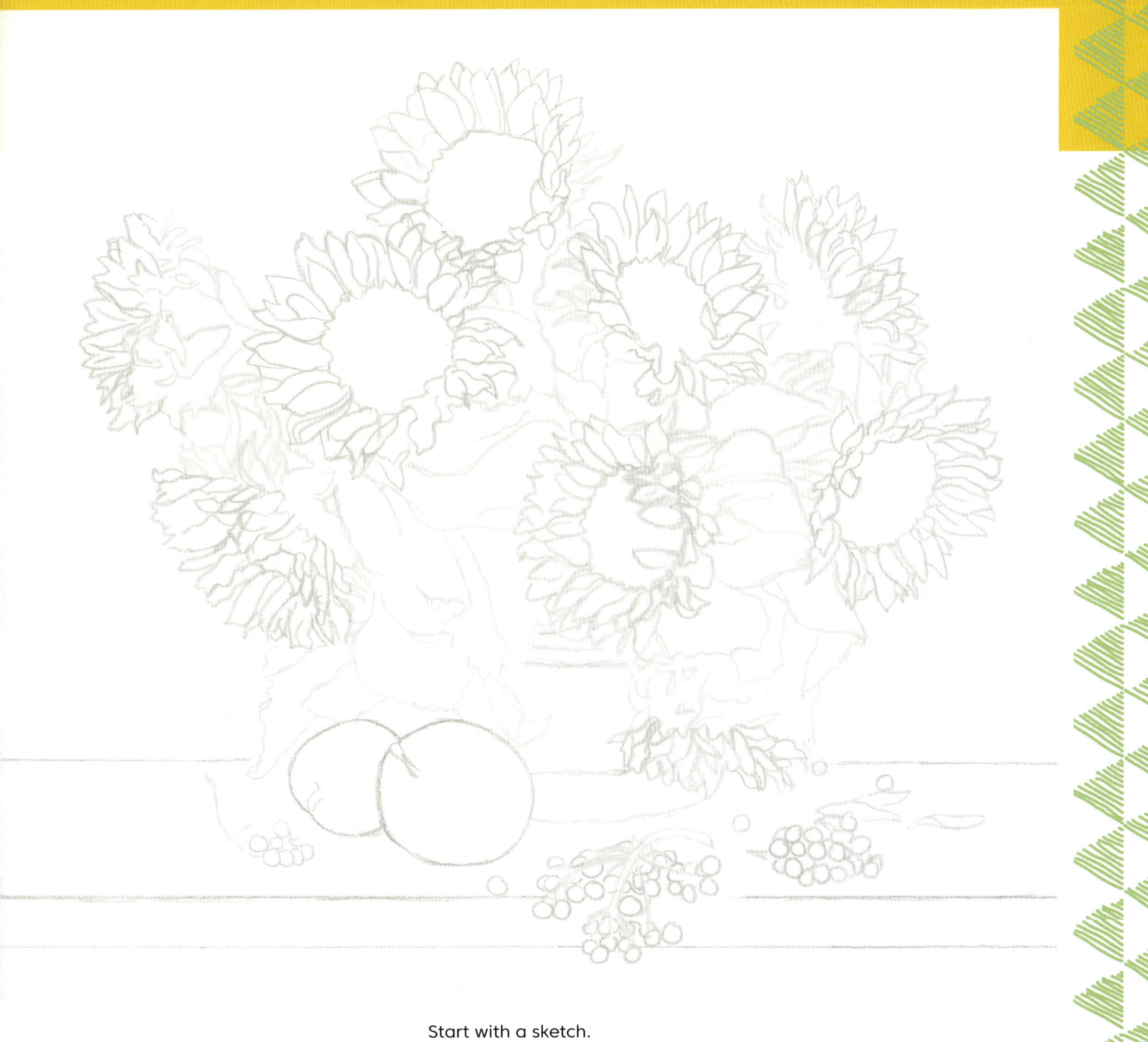

Start with a sketch.

945 Sienna Brown
946 Dark Brown
947 Dark Umber
989 Chartreuse
1002 Yellowed Orange
1005 Limepeel
1028 Bronze
1034 Goldenrod
1052 30% Warm Grey
1082 Chocolate
1083 Putty Beige
1084 Ginger Root
1089 Pale Sage

STABILO All:
8044 Yellow
8046 Black
8052 White

With moderate pressure (2) and linear strokes that overlap horizontally, apply Dark Green followed by Black (1-2). Intensify the darker areas—such as the left, top, and far right—with more Black and moderate pressure (2).

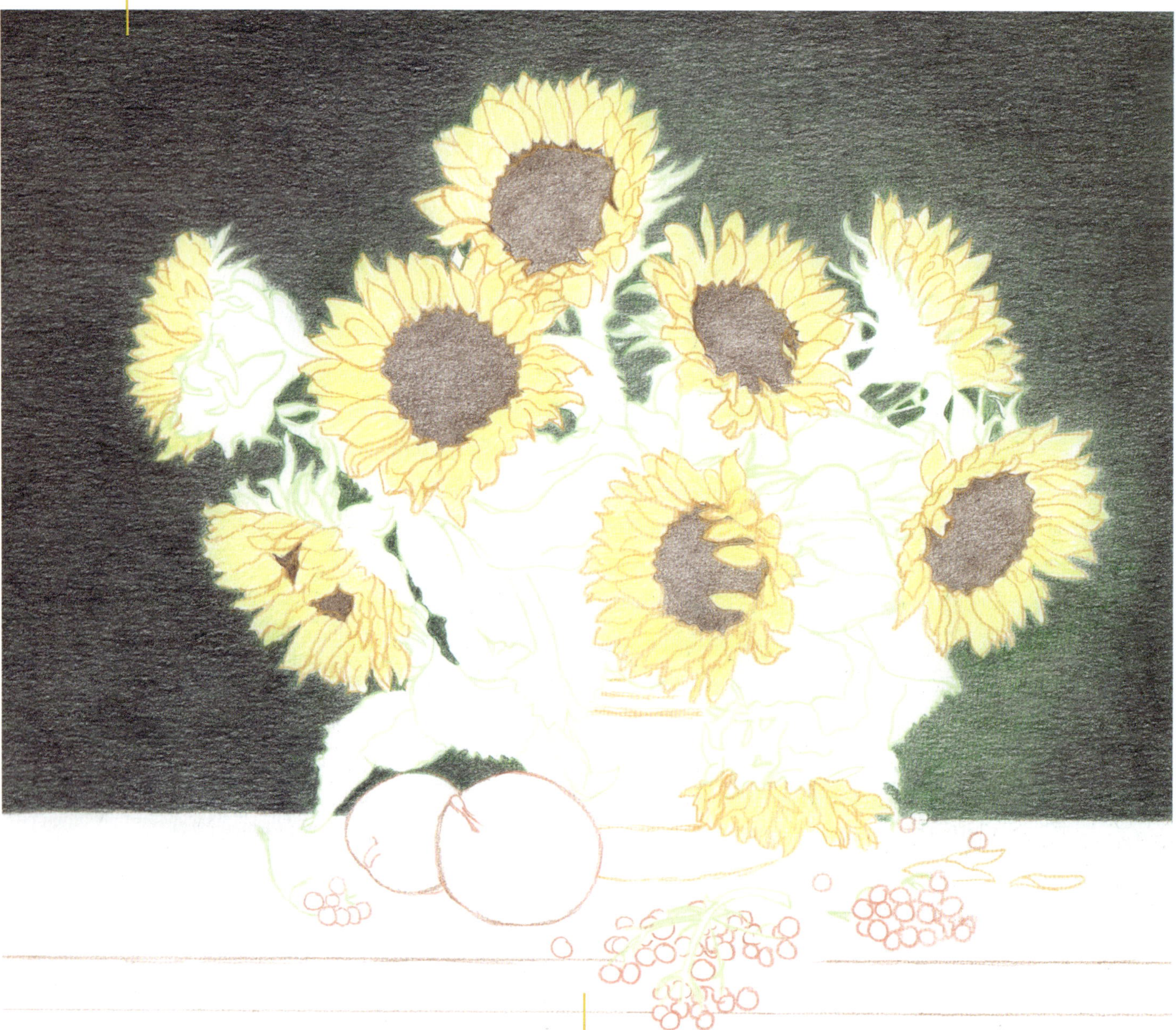

1 Use Lemon Yellow with loose, overlapping, rounded strokes and moderate pressure (2) to color in the petals. You don't need to color each petal separately.

2 Begin the centers with Dark Brown using moderate pressure (2) and rounded, overlapping strokes.

Cover the entire background with Black. This time, burnish the darkest areas using firm pressure (4-5) and tiny, overlapping, and horizontal strokes.

Render the remainder of the background with light to medium pressure (1-3), depending on the darkness of the shadows. Try to achieve the diffused glow behind the sunflowers.

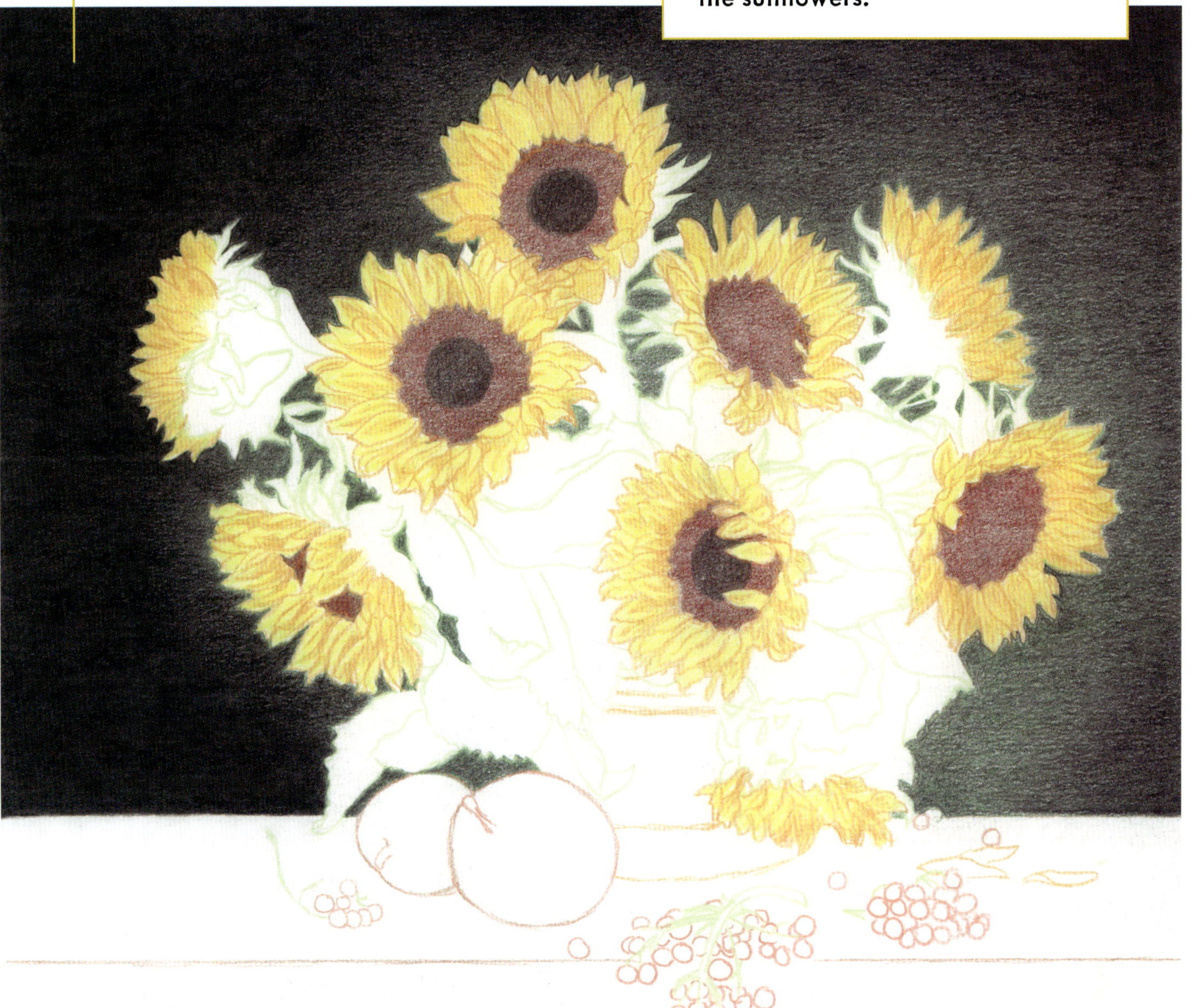

1 Color over the petals with Canary Yellow and moderate pressure (2). Use tiny, rounded, overlapping strokes for even coverage.

2 Color Goldenrod over all but the brightest yellow petals using tiny, overlapping strokes and moderate to medium pressure (2-3).

3 Enhance the sunflower centers with Tuscan Red applied with moderate pressure (2) and small, overlapping, rounded strokes. Color in the three black interiors with Black using the same techniques.

BACKGROUND

1 Color in the two blank areas in the lower-right foliage using a layer of Dark Green (3) followed by Black (2).

2 Burnish all but the very blackest areas of the background with Olive Green using firm pressure (4) and small, rounded, overlapping strokes.

3 With sharp White, tiny and rounded strokes, and medium pressure (3), lighten the highlights on the right. Also do this in the interior areas of the background within the foliage on the right side. Then skim the sharp point of the Indigo Blue pencil over these areas to darken their value.

4 Use Olive Green and Black to seamlessly transition between the green and black. For a smooth, blurred effect, make tiny, overlapping strokes.

5 Seal in the background layers using workable fixative to prevent wax bloom, or simply wipe off the wax bloom that will occur later with a soft cloth.

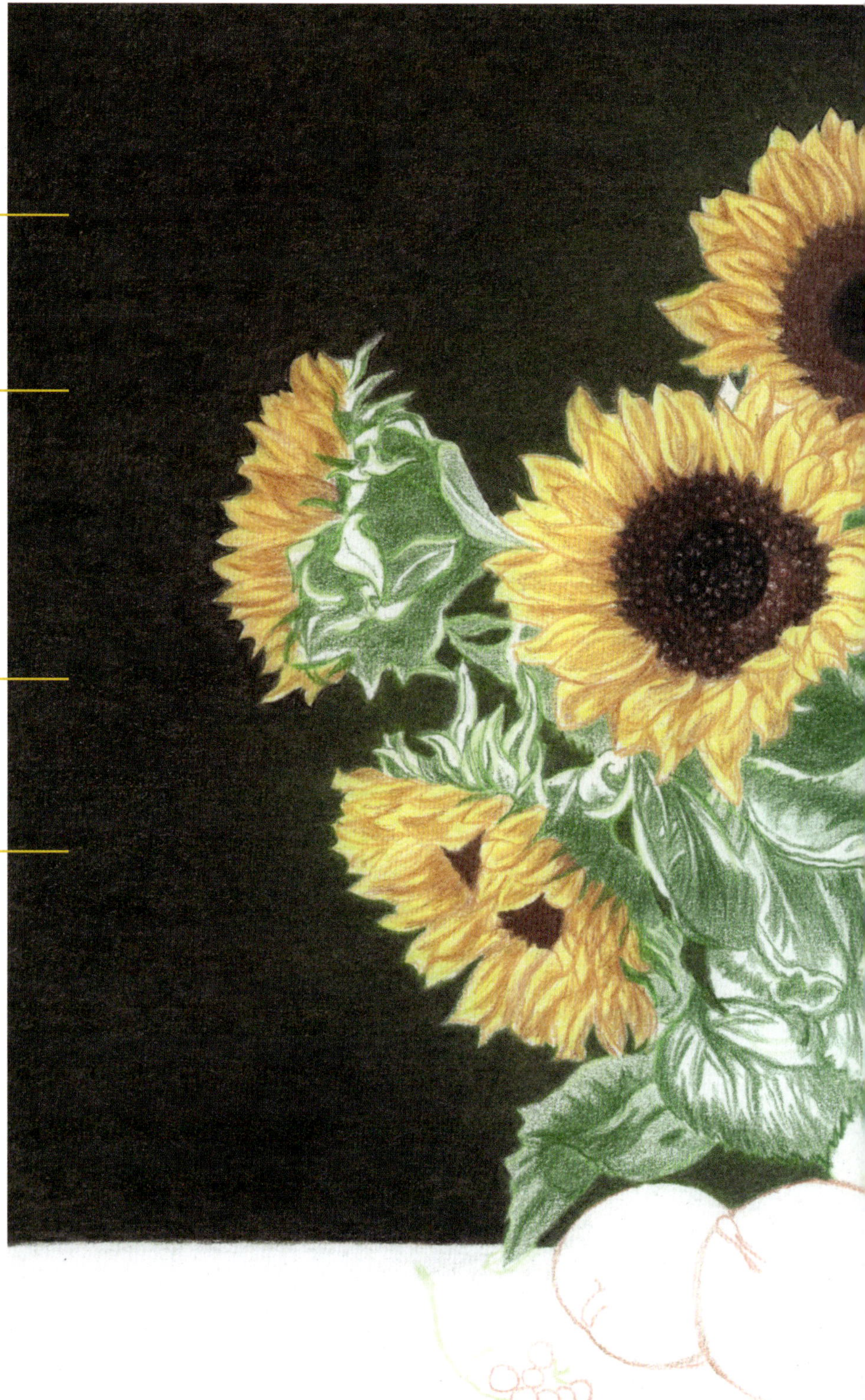

TIP

Do you have a dark waxy blip? If so, nudge it up with the sharp point of your White pencil.

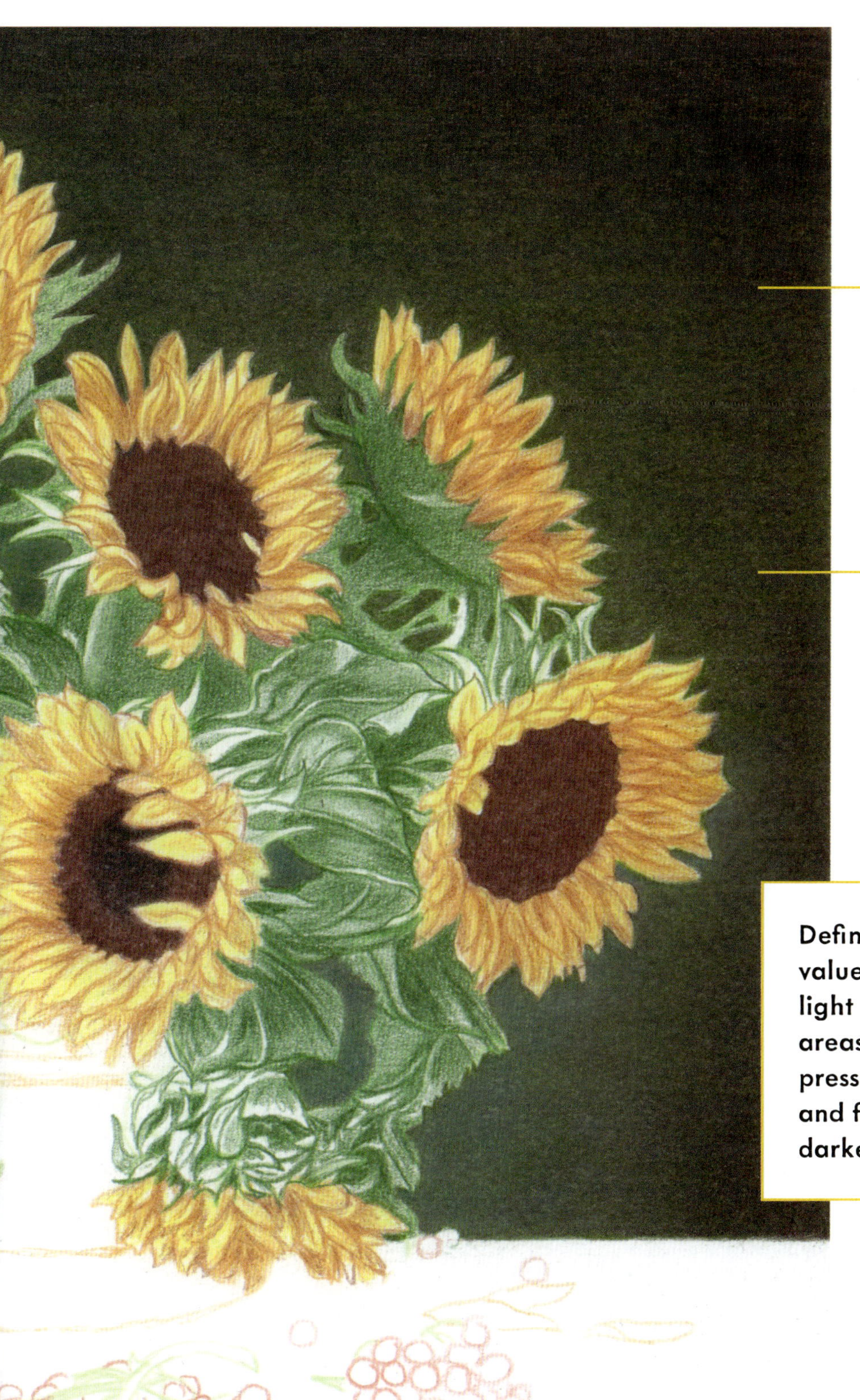

SUNFLOWERS

1 Darken the shadowed areas of the petals with Sienna Brown, varying your pressure depending on the lightness or darkness of each shadow.

2 Burnish the centers with firm to very firm pressure (4-5). For all but the sunflower with the speckled center, burnish Dark Umber over the dark brown areas and Black over the darkest round interiors. Leave a thin curved area lighter above the top sunflower's center.

3 For the speckled sunflower center, leave tiny random dots of lighter color as you travel around the exterior with Dark Umber and the interior with Black. Lightly skim Black (1-2) over all of the brown exterior except for the curved right section.

Define and establish the foliage values with Dark Green using light pressure (1) in the lightest areas, moderate to medium pressure (2-3) in the midtones, and firm pressure (4) in the darker areas.

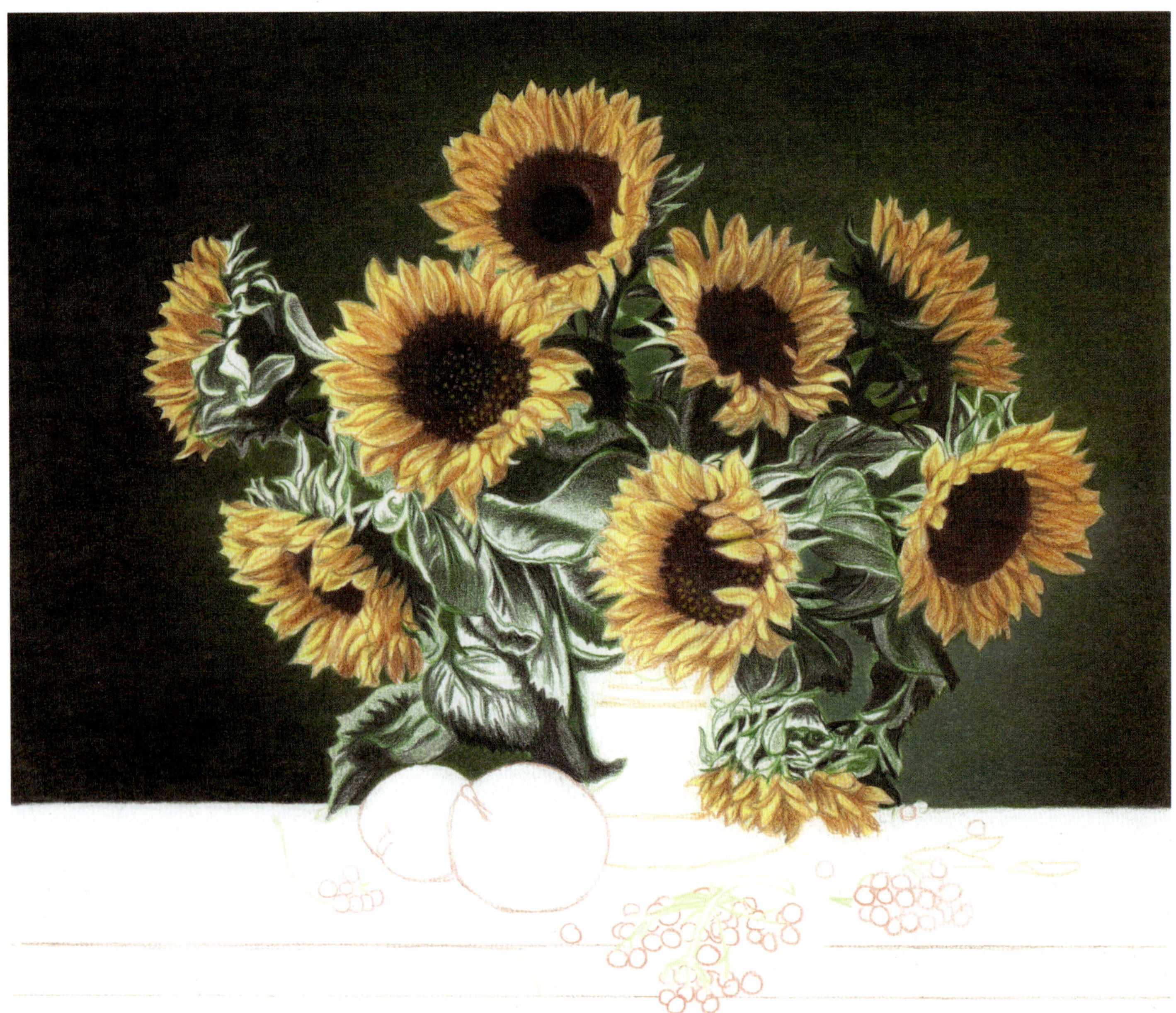

1 Deepen the shadows of the petals with Dark Umber using directional strokes and light to moderate pressure (1-2). Bring in Terra Cotta wherever you see reddish hues.

2 Use firm pressure (4) with Canary Yellow to reinforce and/or create yellow seeds within the two middle sunflower centers. Darken the remainder of the black interior and the other sunflower centers with Black using firm pressure (4) and tiny, overlapping strokes. Lightly color Dark Umber over the interior curve of the top sunflower's center.

Deepen the shadows with Black using medium to firm pressure (3-4) and overlapping directional strokes.

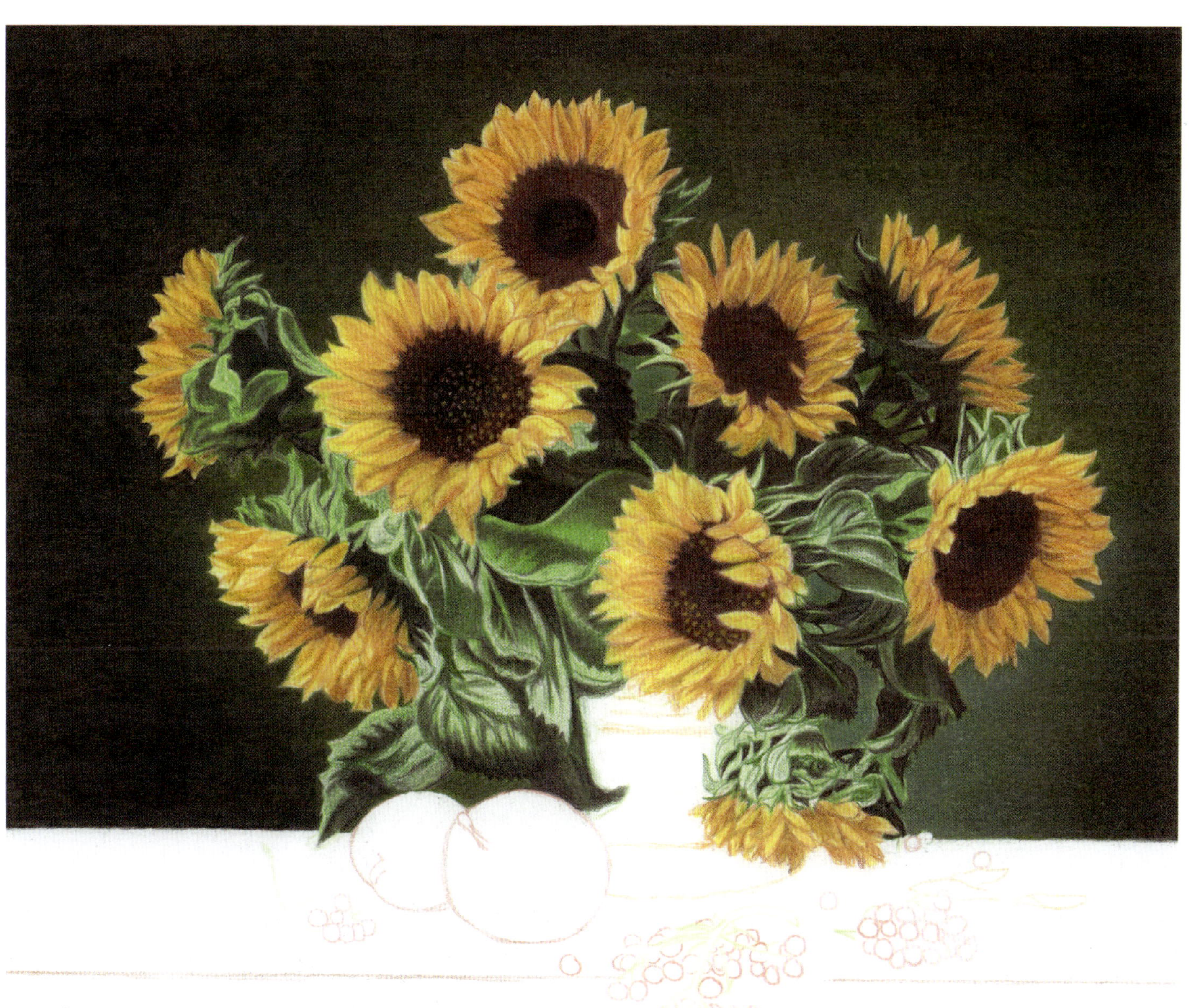

1 Burnish the petals of all but the two center sunflowers with Sunburst Yellow using firm pressure (4).

2 Burnish the two center flower petals with Canary Yellow.

LEAVES & STEMS

Use Apple Green to sweeten the green coloring of the leaves and stems. Apply light to moderate pressure (1-2) over the lightest areas and intensify your pressure over the darker areas. Use firm pressure (4) over most of the large leaf in the center. Tweak the shadows using Dark Green and Black.

1 Reclaim the petal outlines with Sienna Brown or Terra Cotta using moderate to medium pressure (2-3). Lighten and brighten using White and Canary Yellow. Finish the orange-looking petals with Sunburst Yellow and/or Yellowed Orange. Apply touches of Terra Cotta and Tuscan Red to reddish areas. Enhance the darkest shadows with Dark Brown and/or Dark Umber.

2 To darken the flowers at the top and right, complete the petals with yellow-orange hues, and then lightly skim Dark Brown or Dark Umber over the entire section with a sharp point and light to moderate pressure (1-2).

3 Add touches of highlights peeking through with Sunburst Yellow or Yellowed Orange. If the petal borders need more delineation, define them with sharpened Dark Umber and some pressure. Need more red? Use Tuscan Red with a soft touch. Add Canary Yellow with firm pressure (4) to recapture vivid yellow hues.

4 The sunflower centers are each a little bit different. Where you see an obvious inner circle, color it in with Black STABILO. For the others, use Black STABILO to randomly scribble black throughout.

5 Use White STABILO and a 000 round paintbrush for the tiny white dots in the interiors of the centers of the two front flowers. Dip the paintbrush in water and shake off the excess drops; then sweep it across the point of the pencil several times. Touch the paintbrush tip to the sunflower interiors and paint random dots.

6 For the little yellow dots surrounding the black centers of the front two flowers, follow the same process with the Yellow STABILO pencil.

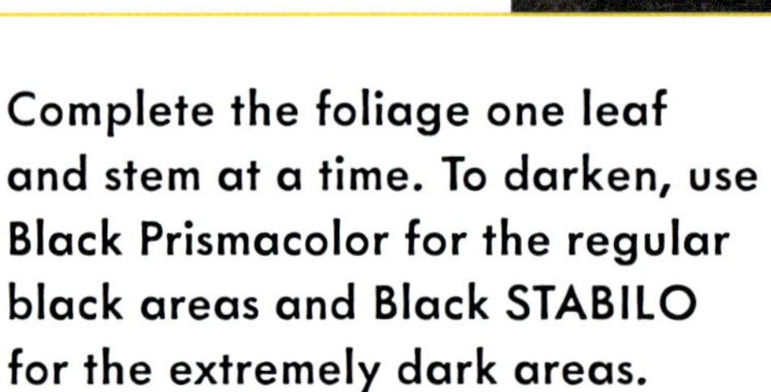

Complete the foliage one leaf and stem at a time. To darken, use Black Prismacolor for the regular black areas and Black STABILO for the extremely dark areas.

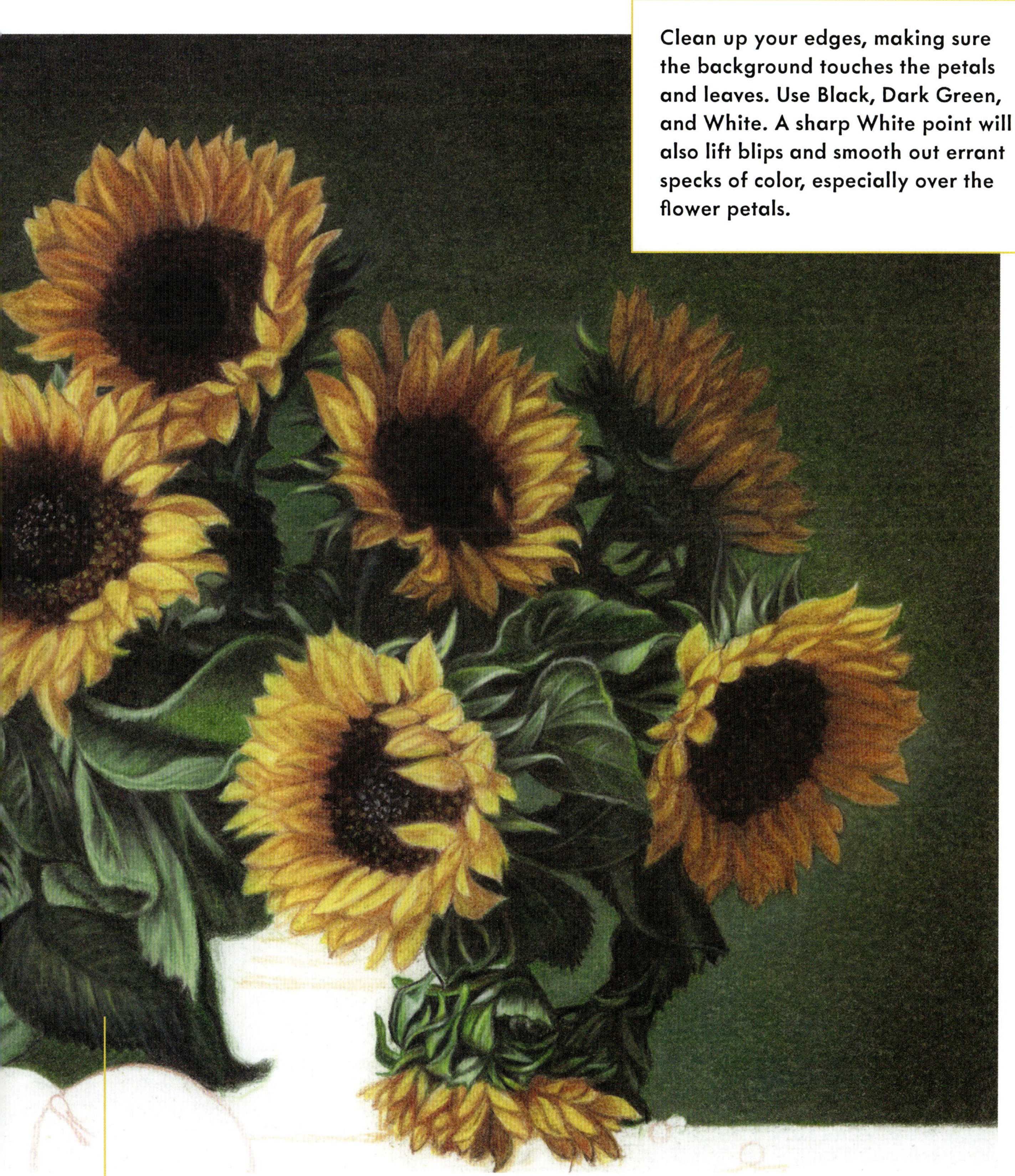

Clean up your edges, making sure the background touches the petals and leaves. Use Black, Dark Green, and White. A sharp White point will also lift blips and smooth out errant specks of color, especially over the flower petals.

Create the very dark green areas with a basecoat of Black followed by Dark Green. Use Pale Sage for the lightest greens and White for highlights. Color the center leaf and right side with Apple Green and/or Chartreuse, and then develop with the light and dark pencils you've already used.

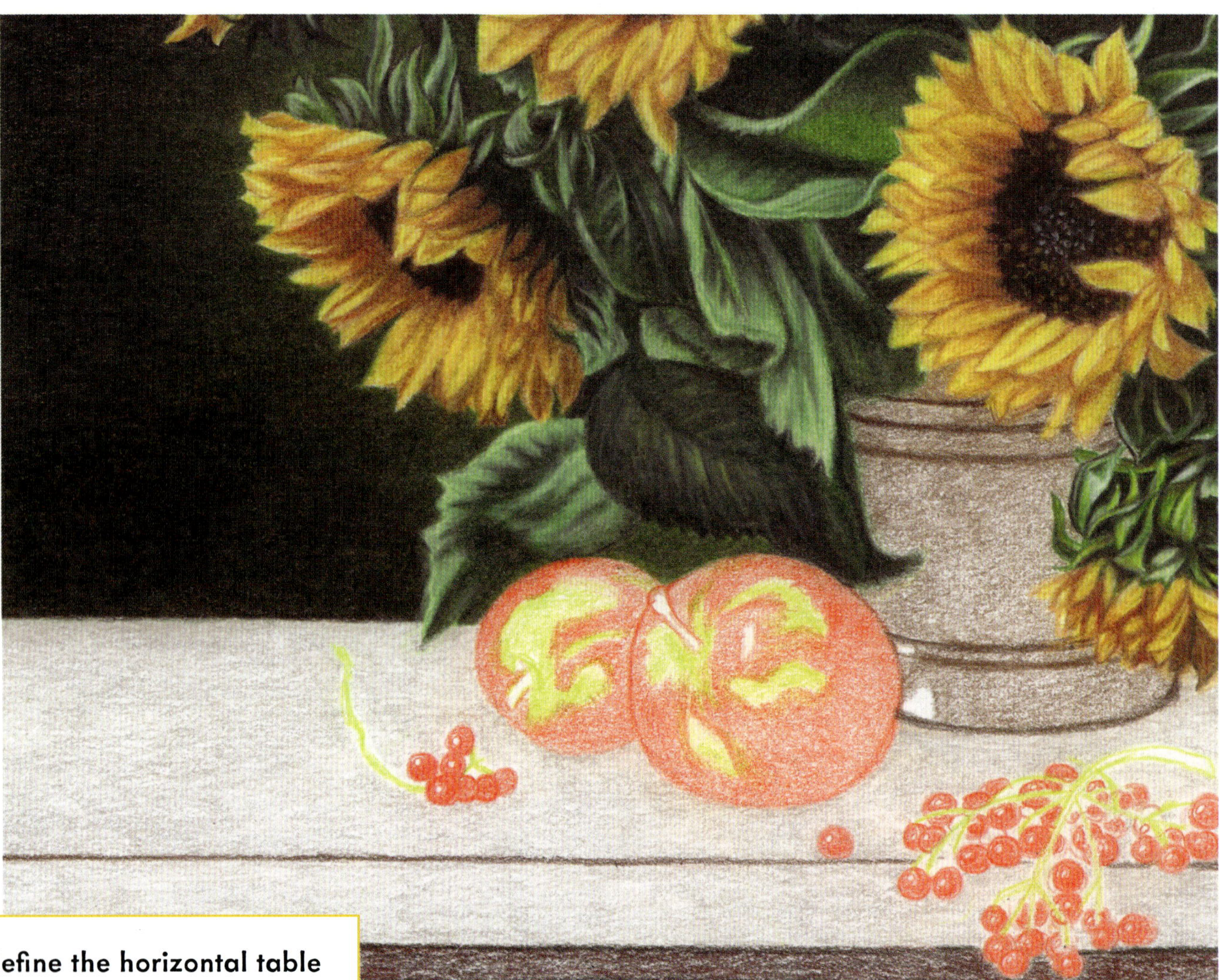

Redefine the horizontal table lines with Dark Umber using moderate pressure (2). Color the top and front edge with Putty Beige followed by 30% Warm Grey using horizontal strokes and moderate pressure (2). Layer the underside of the table with two applications of Black followed by Tuscan Red, using horizontal strokes and medium pressure (2). Darken the edge lines with Black.

1 Reline the apples with Poppy Red, including the stem. Block in the green areas with Chartreuse using moderate pressure (2) and small, overlapping strokes. Apply Poppy Red over the red areas in the direction of the streaks using moderate pressure (2).

2 Sketch the curved lines of the copper container with Dark Umber; then reinforce those lines with firmer pressure (3-4). Color in all but the lower-left highlights with Dark Brown using moderate pressure (2) and overlapping circular strokes.

3 Outline the berry stems with Chartreuse and use Scarlet Lake to outline the berries. Draw tiny highlight circles with Scarlet Lake and then color around them using moderate pressure (2) and circular strokes.

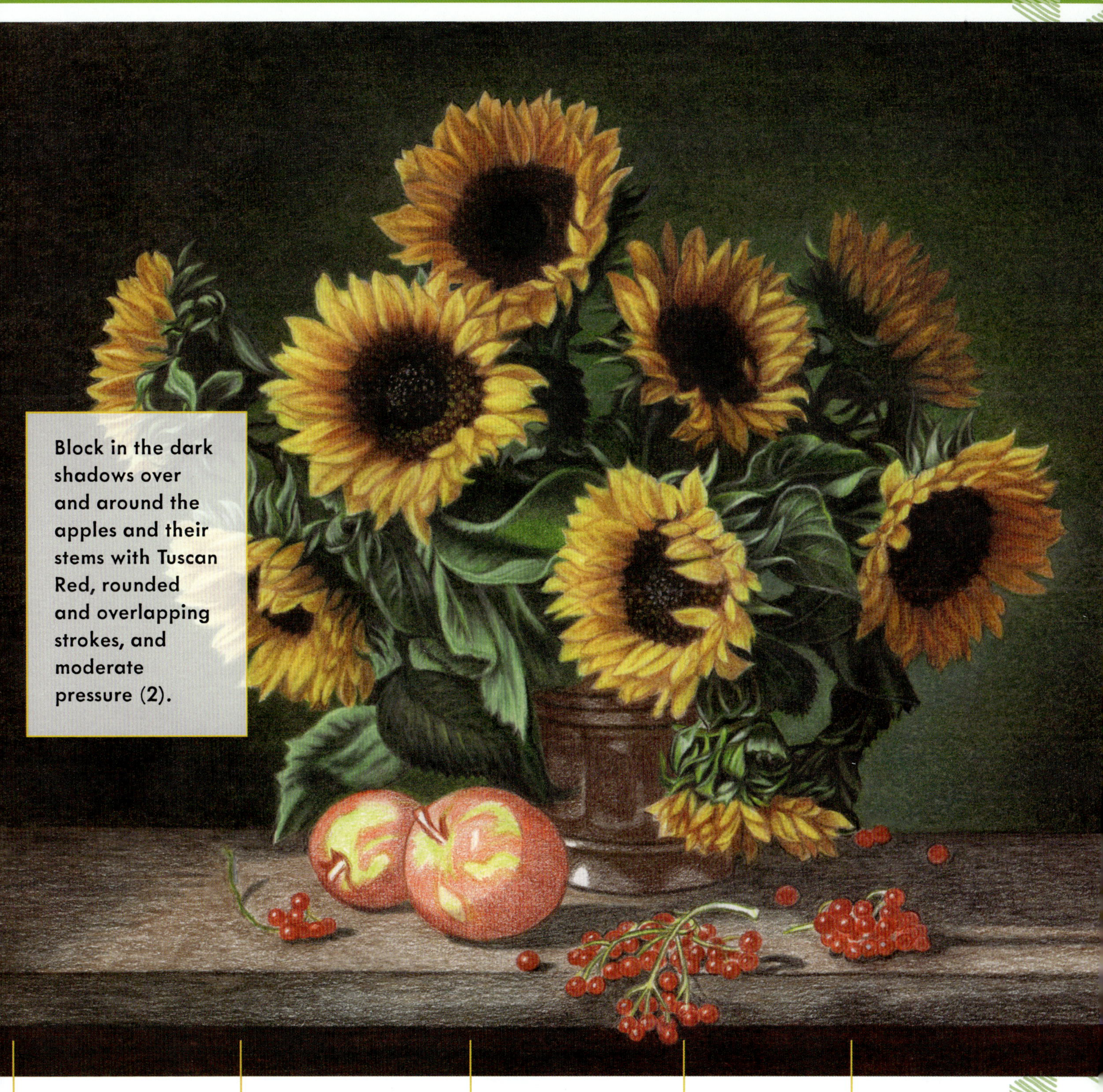

Block in the dark shadows over and around the apples and their stems with Tuscan Red, rounded and overlapping strokes, and moderate pressure (2).

1 Apply Dark Umber over all but the lower highlights of the copper container using moderate pressure (2). Then darken the deeply shadowed areas with more Dark Umber using medium to firm pressure (3-4). Reinforce the curved seam lines with Black (3).

2 Burnish the red sections of each berry with Tuscan Red using medium to firm pressure (3-4). Try to preserve the tiny white highlights, but if you lose them, paint white dots with the 000 paintbrush and White STABILO. Draw the stem outlines with Dark Brown followed by Dark Green. Color in the stem on the far left.

3 Layer Dark Brown over the top of the table and front edge using moderate to medium pressure (2-3) and horizontal strokes. Apply Black over the darkest areas with medium pressure (3) and horizontal strokes.

4 Burnish the underside of the table with Black using firm pressure (4) and horizontal strokes. Apply Tuscan Red overall.

5 Darken the apple shadows and their stems with Dark Umber.

1 Apply Dark Umber over the tabletop with firm to very firm pressure (4-5) in the darkest areas and moderate pressure (2) in the lightest areas. Apply Light Umber over the mid-left section and between the clumps of berries using medium to firm pressure (3-4).

2 Color in the lightest areas with Ginger Root. Darken the fruit shadows with Black using firm to very firm pressure (4-5).

3 Draw streaks of wood grain with sharp Black and moderate to medium pressure (2-3).

4 Apply Black over the darkest areas of the front edge using firm pressure (4); then skim Tuscan Red over the Black with moderate pressure (2).

5 Burnish Chocolate over the entire front edge from left to right with firm pressure (4) and a sharp point. Add a few random Black grain lines throughout.

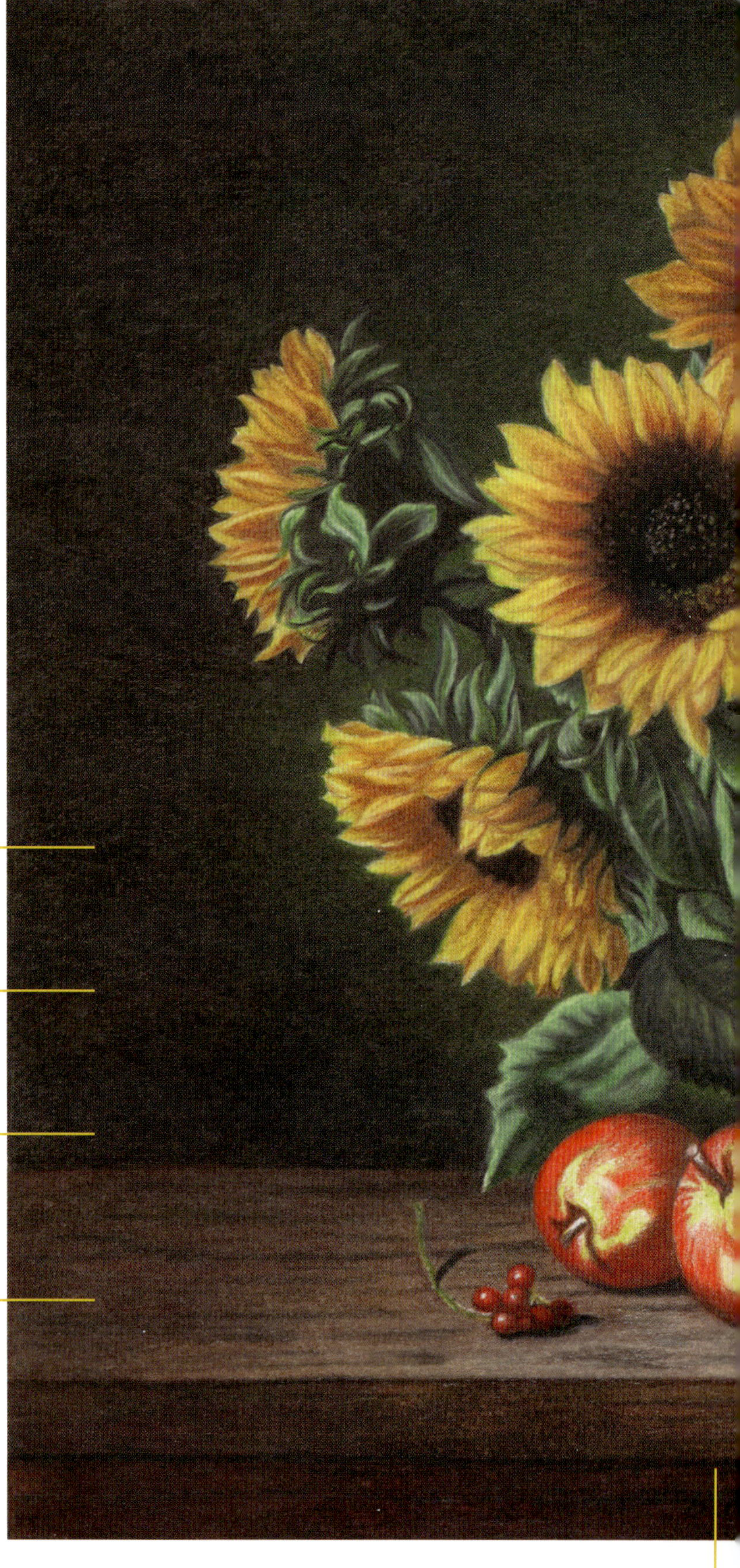

1 Darken the stems and shadows around the apples with Dark Umber using moderate pressure (2) and tiny, overlapping, rounded strokes. Just above the two apples, color in the background area with Black.

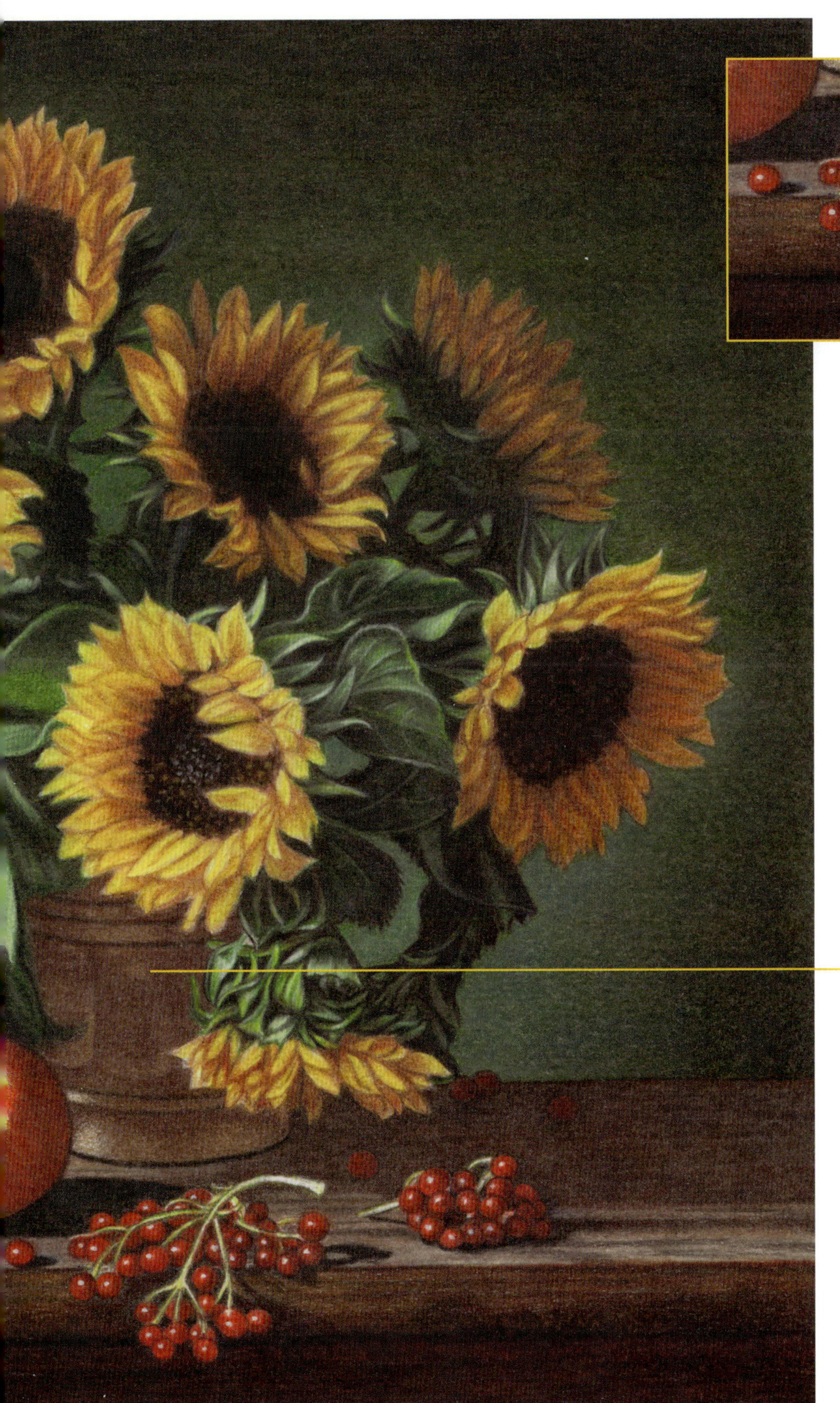

Reoutline and intensify the berries with Scarlet Lake using medium to firm (3-4) pressure and rounded and overlapping strokes. Finish by lightly darkening the shadows with a sharp Black point. If you need to brighten up the tiny highlights, do so with the 000 round paintbrush and White STABILO.

Burnish Bronze over the entire container except the two lower-left highlights. Use firm pressure (4) and rounded, overlapping strokes. Lightly color in the two highlights with Bronze (2).

2 Apply Scarlet Lake over the apples with tiny, curved strokes in the direction of the red pattern. Begin with moderate pressure (2) over the light red areas and intensify (4) over the brighter red areas. Color over the brown shadows as well.

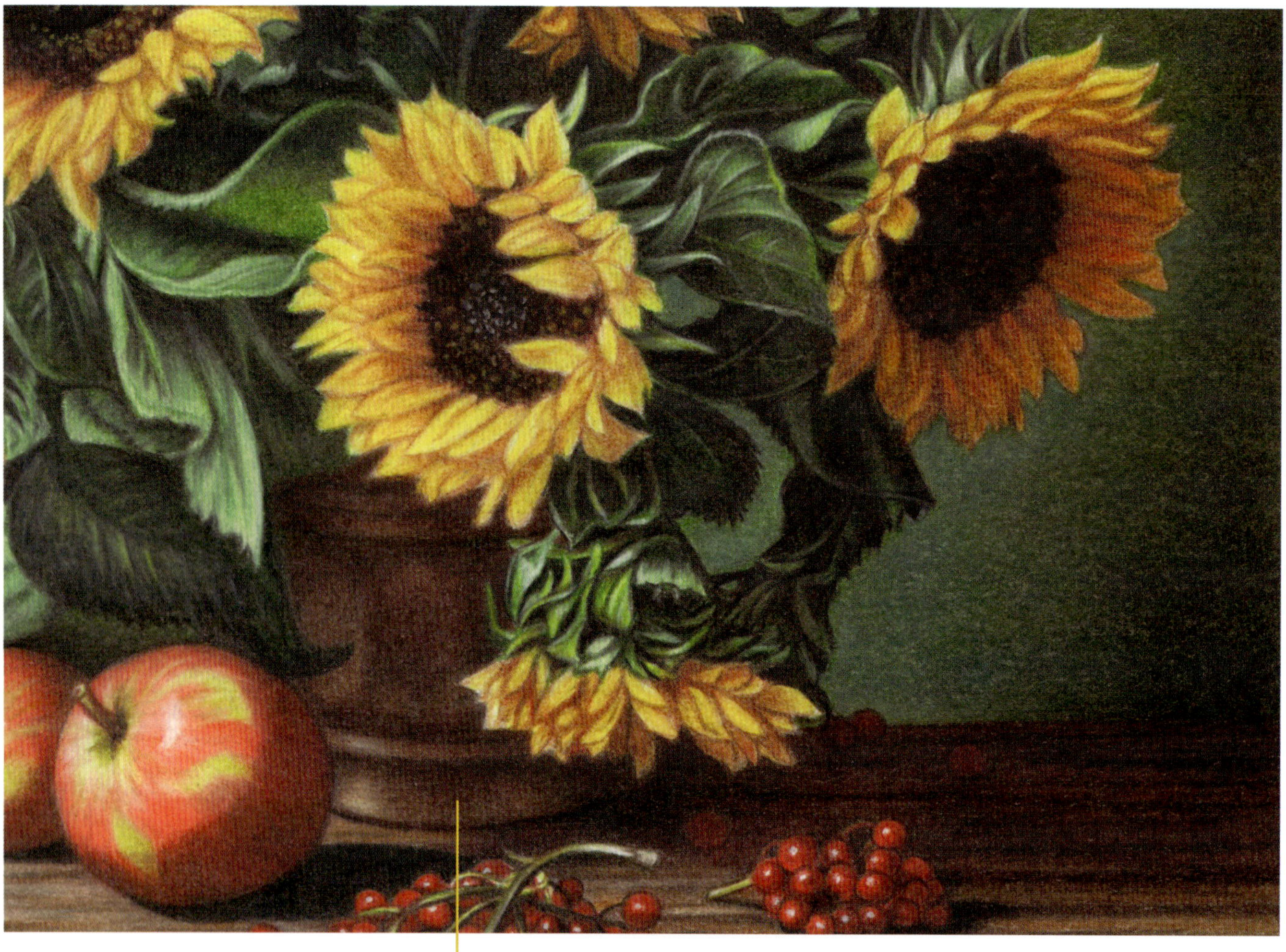

1 Burnish Dark Umber over the darkest areas with firm pressure (4). Redefine the curved black lines with Black.

2 Skim Black over the darkly shadowed areas throughout (2) and apply Tuscan Red over that (2). If necessary, use Black STABILO with light to moderate pressure (1-2).

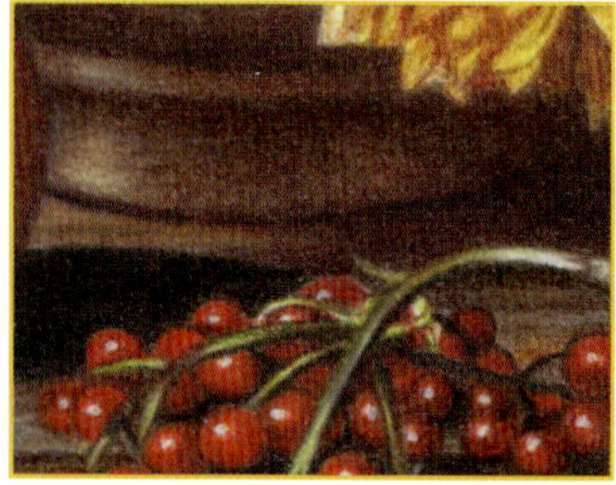

Color Goldenrod over the two lower-left highlights, and then burnish with White for a dull shine (4).

1 Use Chartreuse with medium pressure (3) to enhance the existing greens within the apples. Lightly (2) apply Black over darkly shadowed areas using small, rounded, overlapping strokes for smooth coverage; then blur their upper curved lines with tiny, rounded strokes of Scarlet Lake.

2 Burnish and brighten the remainder of the apples with a sharp White and medium pressure (3). "Carve" in a few curved streaks with White and color some in with Chartreuse. With very firm pressure (5) and White, establish and soften the two curved highlights.

3 Color the apple stems and their bases with Limepeel, and add touches of Dark Umber down the stems. Establish depth with a bit of Black at the very base; then soften with Limepeel.

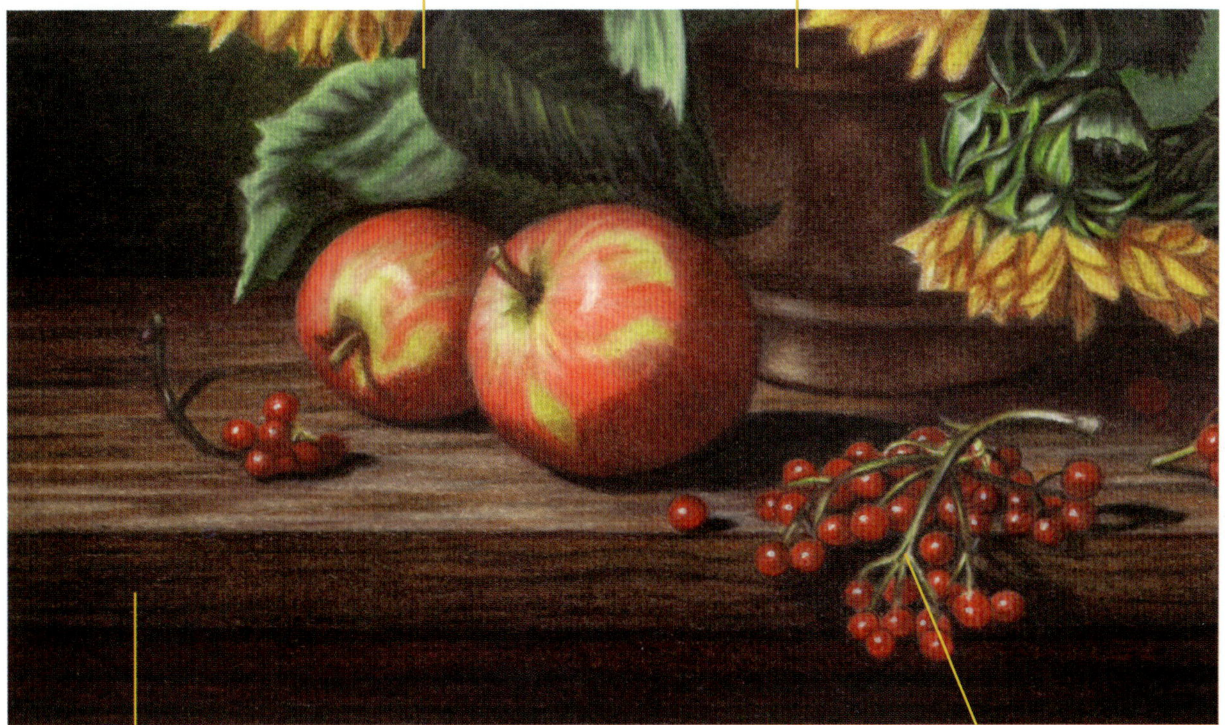

1 Develop the wood grain with streaks of black using Black STABILO with a sharp point. Also skim this lightly (1-2) over the darkest areas of the tabletop.

2 Warm up the darkest hues with a light application of Tuscan Red. Also warm up the midtones of the tabletop and the front edge with Chocolate and blend into the Black. Extend the Chocolate very lightly into the front highlight area, and then add streaks of Ginger Root.

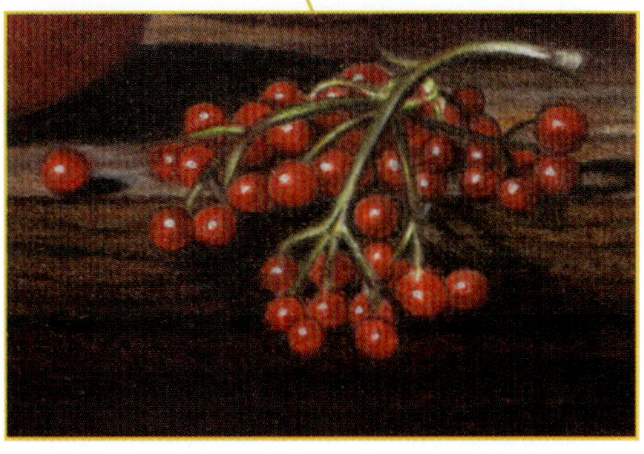

Use Limepeel for the green midtones, White for the highlights, and Dark Umber and Black for the shadows. For the cluster on the right and the tip of the far-left stem, use Tuscan Red.

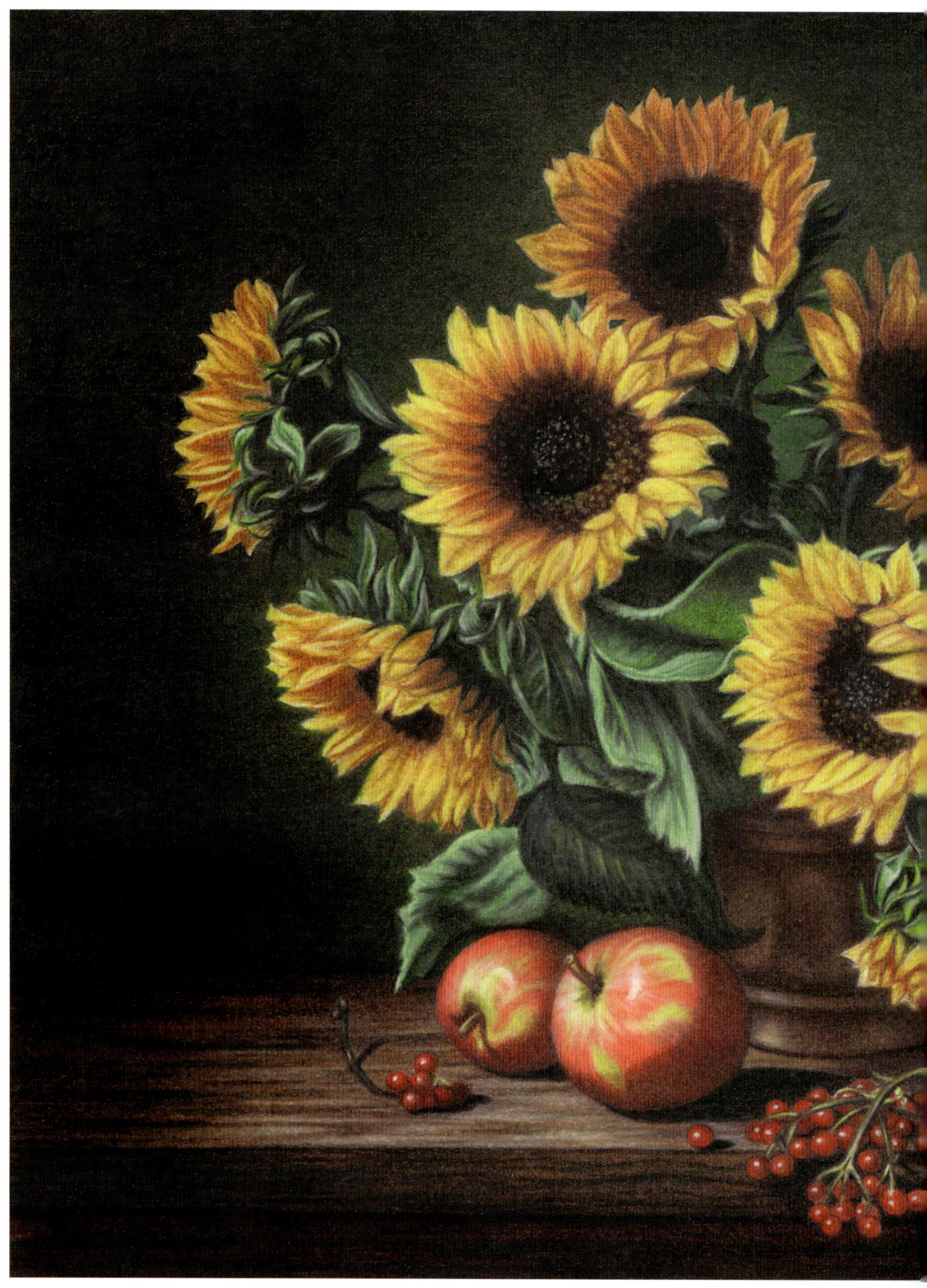

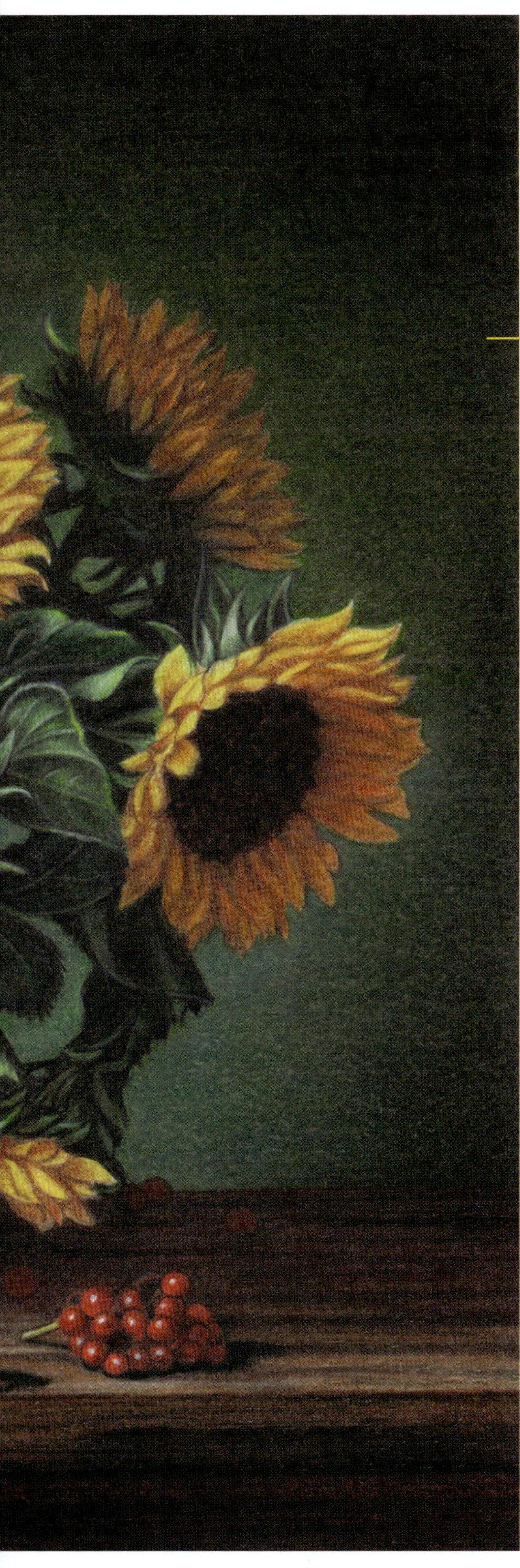

FINISHING TOUCHES

1 I like color and contrast! I chose to skim some Orange over the top sunflowers and deepen the shadows throughout the entire subject with a light skimming of Black.

2 Look over every area to determine if you need to attend to any details. The visual impression of a whole piece comes down to the details, and you want them to be crisp or softly blurred, depending upon the section.

Check for wax bloom and lift with a soft cloth if you notice any. Spray with workable fixative or a final fixative.

Project 5:

Meringues

Glass, especially tinted glass, is a popular texture in still lifes. Throw in some delectable meringues and add a lovely blurred background, and you have a still life that is attractive, modern, and appealing. In this project, I'll show you how to create a unique glass jar, the clustered meringues with their unusual shapes and shadows, and the soft background and foreground. Join me and let's get started creating your next masterpiece!

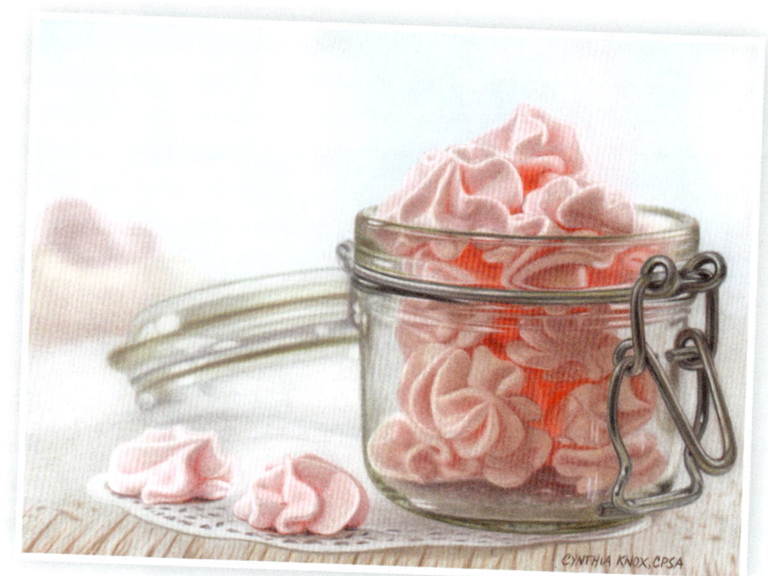

PALETTE

Prismacolor Premier:
923 Scarlet Lake
924 Crimson Red
929 Pink
935 Black
937 Tuscan Red
938 White (x2)
941 Light Umber
943 Burnt Ochre
945 Sienna Brown
946 Dark Brown
947 Dark Umber
988 Marine Green
996 Black Grape
1014 Deco Pink
1017 Clay Rose
1018 Pink Rose
1019 Rosy Beige
1020 Celadon Green
1060 20% Cool Grey
1061 30% Cool Grey
1063 50% Cool Grey
1065 70% Cool Grey
1069 20% French Grey
1074 70% French Grey
1078 Black Cherry
1081 Chestnut
1086 Sky Blue Light
1091 Green Ochre
1093 Seashell Pink
1103 Caribbean Sea

Derwent Drawing Pencil:
7200 Chinese White

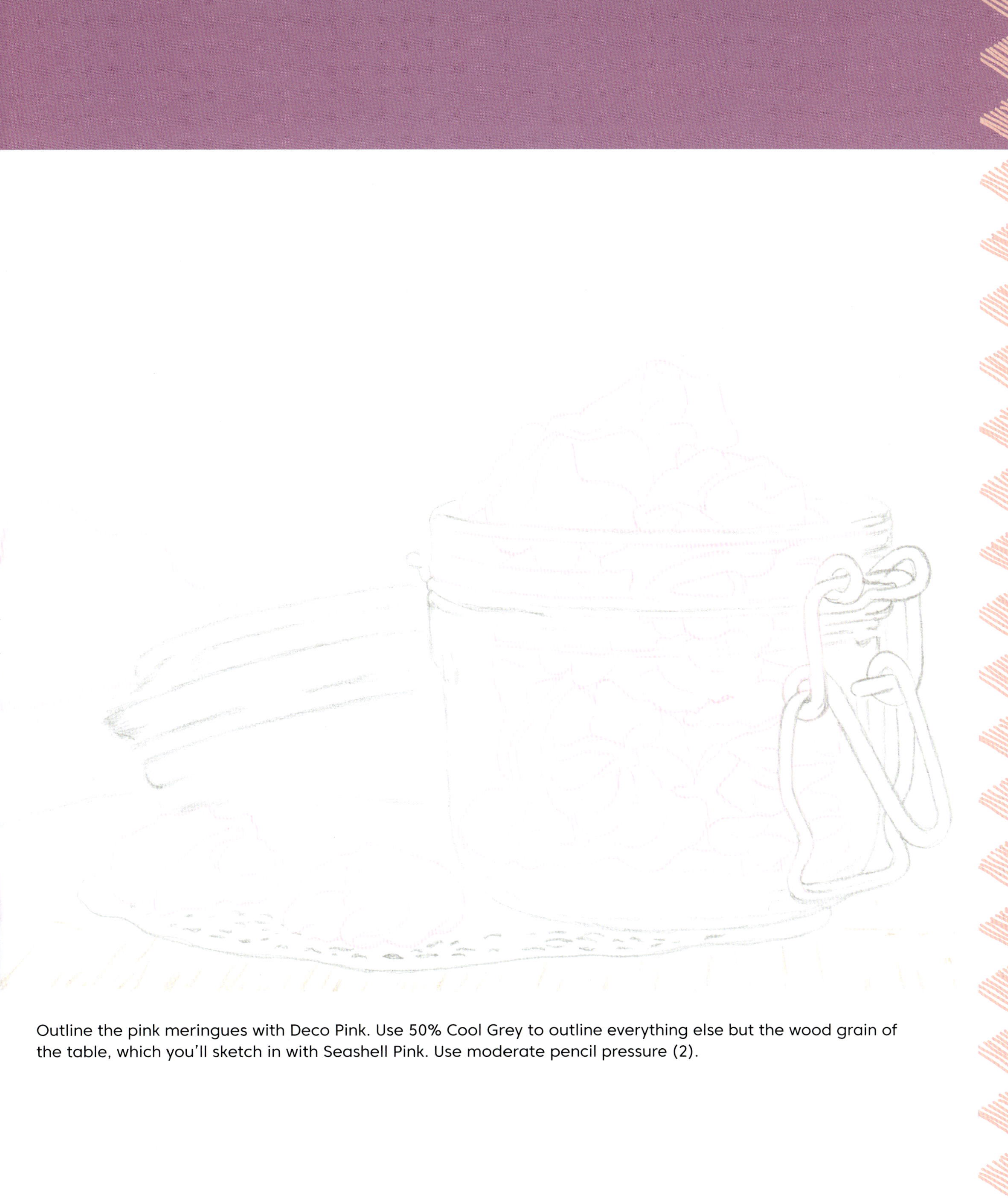

Outline the pink meringues with Deco Pink. Use 50% Cool Grey to outline everything else but the wood grain of the table, which you'll sketch in with Seashell Pink. Use moderate pencil pressure (2).

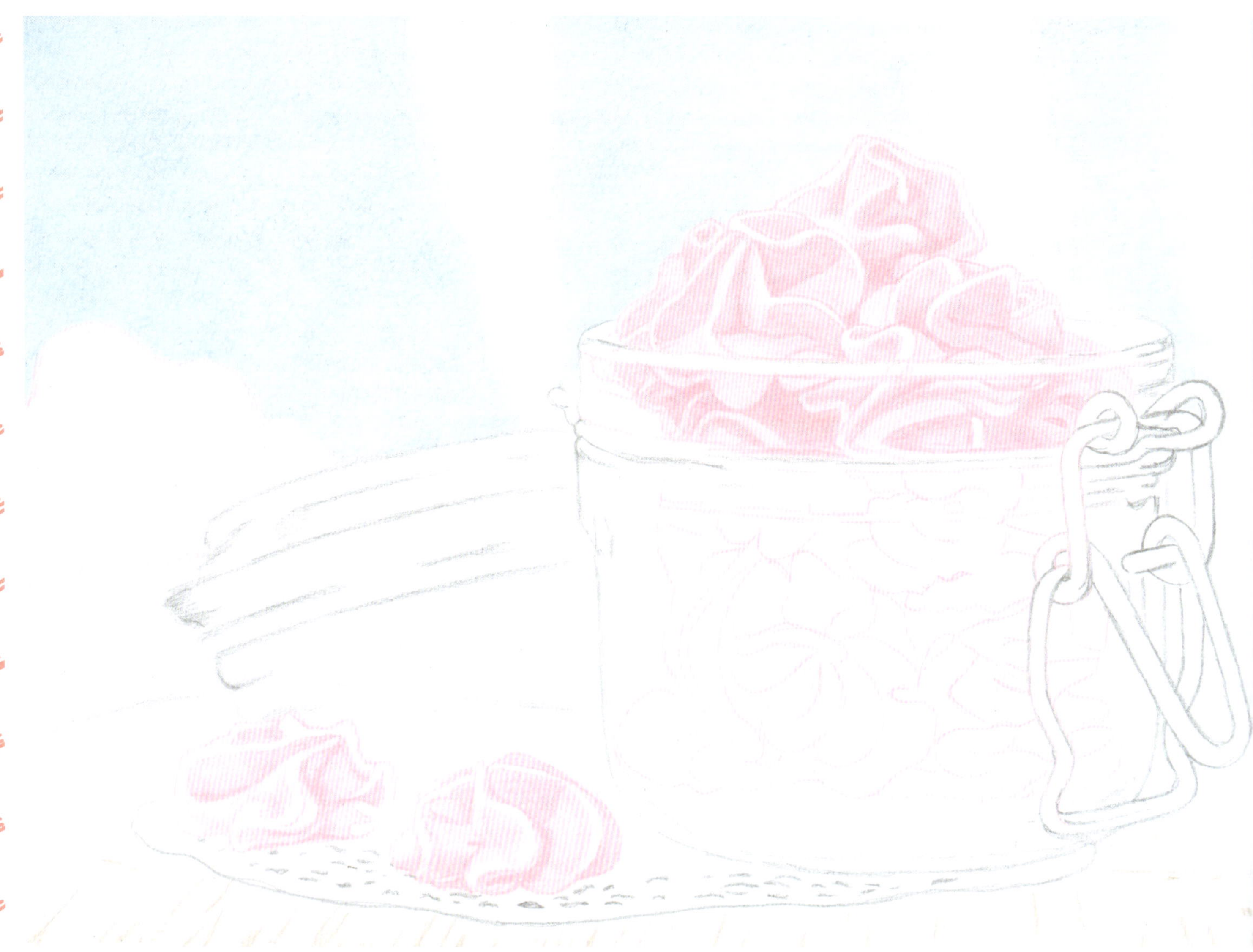

1 Begin the background with Sky Blue Light and lightly (1) sketch a few loose vertical lines to mark off the borders of the whitish-blue sections. Then fill in the blue areas with Sky Blue Light using small, rounded, and overlapping strokes with moderate pressure (2). Repeat with Caribbean Sea.

2 Work with the Deco Pink pencil and an eraser to establish the shapes and values for the meringues. Move from left to right and begin with light pencil pressure (1). As the pink sections darken, increase the pencil pressure.

BACKGROUND

1 Apply Sky Blue Light over just the left blue section with loose, overlapping, rounded strokes and moderate pressure (2). Over the center and right blue sections, apply Caribbean Sea in the same manner.

2 Color in the three white vertical sections with Sky Blue Light (2) and then Deco Pink (2). Repeat with both pencils for deeper color. Use small, rounded, and overlapping strokes with moderate pressure (2).

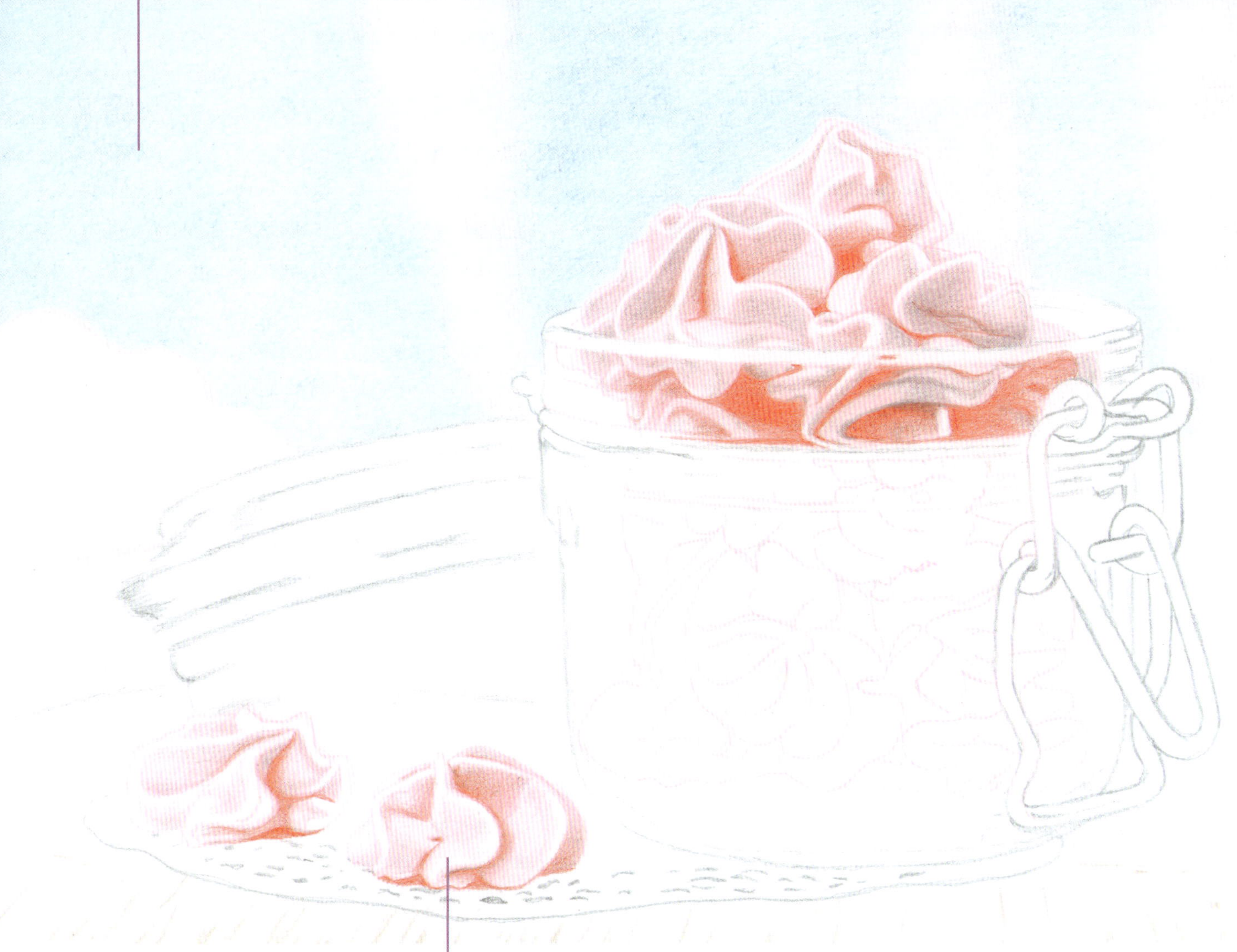

MERINGUES

1 Begin with Rosy Beige to darken the areas that are in shadow. If you make a mistake, use the White pencil to correct or lighten, rather than an eraser. Use small, overlapping strokes with varied pressure.

2 Lightly apply Scarlet Lake in the reddish sections. Start with the obvious lines, curves, and deeply colored sections, and use light to moderate pressure (1-2). Then add layers to deepen the color. Use light pressure (1) to brighten adjacent areas.

3 Fill in the few sections that should be light pink with Deco Pink.

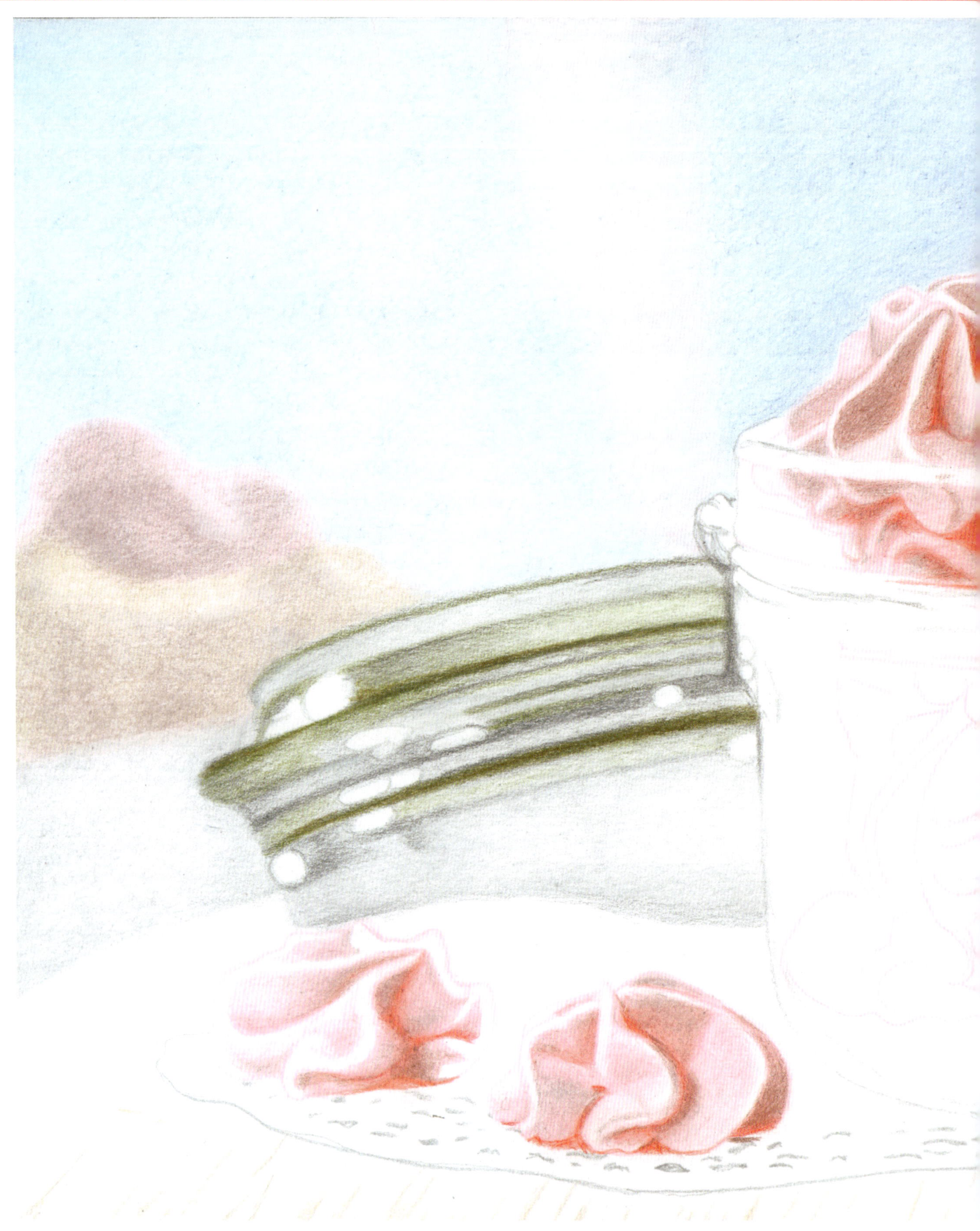

1 For the extremely blurred meringues on the far left, establish the top with Pink Rose followed by Rosy Beige. Use small, rounded, and overlapping strokes with moderate pressure (2). For the lower half, layer with Seashell Pink using small, rounded, overlapping strokes and moderate pressure (2). Over all but the horizontally curved section in the middle, apply Rosy Beige. Use a sharp White to lift and correct misapplied color.

2 Beneath the blurred meringue collection is a curved band of grayish-white color. Fill this in with 30% Cool Grey using rounded strokes and moderate pressure (2).

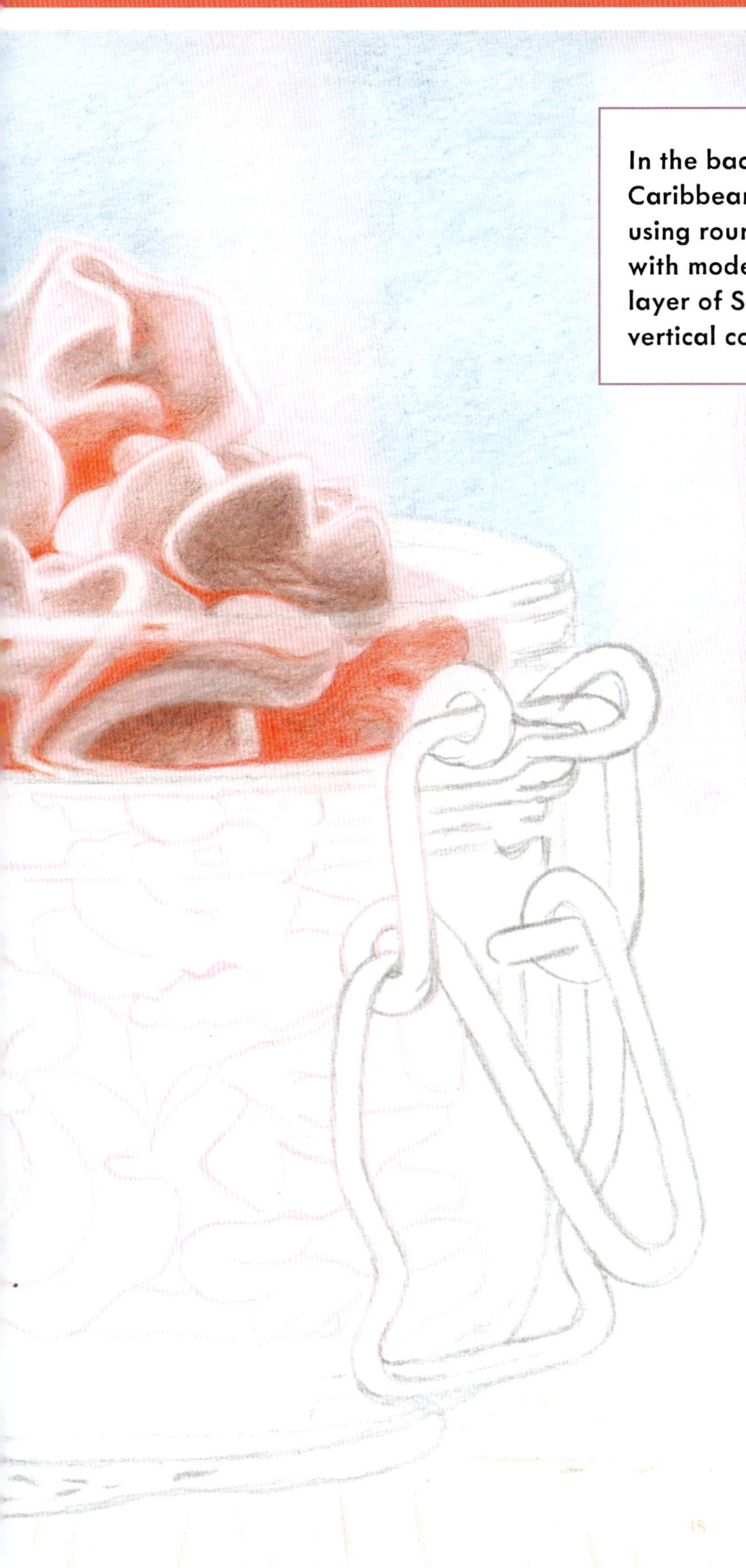

In the background, loosely add more Caribbean Sea to the two blue sections using rounded and overlapping strokes with moderate pressure (2). Apply another layer of Sky Blue Light over the three white vertical columns. Add a layer of Deco Pink.

4 Create each thin band and thicker section of the jar lid rings with Cool Grey. Start the light rings with 30% Cool Grey, midtones with 50% Cool Grey, and dark rings with 70% Cool Grey. Apply Marine Green over the various grays using strokes that are curved horizontally and light pressure (1) in the whiter areas and moderate (2) in darker areas. Use White to correct.

5 If you need more gray to neutralize the green, apply a layer of 30% Cool Grey or 50% Cool Grey. Then sweep Green Ochre over the two dark and prominent green rings.

3 Develop color in the meringues using White to correct, Pink Rose and Rosy Beige for the midtones, Crimson Red for the bright-red areas, and Chestnut and Black Grape for the darker areas. Use loose, overlapping strokes with light to moderate pressure (1-2).

Burnish every background section with White, beginning in the upper-left corner of the blue background. With a sharp White point, start with medium pressure (3) and tiny, overlapping, rounded strokes. Move from left to right and cover the entire background. Overlap all background and lid edges to create a blurred effect.

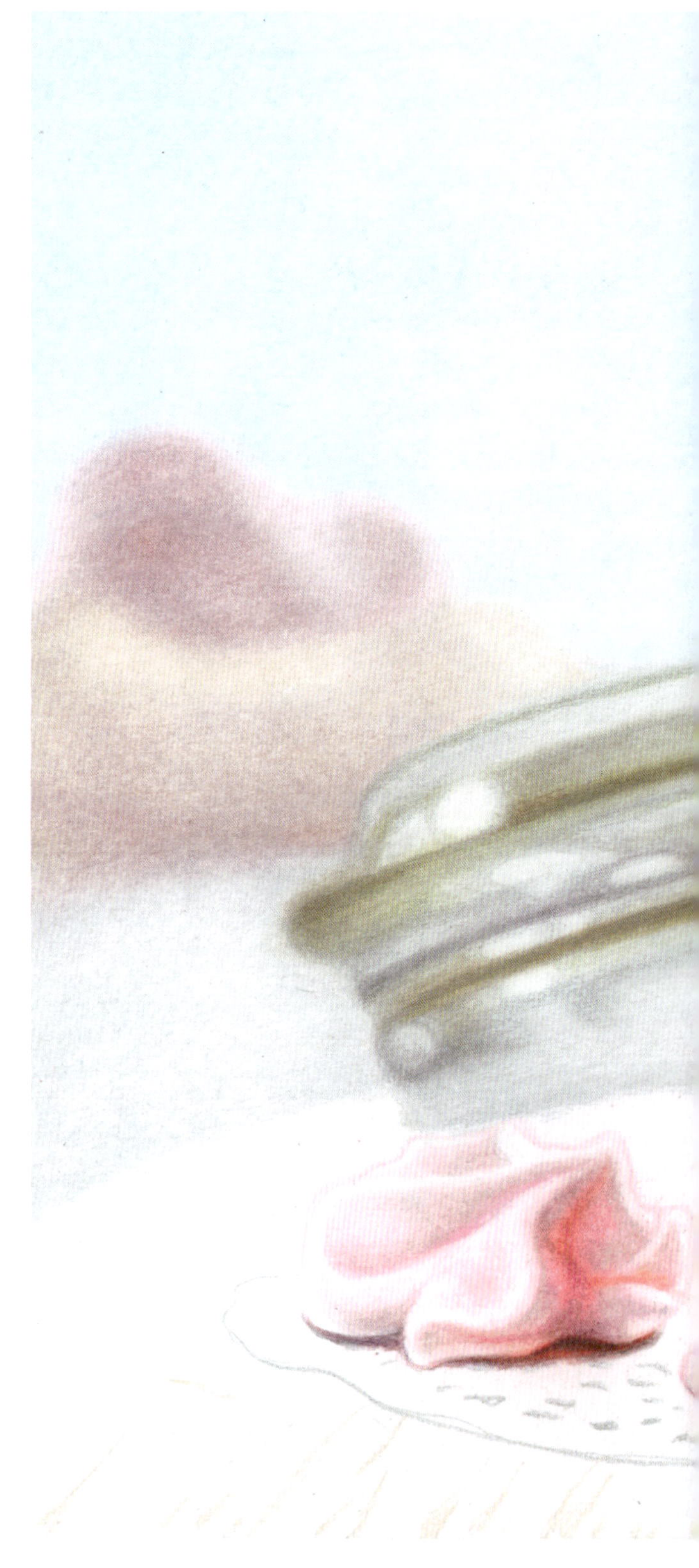

1 Complete the blue background with another layer of Sky Blue Light applied with small, overlapping strokes and moderate pressure (2). Color over the vertical pink areas as well to yield a smooth transition of blues into pinks and vice versa from left to right.

2 Darken the blurred meringue collection a bit with Clay Rose over the pink areas. Use small, overlapping strokes and moderate pressure (2). Soften with White if desired. Work with 30% Cool Grey and White over the slightly darker gray areas.

3 Work from left to right to restore color in the meringues, intensify the darker values, and blend for a smoothly finished appearance. Use the following pencils with a sharp point and light to moderate pressure (1-2): in the light pink areas, use Pink and White; in the moderately shadowed pink areas, use Clay Rose and Pink; in the darkly shadowed pink areas, use Chestnut and Pink; and in the reddish areas, use Tuscan Red and Scarlet Lake. For the deeply shadowed meringues on the right, use Black Cherry and Black Grape. Where the meringues on the table have dark shadows, use Tuscan Red, Black Grape, Scarlet Lake, and Black. Use White and Rosy Beige to transition lighter colors into darker ones. Use sharp points and light pressure (1), or lightly use darker pencils to fill in the blotchy areas.

4 Use Deco Pink to block in and color the remaining pink meringues in the jar. Begin with moderate pressure (2), increasing it in the darker sections.

1 Restore color by applying Dark Brown over the greenish-brown areas of the jar lid and 70% Cool Grey and Black Grape over the purplish-gray areas. Use light to moderate pressure (1-2). Work with 50% and 70% Cool Grey to develop the gray values.

2 Use White liberally to lighten, soften, blend, and transition all colors. Diffuse and blur color by stroking the White pencil diagonally across the curved sections. Pay special attention to the light highlight shapes.

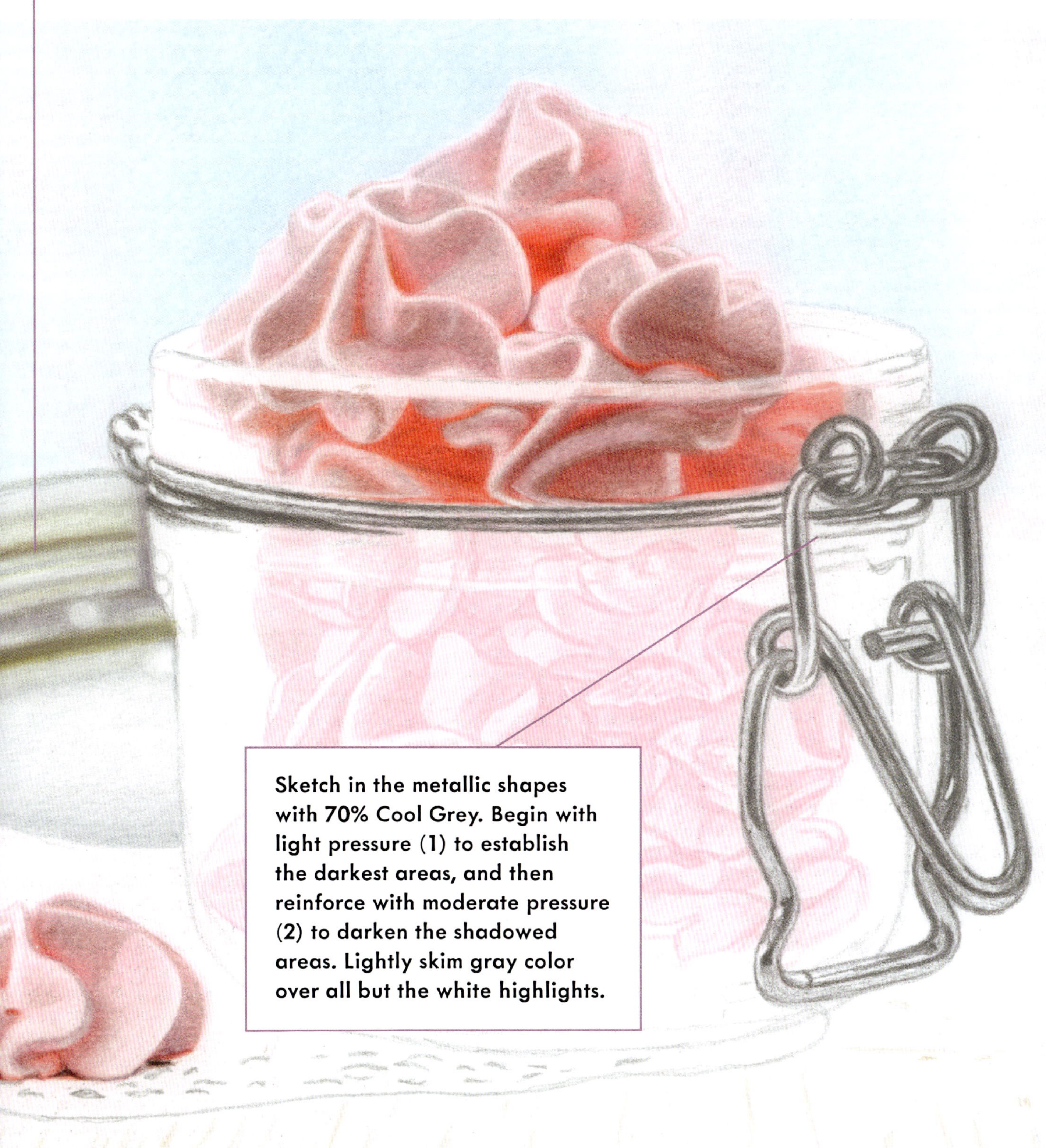

Sketch in the metallic shapes with 70% Cool Grey. Begin with light pressure (1) to establish the darkest areas, and then reinforce with moderate pressure (2) to darken the shadowed areas. Lightly skim gray color over all but the white highlights.

GLASS JAR

1 Work with 50% and 70% Cool Grey along with White to begin developing the jar rims. Use Rosy Beige, Clay Rose, Pink, or Chestnut to bring the various meringue sections right up to the rim edges. Establish the darker border areas down the sides and along the bottom of the jar with 50% Cool Grey. Use several coats for the vertical edging. Color the light interior of the left and right sides with 30% Cool Grey.

2 Skim a few colors over the grays to convey the greenish and burgundy tints observed throughout. Begin with Marine Green skimmed over the areas with a darker greenish tint. Skim Celadon Green over the light gray areas within the main lower portion of the jar. Color Black Cherry over the bottom burgundy section.

3 Apply Black over the darkest shadows of the metallic closure on the right side.

Over the table, sketch the wood grain lines with Burnt Ochre. Color in between these lines with 30% Cool Grey followed by 20% Cool Grey and then 20% French Grey. Use linear strokes with moderate pressure (2).

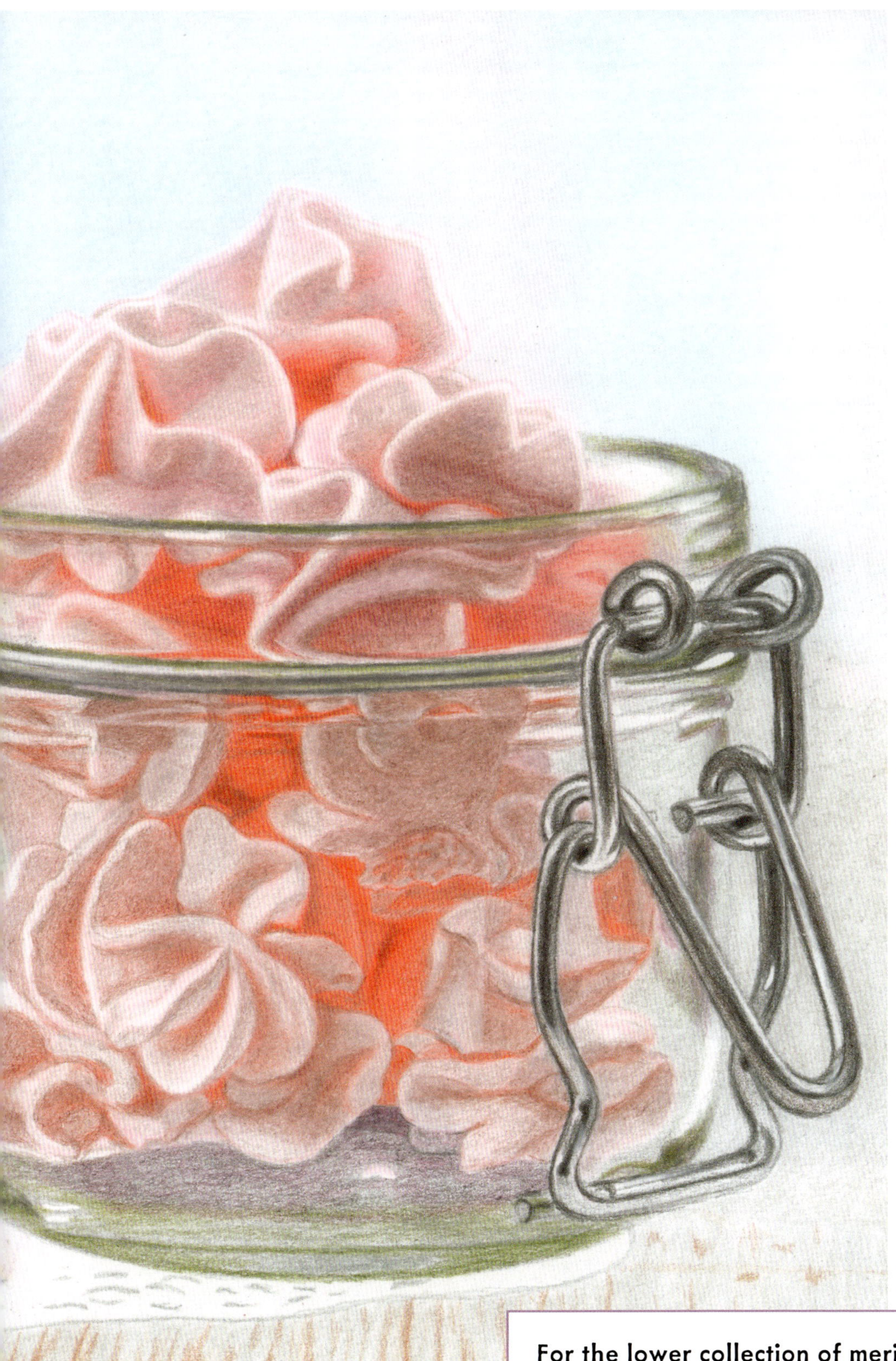

BACKGROUND

1 In the blurred grayish area on the left side and above the far-left meringue, apply 30% Cool Grey with small, rounded strokes and moderate pressure (2). Follow with a layer of 20% French Grey.

2 On the far-right side next to and in between the metallic closure, apply 30% Cool Grey to just below the bottom rung. Use small and rounded strokes with moderate pressure (2). Apply 20% French Grey over that in a similar manner.

For the lower collection of meringues, develop color and value with Rosy Beige applied over all but the lightest areas using varied pressure. Add Scarlet Lake to the reddish sections beginning with light pressure (1) and increasing as needed for brighter color. A light touch of Chestnut darkens shadowed areas. Use light to moderate pressure (1-2). Correct color placement with White.

1 For the lower collection of meringues, use a very sharp White and tiny, circular strokes to blend the layers in each meringue. Use mostly medium pressure (3). This texturizing step transitions the meringues from appearing drawn to painted. Observe how some edges are blurred and some are crisp.

2 To refine the horizontal rings and edges around the jar, establish the reflections, and blend the interior layers, work with White Prismacolor and Derwent Chinese White. Use White Prismacolor to blend the purplish and green areas at the bottom of the jar.

3 Work with White Prismacolor to blend and smooth the grays of the metallic shapes. Keep the point sharp and use moderate to medium pressure (2-3). Also use 70% Cool Grey to refine edges and deepen shadows.

4 Burnish the lower-left background with White to blend and blur the grays. Use small, rounded, and overlapping strokes with medium pressure (3). Then burnish the far-right background next to the jar with White. Restore color with 20% French Grey. Add a bit more Caribbean Sea over the right blue area and soften transitions with White.

5 Develop the reddish-brown table grain with Light Umber using moderate pressure (2). Layer Dark Brown over some of the grain lines to darken. Color more 20% French Grey between the grain lines to deepen the table color. Increase pressure to medium (3).

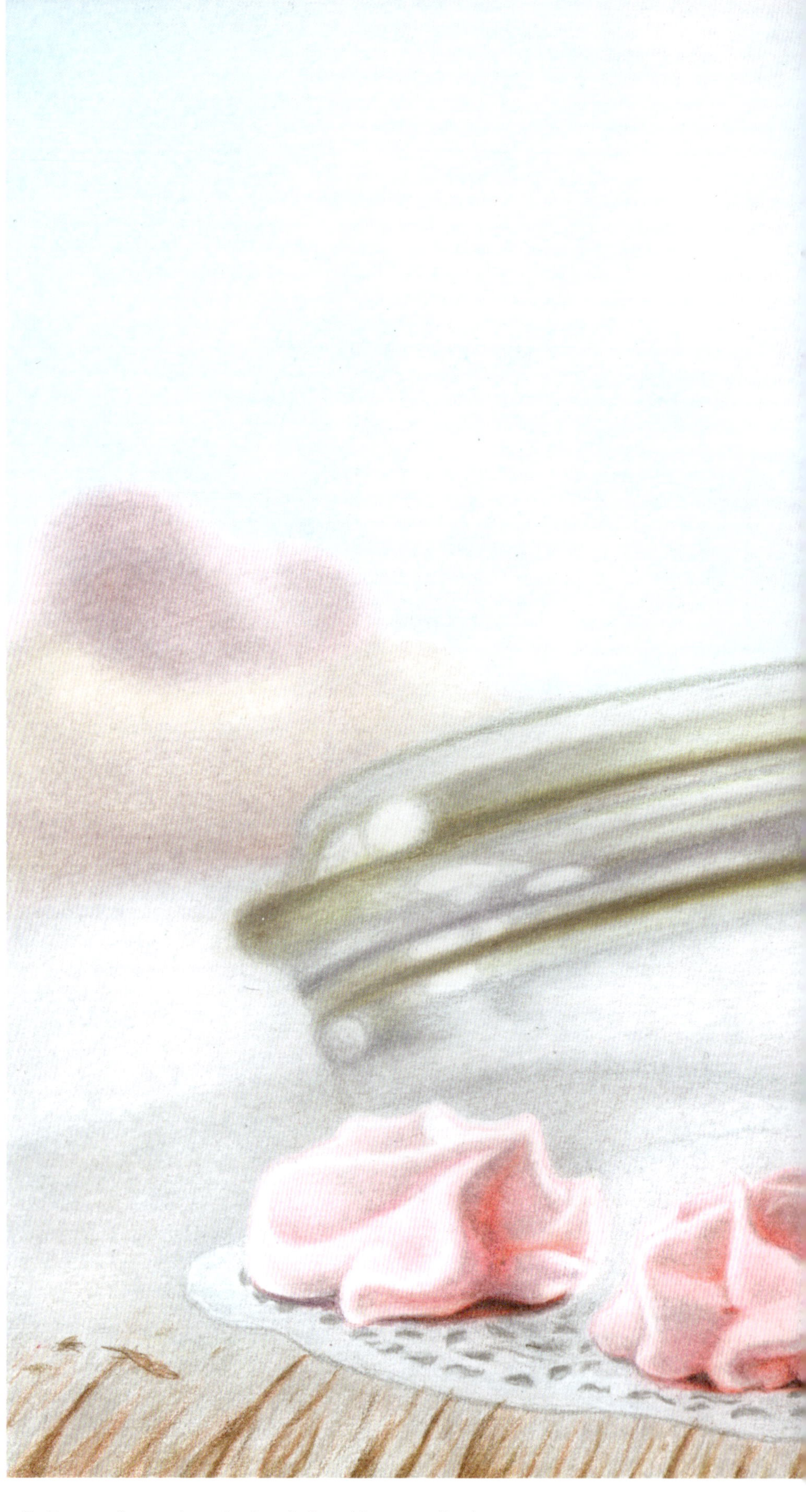

6 Erase all smudges in the doily with a small, clean eraser. Lightly outline the front edge with 50% Cool Grey. Very lightly suggest the fold of the back edge. Next, apply 30% Cool Grey over the entire doily, including the hole markings. Use small, rounded, and overlapping strokes with moderate pressure (2).

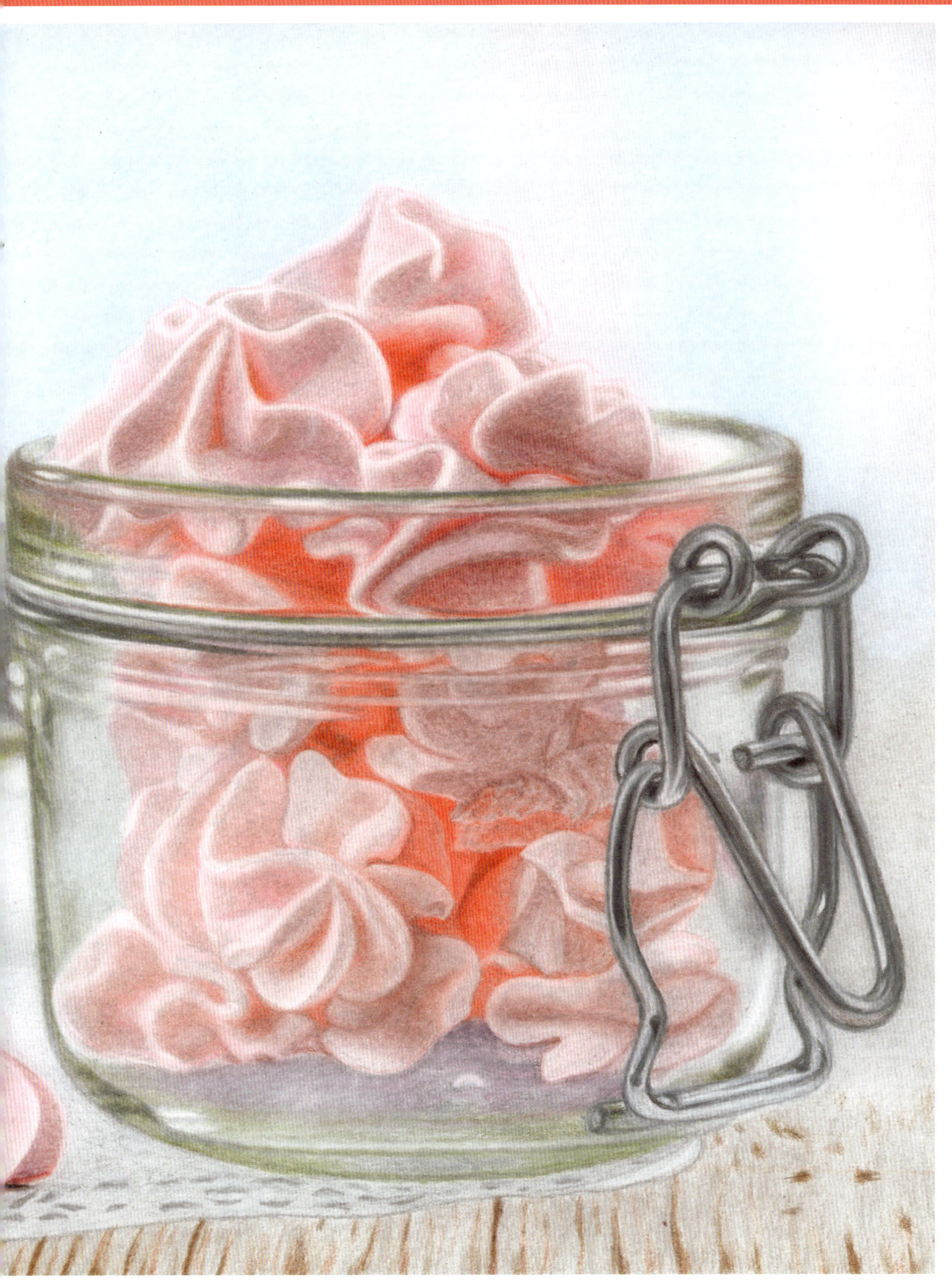

7 Apply another layer of 30% Cool Grey in the shadowed areas of the doily. Over the entire object, add a layer of Sky Blue Light to convey the slightly blue tint. Use 50% Cool Grey with moderate pressure (2) to reinforce the holes within the doily.

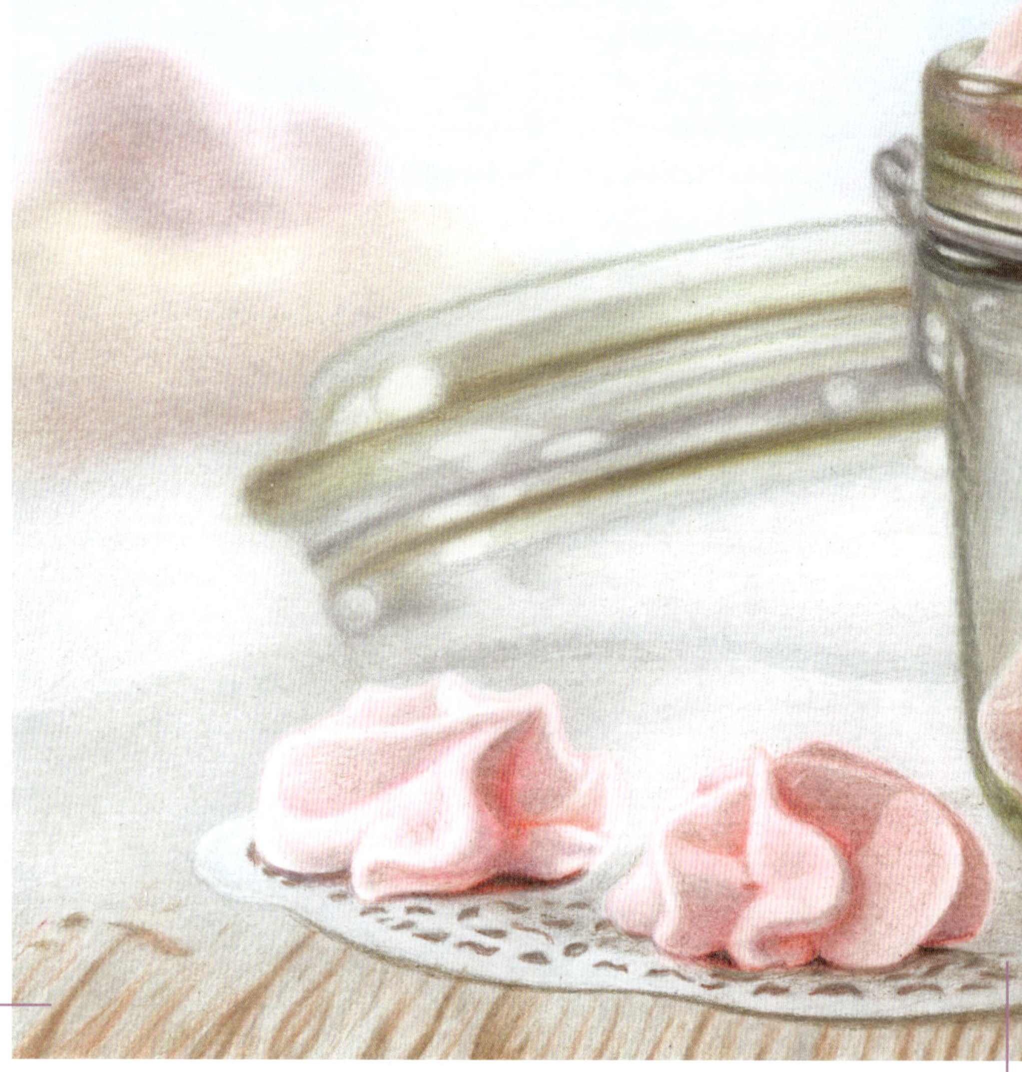

Work with Chestnut to deepen the values of each meringue below the rim, as well as some of the existing shadowed areas. Vary your pressure as you build up color density.

Soften and blur the grain lines into the table by applying White over the entire table in the direction of the grain. Use linear strokes with moderate to medium pressure (2-3). Establish the shadow beneath the doily with 70% French Grey using moderate pressure (2) and darken the left and right sides with another layer.

Burnish the entire doily, except for the holes, with White using medium to firm pressure (3-4) and tiny, rounded strokes. Color in the holes in the left and front with Chestnut using moderate pressure (2). Use 70% Cool Grey in a similar manner on the right side but with very small strokes, because the holes there are barely discernible. Lastly, skim 70% French Grey lightly (1-2) over the shadowed areas of the doily. If your markings are too dark or too large, “erase” using a sharp White pencil with firm pressure.

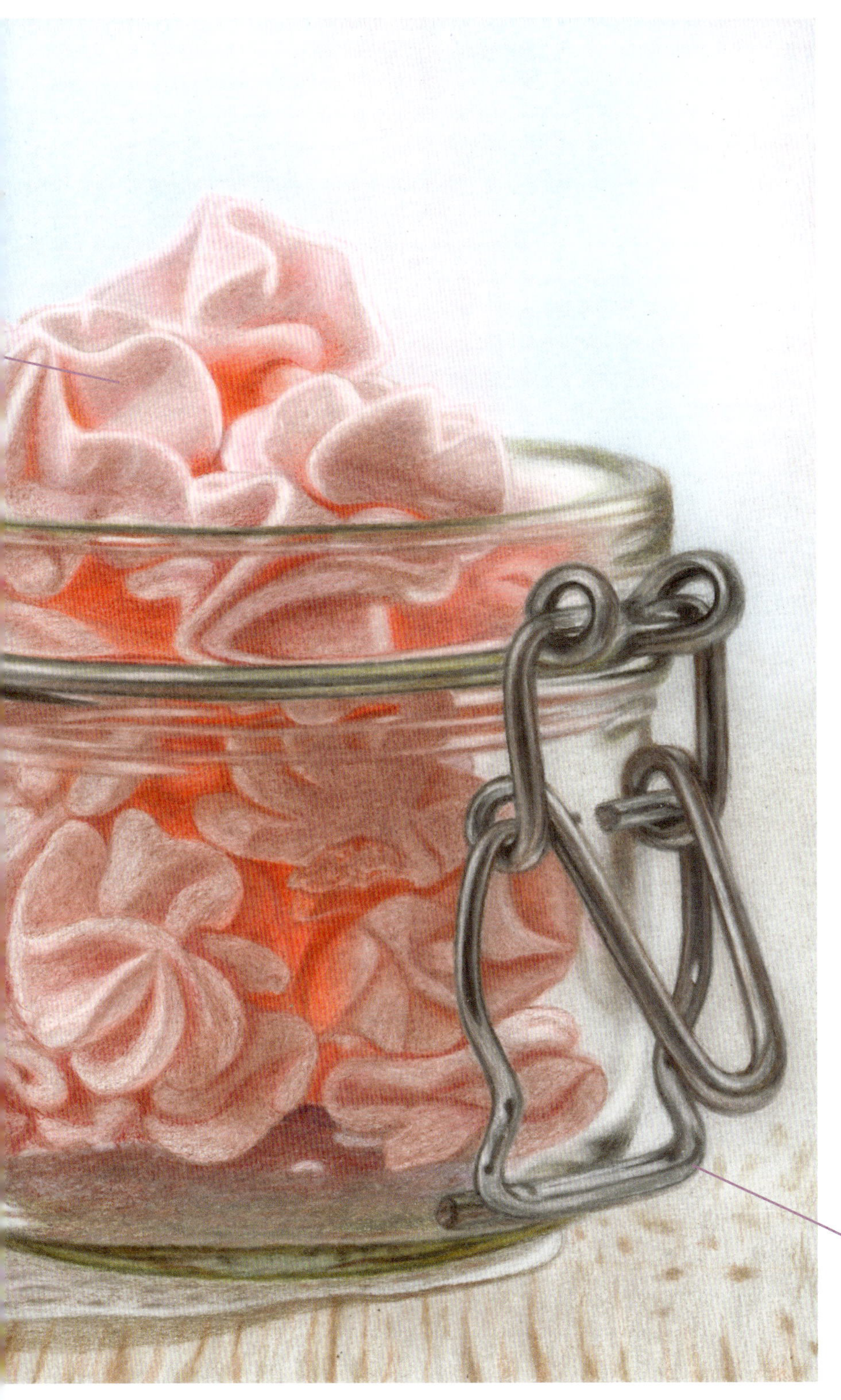

Work with Black, White, 70% Cool Grey, and Dark Umber to complete this section of the jar.

GLASS JAR

1 Develop the rims from left to right using the sharp points of a variety of pencils: Black, White, 70% Cool Grey, Chestnut, Dark Brown, Tuscan Red, Scarlet Lake, Green Ochre, and Marine Green. Aim for a realistic representation of curved rims. Skim lightly with White to soften. Create the thinly curved highlights below the rims with Chestnut, Scarlet Lake, Tuscan Red, and White.

2 Blur the top and side sections with more White. Restore and/or intensify color with Dark Brown, 70% Cool Grey, and Black. Soften and blur with White.

3 Develop the purplish-gray interior base with Chestnut using loose strokes and medium pressure (3). Create a tiny section in the back with Black Grape followed by Tuscan Red, and then apply Tuscan Red between the two front meringues. Beneath that and over the remaining Chestnut, apply 70% Cool Grey.

4 At the very base of the glass jar is a thin greenish section; color it with Marine Green, Green Ochre, and Dark Brown. Draw the thin border lines with Black and the mint-green center with Celadon Green. Use White to blend, soften, and lighten.

MERINGUES

1 Use a very sharp White and small strokes to soften, smooth, and blend each meringue. Deepen color with Chestnut. Darken the reds with Tuscan Red and brighten with Scarlet Lake or Crimson Red.

2 With a sharp and angled point and light to almost moderate pressure (1-2), skim Green Ochre over all but the red and whitest sections of the meringues. Finish by using sharp White and light to moderate pressure (1-2) to soften any obvious lines or blips.

DOILY

Darken the holes with 70% Cool Grey and a touch of Black Grape. Blend and soften the entire doily with White. Work with 50% Cool Grey and White for the left shadow. Use 50% Cool Grey, Chestnut, and White for the remaining shadow. Apply touches of 70% Cool Grey and Black Grape to darken the shadows beneath the two meringues. Carve tiny lines above some of the thin holes on the right with White. Soften by skimming 50% Cool Grey over them.

TABLE

1 Darken the wood grain with Sienna Brown. Apply Dark Umber over the darker grain. Soften and blur the entire table with a sharp White using vertical strokes and medium pressure (3).

2 Blur the shadow beneath the doily with horizontal strokes from left to right. Darken the shadowed areas on the left and right with more 70% French Grey. Soften and blend with White.

3 Where applicable, apply the grain lines up to the doily rim and over the shadow areas using Sienna Brown and Dark Umber. Skim Green Ochre over the front center with light to moderate pressure (1-2).

4 To finish and join the lower background to the table, apply 50% Cool Grey over the grayish area next to the jar lid, and then 30% Cool Grey on the right side of the Green Ochre. Begin with light pressure (1) and increase. Use White to smooth.

GLASS JAR

1 Work with the grays, Green Ochre, Dark Brown, and White to complete the glass jar. Apply the colors used for the meringues over a portion of the reflections as well.

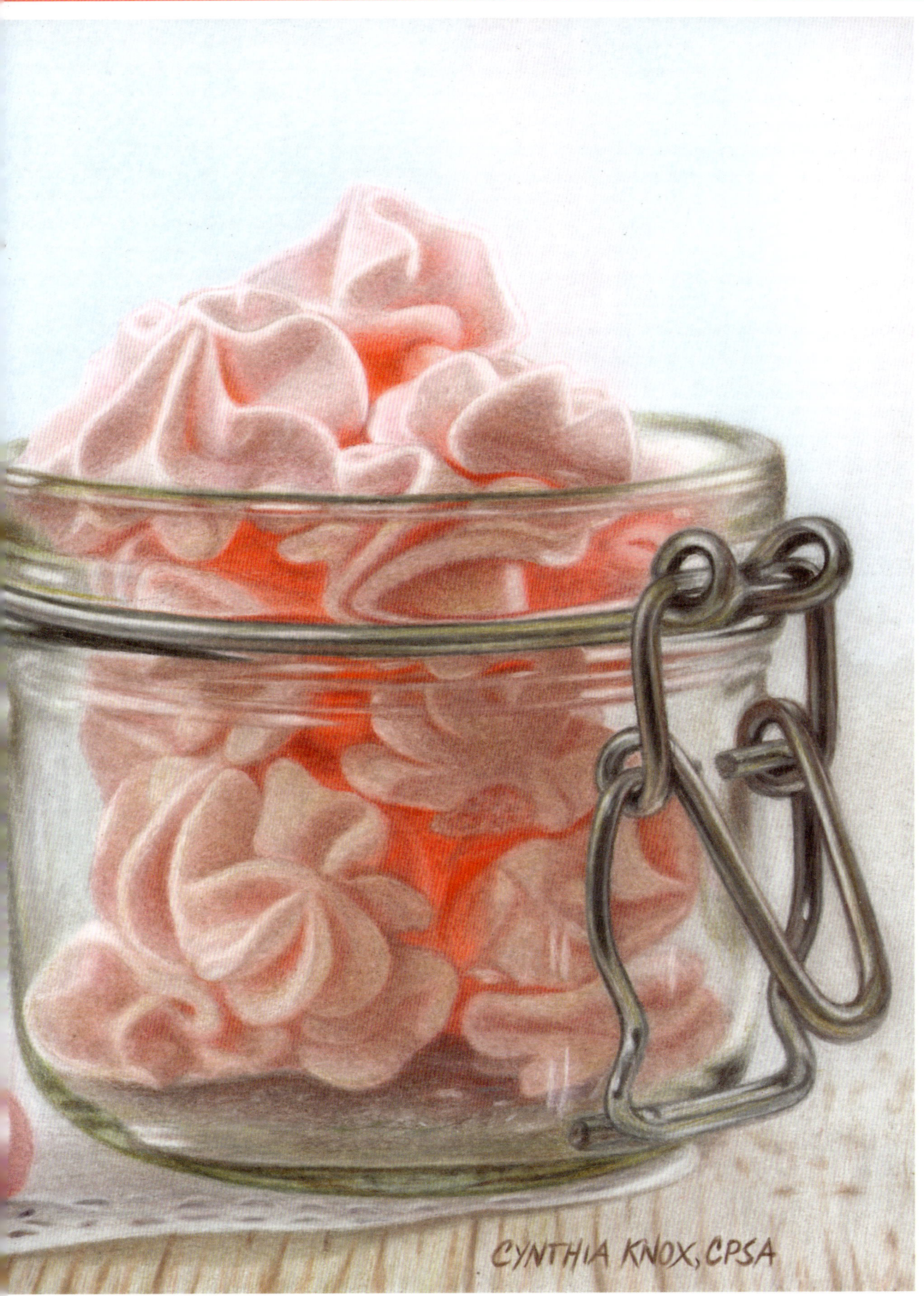

2 Over the bottom, apply Green Ochre. Burnish existing layers with White using medium to firm pressure (3-4). Darken the shadowed areas with 70% Cool Grey and Dark Umber. Just below the bright red meringue, use Black Grape, Dark Umber, and Scarlet Lake. Add a touch of Marine Green to the lower half of the curved bottom. Use sharp White to create random dots and markings over the bottom, as well as short vertical highlights.

3 Lightly add touches of Scarlet Lake and Green Ochre for the metallic reflections. Use a sharp White Prismacolor or Chinese White Derwent Drawing pencil to reinforce the white highlights.

FINISHING TOUCHES

Now view the entire piece. Squint. Observe your values, which are actually more important than your colors. Check out your edges. Some should be blurred—primarily in the background—and some should be crisp. Are there any waxy blips that need to be eliminated? Use a sharp White point. Once you are satisfied, sign your name with a sharp point, patience, and precision. Spray with workable or final fixative to seal in the wax layers. Congratulations! You have completed this lovely contemporary still life and hopefully have learned a few new things in the process.

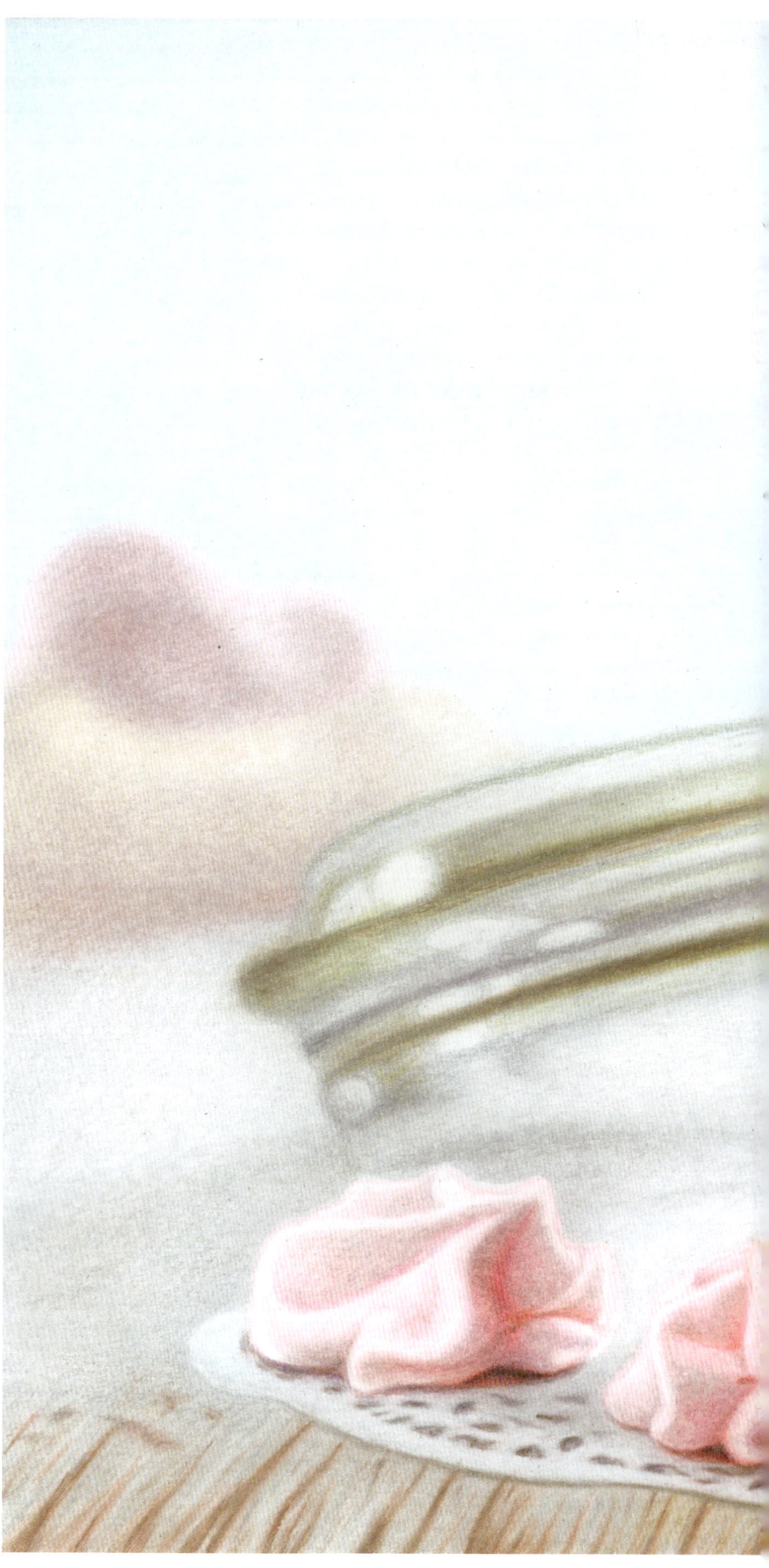

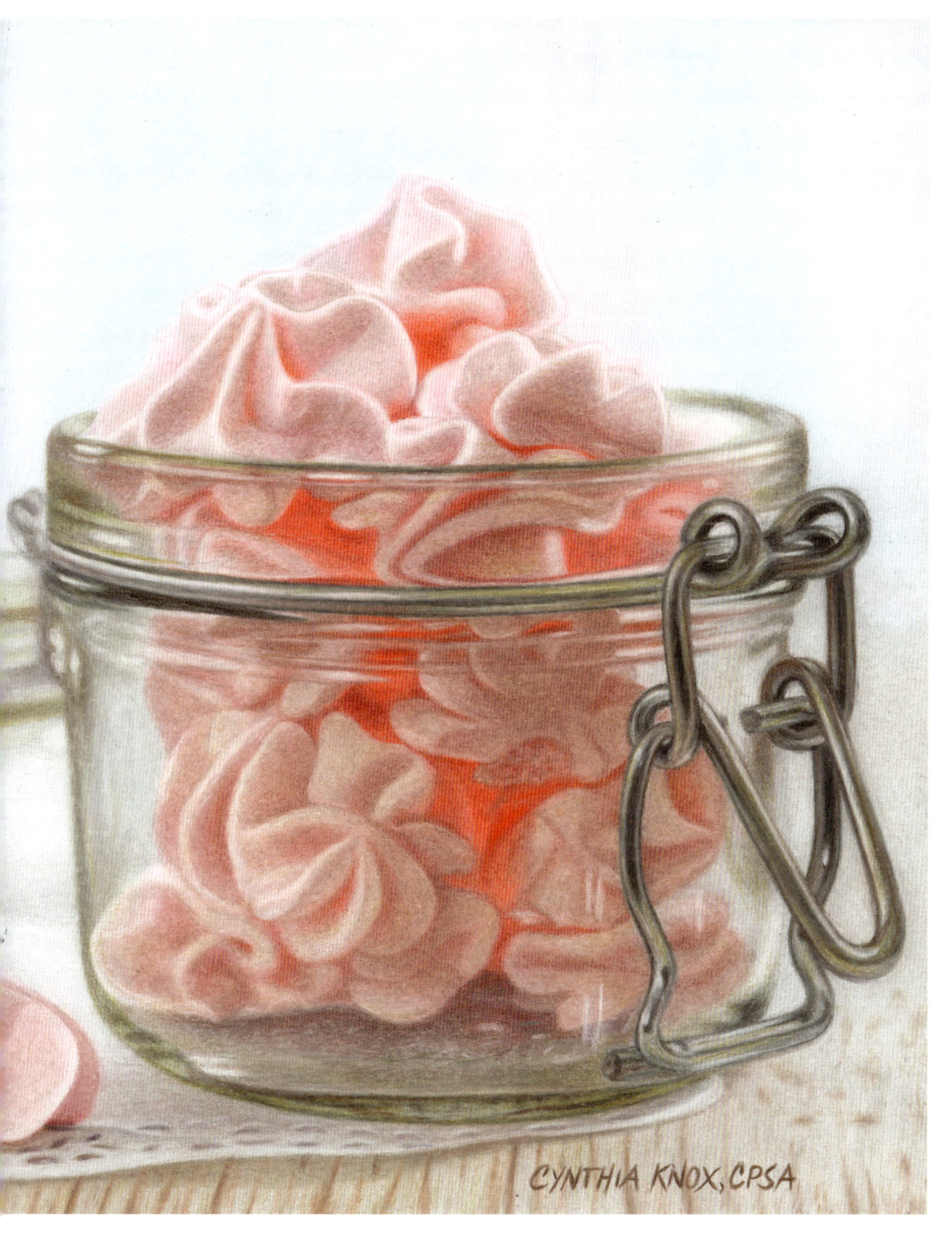
CYNTHIA KNOX, CPSA

About the Artist

CYNTHIA KNOX

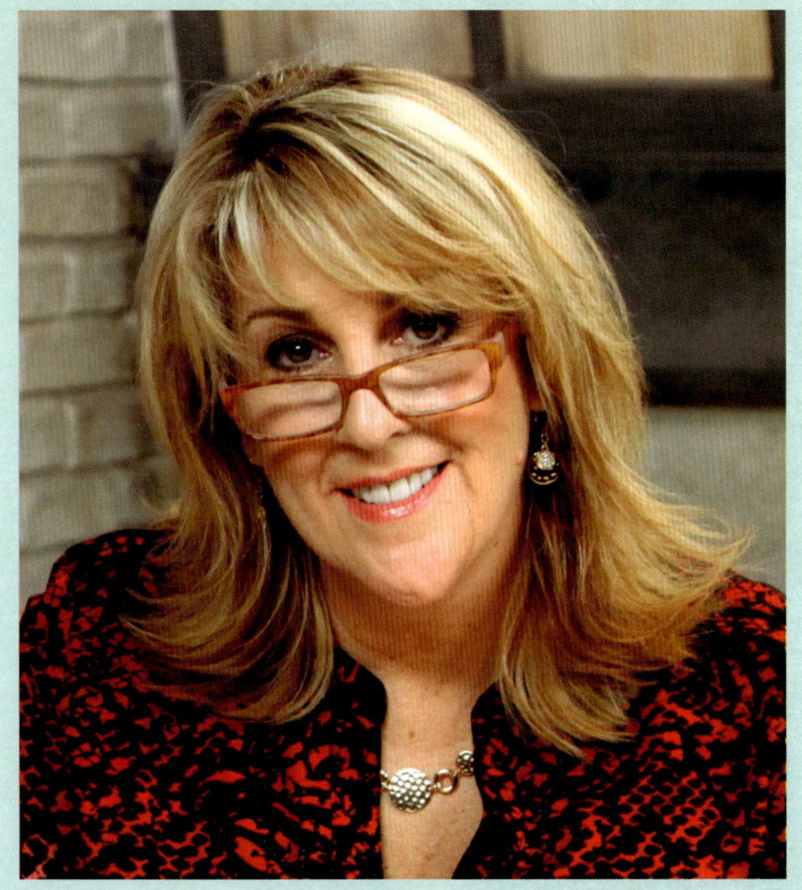

Cynthia Knox, CPSA, is a professional colored pencil and graphite artist who lives in New York with her family. Her artwork has received numerous awards in national and international juried exhibitions, and she has authored 15 art-instructional books. Cynthia teaches art workshops to individuals and groups throughout the United States, internationally, on cruises, and online with Bluprint (formerly Craftsy.com). She is a signature member of the Colored Pencil Society of America, juried member of The International Guild of Realism, and commissioned portrait artist. Cynthia credits her passion and artistic inspiration to a deep love for God and her family. View her resume, artwork, books, testimonials, and teaching schedule at www.cynthiaknox.com. She is on Facebook as Cynthia Knox, as well as Cynthia Knox Fine Art, and on Instagram as cynthiaknox.artist.